Horror Fiction in the Protestant Tradition

First published in the United States of America in 1988

Printed in Hong Kong

ISBN 0–312–01241–1

Library of Congress Cataloging-in-Publication Data
Sage, Victor, 1942–
Horror fiction in the Protestant tradition.
Bibliography: p.
Includes index.
1. Horror tales, English—Protestant authors—
History and criticism.   2. Protestantism and literature.
3. Theology in literature.   4. Catholic Church in
literature.   5. Gothic revival (Literature)   I. Title.
PR830.T3S24   1988   823'.0872'09382   87–23452
ISBN 0–312–01241–1

HORROR FICTION IN THE PROTESTANT TRADITION

To all the students . . .

Contents

List of Plates

Acknowledgements

The author and publishers would like to thank the following who have kindly given permission for the use of copyright material:

Butterworths, Law Publishers Ltd, for the extract from *The English Legal System* by G. R. Y. Radcliffe and G. Cross;

John Calder Ltd, for the extract from *Molloy, Malone Dies, The Unnameable* by Samuel Beckett;

Cambridge University Press, for the extract from *Fourscore Years* by G. C. Coulton;

Jonathan Cape Ltd, for the extract from *Fox's Book of Martyrs and the Elect Nation* by W. Haller;

Chatto and Windus Ltd, for the extract from *Philosophy and the Historical Understanding* by W. B. Gallie; and the extract from *The Rise of the Novel* by Ian Watt;

Collins/Fontana Ltd, for the extract from *On Religion* by David Hume;

Columbia University Press, for the extract from *Some Problems of Proof under the Anglo-American System of Litigation* by Edwin Morris Morgan;

Curtis Brown Ltd, for the extract from *Natural and Supernatural* by Brian Inglis, © Brian Inglis;

Faber and Faber Ltd, for the extract from *The Growth of Philosophic Radicalism* by Elie Halévy;

Victor Gollancz Ltd, for the extract from *Great Horror Stories of Europe and America* edited by P. Haining;

Miss Olwyn Hughes, for the extract from *Ariel* by Sylvia Plath;

Harvard University Press, for the extract from *The Genesis of Secrecy* by Frank Kermode;

The Macmillan Press Ltd, for the extract from *Historical Essays* by Hugh Trevor-Roper;

Oxford University Press, for the extract from *Everywhere Spoken Against* by Valentine Cunningham; for the extract from *William Cowper: Letters and Prose Writings* edited by James King and Charles Ryskamp; for the extract from *Grace Abounding to the Chief of Sinners* edited by R. Sharrock; for the extract from *Melmoth the Wanderer* by C. Maturin; and for the extract from *The Italian* by Ann Radcliffe;

Penguin Books Ltd, for the extract from *Heroes and Villains*, © Angela Carter; and for the extract from *Radcliffe*, © David Storey;

Rutgers University Press, for the extract from *Poe: The Detective* by John Walsh, © 1968 by Rutgers, the State University;

Transworld Publishers Ltd, for the extract from *Uncle Silas* by Sheridan Le Fanu;

Weidenfeld and Nicolson Ltd, for the extract from *The Revolution of the Saints* by M. Walzer; and for the extract from *Evidence, Proof and Probability* by Sir Richard Egglestone;

University of Wisconsin Press, for the extract from *The Eloquent 'I': Style and Self in Seventeenth-Century Prose* by Joan Webber.

Preface

There is something about horror fiction which has always provoked readers to *account* for it. The extremity of the genre, the recurrence of its symbols, and the *déjà vu* effect of its language seem to demand a broader explanation than other, apparently more self-justifying, literary forms. Contemporary reviewers of the 'Gothick' novels, although they differed sharply as to what interpretation to give them, were in no doubt that they were a species of political writing. The Marquis de Sade was perhaps the most influential of these commentators. He took the novels of Lewis and Mrs Radcliffe as a response to the political trauma of the French Revolution: 'let us agree that this species of writing, whatever one might say about it, is assuredly not without merit. It became the necessary fruit of the revolutionary tremors felt by the whole of Europe.'

In the 1930s, the French surrealist André Breton developed this view of de Sade's, integrating it with a Freudian perspective:

The pleasure principle has never revenged itself more obviously upon the principle of reality. The ruins appear suddenly so full of significance in that they express the collapse of the feudal period; the inevitable ghost which haunts them indicates a peculiarly intense fear of the return of the powers of the past, the subterranean passages represent the difficulty and perils of the dark path followed by each individual towards the light; in the stormy night can be heard the incessant roar of cannon. Such is the turbulent background chosen for the appearance of the beings of pure temptation, combining in the highest degree the struggle between the instinct of death on one hand, which, as Freud has shown, is also an instinct of preservation, and, on the other, Eros who extracts after each human hecatomb the glorious restoration of life. I insist on the fact that the substitution of one kind of scenery for another (scenery of the romantic type for realist scenery) has in no way been determined by the authors of the 'romans noirs' and still less contrived by mutual consent. Their undoubted innocence in this respect gives even greater importance to their sensitive testimony.[1]

A direct connection is made here between the essentially random

activity of the individual subconscious and the determining
pressure of the political culture. Surrealism, thought Breton,
worked in an analogous fashion, subversively exposing the
collective myths of the modern period, and this is in part why he
sees the English Gothic novelists as such an important precedent for
his own artistic programme.

These remarks are suggestive, and they have proved influential in
modern views of the subject. But Breton is also unnecessarily
reductive: his insistence on a purely unconscious response by these
writers lacks a certain explanatory power. Why does the genre
survive, for example, as a demonstrably recurrent strain in
nineteenth-century fiction long after the French Revolution? And, if
we are to accept the significance of the unconscious as a factor in the
explanation of the recurrence of the literary genre, exactly how do
the materials of this tradition become available to the individual
writer's imagination? The idea in itself that the unconscious is a
timeless activity, unmediated by other cultural and ideological
factors, yields no real possibility of giving a convincing, or even a
detailed, account of the interaction between this kind of writing and
the cultural context in which it may appear.

The availability of literary materials is a notoriously difficult
question, especially when one has the problem of a species of
writing that appears over a vastly extended historical period.
Breton's Freudianism is, as I have suggested, unacceptably
reductive in the context of the whole tradition of horror. Another
application of Freud, perhaps even more inhibiting, is visible in the
Breton passage. The horror genre itself is seen as 'fantasy', and it is
opposed, on the analogy of the pleasure and reality principles, to
'realism'. Thus Breton comments on the choice of genre, as if it too
were an unconscious factor. This view is still quite widespread. The
horror novel is portrayed as the dark unconscious of the nineteenth
century, which surfaces periodically in a struggle with an 'official',
'dominant' or 'bourgeois' mode of realism.[2]

The curious effect of this is to confine discussion to a new kind of
literary formalism which again fails to take account of the real
complexity of determining factors in the culture. The psychoanalytic
dichotomy between conscious and unconscious meaning has, in
this account, become a rather crude a-historical metaphor for
competing literary forms. This loose adaptation of Freud defeats its
own ostensible purpose: it gets rid of the notion that anxiety is
common to art and life. In the act of trying to open up discussion of

the subject, we find at the outset that horror fiction is sealed into an opposition with other literary forms. The notion that it is 'subversive' is robbed of its efficacy by the implication that the only major thing it subverts is 'realism', another literary genre.

But de Sade, Breton and Freud were originally right, to this extent: that horror is not a literary genre, in the narrow sense, at all. It is a cultural response, which implies a broad series of relationships with the whole of the culture in which it is produced. The narrower the conception of genre, the more one is moving away from the possibility of explaining it.[3]

The French Revolution is by no means the only political event which has been cited as a determinant of the Gothic novel. After reviewing the remarks of de Sade and Breton, the French critic Maurice Lévy came to the conclusion that the social and political revolution more importantly related to the Gothic writers was the so-called 'Glorious Revolution', the Protestant Settlement of 1688, the event which, arguably, saw the foundation of the English political state in its modern form.[4]

M. Lévy had no space to demonstrate the implications of this view, and, curiously, the suggestion has never been taken up in any sustained fashion in modern discussions of the subject. And yet it seems obvious that the penetration of Protestant theology into every aspect of English culture since the Settlement acts as a most intimate, and at the same time a most objective, conditioning factor in both popular belief and literary culture. Theological assumptions are *points de répère*, demonstrably present in the broad spectrum of the culture's language, whether at the popular or the literary end of it.

But when we speak of a Protestant tradition, we are apparently speaking of a common set of doctrines which hold English culture together. There is an important sense in which theology is, by definition, conservative: it must preserve itself and its limits. To be a social cement, it must be recognisable and it must transmit a set of values from generation to generation. This is true of both established and dissenting Protestantism.

On the other hand, Protestantism in its social and political aspects is notoriously hydra-headed. It is always in the process of re-forming itself, re-aligning its sympathies in relation to local

economic and political changes. Neither of these levels, I have
assumed, is more 'objective' than the other, for they are constantly
interacting.

Let me take a famous example: the reception of Lewis's *The Monk*.
An obvious rhetorical tactic to gain acceptance with his audience is
the book's almost ritual element of anti-Catholic pamphleteering.
Lewis could assume a united audience for this: his rhetoric
presupposes a bundle of psychologically far-reaching popular
prejudices which reinforce the theological identity of different parts
of his readership. Superstition was evident to all, except Catholic
sympathisers.

But the reception of the book reveals a much more complicated
relation between dominant theology and social and political
pressures. The Anglican Coleridge, for example, who initiated the
charge of blasphemy against it, completely ignored Lewis's
titillation of his own vehement anti-Catholicism. Blasphemy was a
serious political charge at the time, and Lewis was a Member of
Parliament. Papers were secretly drawn up against him, it seems,
and he was forced to bowdlerise and censor his own text, in order to
escape prosecution for 'violation of the King's peace'. In other
words, the theology on which Lewis relied to exploit a popular
prejudice underwrote the law which made his book into a
dangerous and subversive political phenomenom. Theology, as a
cultural determinant in the situation, has the capacity to swivel and
face in another direction, to present itself in another aspect, while
remaining a continuous factor. It plays a role at the level of cause,
and of effect.[5]

Popular prejudice and constitutional and legal prohibitions seem
as far apart as opinion and fact, and yet they merge. But where shall
we say that these powerfully linked, yet on this occasion,
contradictory factors meet? Certainly it is not enough to say simply:
the text. We are dealing with a whole *gestalt* of expectation into
which Lewis's text was inserted. Nor is it enough to point to the
psychology of prejudice alone to define those expectations, to make
them merely part of the implied reader's subjective equipment,
because in this case the theology which produces the popular
stereotype is also acting as the guarantee of 'objective' political and
legal prohibition; it is part of the fabric of consequence.

The literary example here is only a special case of the broader
problem of defining the role of a dominant theology which creates
cultural homogeneity beyond its own merely external political

dominance. The Protestant assumption of internalised conscience, for example, is the badge of identity in English culture: it was shared by Dissenters and Anglicans alike, *if* opposed to Catholics. Sterne wrote a brilliant skit on this major theological and psychological difference in the reactions of the Protestant Walter and the Catholic Dr Slop to the sermon read by Trim in *Tristram Shandy*. Their responses to minute theological points are monitored in such satirical ways that dissenting and high-church readers alike could join in a common guffaw at the superstition of the Catholic Doctor. Thus a theological assumption, if broad enough, could invite an audience to forget its differences.

But such homogeneity appears as a mirage if these groups are considered in the aspect of their social and political opposition to one another. Just how radically internalised *was* the conscience for established Churchmen, compared with Dissenters, for example? Even Dissenters accept the doctrine of Calvin on the internalisation of the conscience differently, dependent on what social and political groups they belong to – Huguenots and Baptists, for example. The elasticity of this theological doctrine can unite groups socially and politically, and yet lock them into a mutually-agreed isolation. And this is true at an individual psychological level, too. Bunyan tells the story, for example, of going to see a dissenting Elder, because he suspected that he had committed the sin against the Holy Ghost, the sin without a name. Upon enquiry, the reply was, unexpectedly, that the man thought that he probably had. Bunyan reports, dryly, that he had 'cold comfort' from this comment. But his disturbance gradually abated, as he pondered upon the relation between the man's judgement and his character. And Bunyan eventually came to the conclusion that he was probably not a very good Christian anyway, and decided to ignore his opinion.[6]

The amusing thing about the story to a modern reader is the snobbery of conscience it reveals: Bunyan can always rationalise his vanity, by reference to the superior scrupulousness of his own conscience. Thus even within a sect, or united group, the doctrine specifically promotes the isolation of the individual, the private judgement necessary to his faith. Yet at the same time, by the token of their acceptance of this situation, it acts as a grid, holding individuals in a social relationship to one another.

This universal doctrine of the conscience thus has a complex political significance as well as a social and psychological meaning in Protestant culture. It may appear more or less 'internalised', dependent on social factors. The conscience is part of what Luther originally formulated as the 'separation of the office and the person' and it was accepted and developed by Calvin. This is the point at which the individual Protestant need not accept, on the grounds of conscience, the law of the society in which he lived, if he considered that law to be unjust. Professor Walzer suggests that seventeenth-century French Huguenots brought the conscience much nearer to the office, virtually exteriorising it, as a form of social duty.[7] Such an interpretation of Calvin's doctrine is determined in part by the class and social affinities of the group: aristocratic, wealthy and influential, and to that degree implicated in the administration of their own social position, despite their position as outsiders. For Scottish Presbyterians, however, or again eighteenth-century English non-conformist Calvinists, there tends to be a characteristically severe separation of the office and the person, so that the internalisation of the conscience appears that much greater. Hogg's *Confessions of a Justified Sinner*, for example, is a satire on this latter position.[8]

Yet at the level of popular prejudice, there is a homogeneous identity: it is Calvinism which remains the common factor, whether stigma or advantage, between these social groups, if we compare them with established Anglicans on this issue of the conscience; just as it is Protestantism which links *all* these groups, if we compare them with Catholics, on the same issue.

The rhetoric of the horror novel is demonstrably theological in character. And theological assumptions play the role, again demonstrably, of organising and determining factors in the psychology of individual writers throughout the nineteenth and early twentieth centuries. That is to say, such assumptions, common to literary and non-literary contexts, are available in the culture at large. Horror fiction gives the reader a unique insight into the way these factors operate, because the interaction between cultural homogeneity and political divergence is displayed in a peculiarly clear form in the language of these texts.

But perhaps this is also a point at which we can rescue analysis of the subject from several of its reductive pressures. Freud attempted to eradicate 'intellectual uncertainty' as a cause of the horror experience, because of the commitment of such an idea to the conscious mind. The nature of popular stereotypes in the Protestant tradition suggests that the transmission of anxiety and fear is a simultaneously subjective and objective business. Thus one needs to retain all Freud's mechanisms of condensation and substitution in language, in order to describe the interaction involved between conscious and unconscious assumptions. But it is my contention here that the cause and the effect of the horror experience in English culture is a form of 'theological uncertainty', an anxiety which is recognisable at many different levels of consciousness.

This commits us to a cultural analysis, but not at the risk of neglecting unconsciously available assumptions in writers and their readers. Protestant theology contains, at the subjective level, a complete pre-emptive description of the most obscure processes of the mind; it also consists, at the outward or objective level, of a sophisticated set of models for the recognition and control of social behaviour.

This tradition is continuous: the reprinting of certain texts, for example, often seventeenth-century or earlier Reformation works of theological interest, throughout the eighteenth and nineteenth centuries, conditions the availability of popular images in the horror tradition and provides later, nineteenth-century writers with their materials. That reprinting is itself often determined by the contemporary politics of belief. Fox's *Acts and Monuments*, for example, is an almost universally known text, which became the *Book of Martyrs*, a favourite production for children. This book assumed a new life in the nineteenth century running through many cheap editions, and illustrated with graphic engravings of the sufferings of the Protestant martyrs, because it became the weapon of dissenting propaganda, transformed from its earlier role as the second Bible of the established English church. The Abbé Calmet's *The Phantom World, or the Philosophy of Spirits, Apparitions, etc.*, written by a seventeenth-century Benedictine and translated into English in the early eighteenth century, went on being reprinted throughout the nineteenth century. Dickens had a copy of the edition of 1850 in his library, reissued during the Tractarian scare. Calmet's original work had been written as Roman propaganda against the Greek Orthodox Church, but it was reissued in a Protestant edition in England as propaganda against the author's own Roman Catholic Church. The 'vampire myth', widely disseminated, though actually condemned by this book, was never neutrally inherited; it was always an element in the contemporary politics of belief.[9]

The availability of a text may be a conditioning factor in the imagination of the individual writer. The doctrine of the

Resurrection, for example, one major source for which is the Epistle
to the Corinthians of St Paul, is a determinant of the literary
mode of horror. This doctrine organises the fear of human death at
the subjective psychological level. But in noticing this, we have an
immediate political reflex to contend with. The choice of the
Protestant interpretation of St Paul generates further psychological
and political fear of the heresy and superstition implied in other
interpretations. These second-order fears, as it were, produce
images of the unthinkable, which are strongly related to conscious
caricature often practised in the popular media. Indeed, theology
itself remained a popular language in the nineteenth century, and it
was certainly available as such up to the Second World War. It is the
interaction between the survival of this complex and rich popular
language and the horror tradition which conditions the survival of
the latter and helps to throw some light on the continuity of its
content and form.

Each of the five chapters below takes the form of an essay, which
can be read independently in any order. If taken in order, however,
they are meant to have a progressive, linking structure. A simple
analogy is the slices of a cake: the slice implies the cake, and it
touches its fellows at a point near the centre. Just as each slice
occupies a different position on the circumference, so each chapter
takes a different angle to start from. Each chapter is organised
around a key concept, and the number of concepts in play increases
as the book goes on.

The first chapter traces a theological source for the image of the
dark and ruined house which is at the centre of so many horror
novels, and shows how the theological metaphor is hidden in the
'atmospheric' and picturesque descriptions of domestic architecture
in nineteenth- and twentieth-century novels. The German word
heimlich literally means 'belonging to the house or home' and it was
assumed by Freud and his translators that there was no direct
equivalent in English.[10] But the term 'uncanny' has the effect of
losing this rich metaphorical root. The *heim* literally and
metaphorically represents a space of security, a place, as Grimm's
dictionary has it, 'free from ghostly influences'. Interestingly,
several of the original contexts in the dictionary quotations from
which Freud derived his philological evidence in the essay appear to
be religious, such as, for example, 'To veil the divine, to surround it
with a certain *unheimlichkeit*'; 'a holy *heimlich* feeling'; or 'The
Protestant rulers do not feel . . . *heimlich* among their Catholic

subjects.' These examples demonstrate Freud's dialectical transition between antitheses in the pattern of usage, but their religious context gives the metaphor a further, more specific cultural and historical significance. The fullest descriptions of the *unheimlich* in English are contained in the horror novel and story, and one of the identifying features of this genre, the thing that often leads us to the shorthand label 'Gothic', is the presence of a dark, embattled, characteristically decaying house – an *unheim*, so to speak. Thus the 'picturesque' in this instance is not decorative, but the vehicle of a theologically induced foreboding.

The next chapter expands this consideration of theological doctrine; to show the role of the Resurrection and the Eucharist in the formation of popular anti-Catholic stereotypes, and their appearance in the texts of the horror tradition: the aliens, invaders and walking dead of nineteenth- and early twentieth-century horror omnibuses. The Protestant tradition of testimony by internalised conscience is a highly significant thread in the popular rhetoric of anti-Catholicism, and is often cited as the source of the popular horror of Romish superstition and arbitrary authority. These doctrines postulate a theological relation between individual identity and national sovereignty, and hence reinforce the continuity of the stereotype of the invader.

But this authoritative thread in the rhetoric, the assumption of an internalised conscience, is *itself* a source of horror from another angle, and Chapter 3 takes up some of the characteristic shapes of this interiorised act of witnessing, which acts as a frequently unspoken guarantee in the popular propaganda war of Chapter 2. The logic of the doctrine of internalisation is ultimately paradoxical. The nineteenth-century horror story, the frequent *doppelgänger* form, for example, relies on a pastiche of orthodox Protestant confessional autobiography, particularly in its Puritan form. These fictional versions reveal the monstrous nature of absolute self-scrutiny, tilting the traditional confession into a form which exposes its latent paradox. The 'double' throws into the foreground, often ironically, the anxiety and self-loathing which this doctrine, in its most extreme Puritan form, exploits for its effectiveness.

Chapter 4 takes another journey outwards, exploring the external projection of the notion of testimony. Witnessing has an 'objective', almost scientific significance, as well as an overtly religious sense. These two contexts overlap, especially in the eighteenth century, where the assimilation of faith to reason reduced belief to an epistemological matter. 'Testimony' is a matrix of different contexts, and it reveals 'authority' in actuality as a form of mutual borrowing between law and theology.

The narrative form of horror fiction is demonstrably 'legalistic' – it calls attention to itself as testimony, and employs a corroborative principle in its narrative, which 'authorises' its content. The ambiguity of testimony lies in the fact that it has a simultaneous relationship to the foundations of the Protestant faith, and the rules of evidence of the English Common Law, which in certain respects acts as the outward image of that faith.

There is a historiographical overlap between popular prejudice about the Catholic Inquisition, and the English view of the inquisitory legal systems of contemporary Europe in the eighteenth century: both derive, in popular historiographical myth, from Rome and are viewed with suspicion. The horror novel, in employing the form of testimony to a marked degree thus arouses a flux of 'subjective' and 'objective' expectations at the same time in the reader, giving authority to some of the fictions considered in earlier chapters.

Chapter 5 extends this exploration of the legalistic form of horror fiction into the nineteenth-century short story form: the format of the 'strange case'. This format is a favourite one for horror writers, because it reinforces both anxiety and faith. This story form is a point at which the continuity of the transaction between theology and law shows itself; it is a transaction which 'guarantees' the credibility of any relating or recounting in language of an experience. Thus the apparatus of proof and scepticism is used to promote an inverted form of faith against the bogey of scientific empiricism. The literary form, again parasitic upon other cultural forms, resolves the apparent paradox of a scepticism which generates faith.

It remains to say a word or two about terminology. The word 'horror' is tricky, because it belongs to a class of apparently descriptive psychological terms which are often used covertly by writers to arouse the very emotion they purport to describe. Like its cousin 'sublime', 'horror' is not only a label, it is also a trigger. A standard example of the process can be seen in Milton's allegory from *Comus* of 'this drear wood',

> *The nodding horror of whose shady brows*
> Threats the forlorn and wand'ring passenger.

'Horror' here acts as a target, a kind of black hole for the emotions it arouses, as the reader casts around in vain for its referent. 'Horror', as Macbeth felt earlier and Poe said later, is 'objectless', and yet the reaction seems to imply a source, palpable in the sound and rhythm of this famous line which mimes a sinister movement just beyond our field of perception. This curious effect derives in part from the double function of the term 'horror' which purports to describe what we seem to perceive, and also suggests the emotion we are to have when confronted with this type of experience. The literal base of the word is physiological – it means 'the standing on end of the hair' (*cf.* 'horrid') – and it comes by transfer to denote the recoil, inner and outer, of the whole organism. Milton the allegorist has provided us with a play on 'nodding' and 'brows', so that, as forlorn passengers, we are sure to search the masses of dark, waving trees and think we see, momentarily, the staring grimace of evil. And in that moment of mental threat, Milton's theology asserts itself, for all passengers are 'forlorn and wand'ring' without God's providence as the plot of the masque shows. When I speak of the 'horror tradition', I do not mean that there is always present this kind of theological sting in the tail, but it is this complex of emotional effects I am thinking of when I use the term. In many cases, the writers I quote perform the service for me of unmasking the function of the term; but in other examples I have ventured to use the term myself, because it seems to fit the emotion, though the context may not be so explicit or obvious. Here I do not mean to imply a neutrality I do not feel: my use of the term indeed cannot escape its emotive reflex, and is not intended to.

The term 'Gothic' is awkward in a different way. Many will say it has too many ambiguous historical connotations to be useful, a cluster to which I have, if anything, added, especially in Chapter 4. Yet in literary contexts the term continues to be used with some confidence, largely because of the currency given to it in the postwar period by pulp magazines, the cinema and the novel, much of which is a form of recycling of traditional motifs. Its meaning has stabilised at something like 'lurid or melodramatic fantasy with a decorative metaphysical or graveyard feeling' perhaps. My use of the term is fairly consistent and simple, I think; though it bridges the aesthetic and the theological: 'Gothic' connotes a whole complex of popular theological ideas of a predominantly, if not exclusively, Protestant variety. There may be a case for noting here the complexity of the iconography at certain historical points, which may seem at first sight misleading to the reader: nineteenth-century visual and literary senses of the term tend to polarise into opposites. Much Victorian neo-Gothic architecture, for example, has strong Oxford Movement and Catholic associations, whereas I am particularly concerned in this book with the survival and transformations of a popular Reformation tradition, in which anxiety about 'superstition' of all kinds (Tractarianism in particular) is a regular component, and a mortuary sensibility to which decay itself is the ultimate 'Gothic' style, endlessly at hand, endlessly renewing itself. For such authors, civilisation is, to quote one of them, a 'gigantic memory of rotten stone', and the past is always returning into the present. It is in rendering the sometimes concealed presence of this vague yet powerful complex of traditional elements that I feel the term 'Gothic' is more useful.

It is a pleasure, finally, to record here some of the innumerable debts to friends and colleagues I have incurred during the writing of this book. Needless to say, my errors are in no way their responsibility. I am particularly grateful to Professor Nicholas Brooke for his patient encouragement, and for some invaluable editorial suggestions; to Lorna Sage for her confidence and tactful support; to James Grant for a delightful series of indoor and outdoor perambulations round the subject; and to my old friend Snoo Wilson for invigorating doses of Victorian high-spirits. These good people have helped me negotiate the rapids of obsession and make sense of what I wanted to say. My thanks also to those colleagues who have read portions of the manuscript, corrected errors of fact and made helpful and encouraging suggestions: Professors John Broadbent, Paul Kennedy and Robert Ashton; Dr Geoffrey Searle; Colin Clarke; Jon Cook; Tony Gash; Dr Thomas West; Dr Tim Marshall; Dr David Aers and Richard Webster.

Special thanks for their unfailing courtesy and help to the staffs of the British Library; the London Library; the Senate House Library of London University; Lambeth Palace Library; the University of East Anglia Library; in particular sadly to the late John Kimber, who far exceeded the call of duty. Lastly, my gratitude to Jeanetta Pollok, for leading this horse to the water and cajoling him, expertly, into drinking.

1
Dark House: Theology and the Picturesque

Christian iconography commonly represents the body metaphorically as the house or mansion of the soul. The satisfactions of this metaphor are profoundly ambiguous. In the rhetoric of popular Pauline 'consolation', for example, a tradition which stretches from the seventeenth century to the nineteenth, a loving emphasis is placed on the decay and darkness of the house. Here is an example from Charles Drelincourt's *Christian Man's Consolation against the Fears of Death*, written by a seventeenth-century French Huguenot, and reprinted throughout the eighteenth century. I quote from the 28th edition of 1811:

> Death labours to undermine this poor dwelling from the first moment that it is built, besieges it, and on all sides makes its approaches; in time it saps the foundation, it batters us with several diseases and unexpected accidents; every day it opens a breach, and pulls out of this building some stones.[1]

Of course, Drelincourt goes on to develop the necessity to be vigilant and repair these breaches with a sword in one hand and a trowel in the other, as did those who raised the walls of Jerusalem. But the main point of the allegory is to flatter the departing guest, the soul. The popular technique of rhetorical sermonising pursues the extended metaphor with zest through all its suggested correspondences:

> when we have packed up our bag and baggage we are ready to depart out of this wretched abode, where we endure all manner of calamities; for in this house defluxions fall down, vapours arise, the pillars and foundations tremble, the joints open, the windows are darkened, and the burning fevers, like violent fires, consume it.[2]

1

The innocent-looking 'bag and baggage' is a discreet reference to conscience (since we could not take a will with us). 'Defluxions', 'vapours' and 'joints' are all metaphors which perform a transaction between medicine and architecture, as part of the elaborate *figura*; but 'windows', the non-technical term, is felt to be metaphorical enough already.

The rhetoric of this tradition of mortuary consolation extends the metaphor of the house in several different directions at once. James Hervey's *Meditations Among the Tombs* (1745), for example, one of the most popular texts of the eighteenth century, rings many changes on the image. In the opening, he exhorts his reader to 'set, not their house only, but which is inexpressibly more needful, their souls in order'. But the tombs themselves provide the rhetorical occasion for theatrical embroidery of the theological metaphor of the house:

> I flatter myself, that the thoughts conceived among the tombs may be welcome to the serious and humane mind: because, as there are few, who have not consigned the remains of some dear relation, or honoured friend to those silent repositories; so there are none, but must be sensible that this is the 'house appointed for all living' and, that they themselves are shortly to remove into the same solemn mansions – and who would not turn aside, for a while, from the most favourite amusements, to view the place where his once loved companions lie? Who would not sometimes survey those apartments, where he himself is to take up an abode till time shall be no more?[3]

The theological content of the image ultimately derives from various biblical sources, the most important of which is perhaps St Paul's Corinthians.[4] The ghoulish domesticity of 'apartments' conveys the 'symbolic' interpretation of St Paul. But it also sugars it almost to the point of overt paradox. Our *spiritual* consolation depends here upon a metaphor of domestic ease that is material. The body rots away in the grave, and the soul is freed for spiritual resurrection. As with Drelincourt, the dwelling upon the decay and darkness of this 'house' carries a theological charge – it is assumed that such a stress will serve to remind the reader of the urgency of finding and maintaining a consolation against the inevitable horror of physical decay. The Methodist Hervey, perceiving that some of his dead are premature, produces the same elaborate *figura* as the Huguenot, Drelincourt:

These, I would hope, 'remembered their Creator in the days of their youth' – Before their strength became labour and sorrow:- Before that low ebb of languishing nature, when 'the keepers of the house tremble, and those that look out of the windows are darkened.'[5]

And in case they should miss the allegory, Hervey provides his less pious readers with a footnote:

(Eccles. xii 3,5)   I need not remind my reader, that by the former of these figurative expressions is signified the enervated state of the hands and arms; by the latter, the dimness of the eyes, or the total loss of sight.[6]

Sin, however, makes this state of mind and body into a dungeon, a permanent prison:

The wicked seem to lie here, like malefactors, in a deep and strong dungeon, reserved against the day of trial. 'Their departure was without peace.' Clouds of horror sat lowering upon their closing eyelids, most sadly foreboding the 'blackness of darkness forever.'[7]

The fantasy here of burial alive, the image of arrested decay and the rhetorical insistence of the darkening, decaying, isolated aspect of the house is meant to have the effect of guaranteeing the safe departure of its (virtuous) occupant, the reader.

Isaac Watts, another Methodist, is positively ecstatic about the destruction and ruin of this dark house, again mixing the metaphor for the body and the grave together with delighted abandon: the following extract comes from one of his youthful effusions:

WHEN I enter into a Church-Yard, I love to converse with the Dead. See how thick the Hillocks of Mortality arise all around me, each of them a Monument of Death, and the covering of a Son or Daughter of Adam. Perhaps a Thousand or Ten Thousand pieces of Human Nature, Heaps upon Heaps, lie buried in this Spot of Ground; 'tis the old Repository of the Inhabitants of the neighbouring Town, a collection of the Ruins of many Ages and the Rubbish of Twenty Generations.

I SAY within myself. What a Multitude of Human Beings, noble creatures, are here reduced to Dust! *God* has broken his own best workmanship to pieces, and demolished by Thousands the finest earthly Structures of his own building. Death has entered in.[8]

The bodies of the dead, in this hyperbole, become a vista of ruined buildings. But the theological point of all this rhetorical bravura is contained in the phrase 'earthly Structures' where the pious young reader is meant to locate the consolation of the metaphor: earthly ruins imply their opposite, heavenly mansions.

But the poet Cowper, who was converted to Evangelical Protestantism, reveals how close the *induced* horror of the image, and the real horror of perpetual damnation can be:

> Man disavows and Deity disowns me,
> Hell might afford my miseries a shelter;
> Therefore, Hell keeps her ever-hungry mouths all
> Bolted against me
>
> Hard lot! encompassed with a thousand dangers;
> Weary, faint, trembling with a thousand terrors;
> I'm called, if vanquished! to receive a sentence
> Worse than Abiram's.
>
> Him the vindications of angry Justice
> Sent quick and howling to the centre headlong;
> I, fed with judgement, in a fleshly tomb, am
> Buried above ground.[9]

The whole of this popular rhetorical tradition courts this terrifying image as a part of its motivation; to demonstrate the necessity of imagining something further than the 'fleshly tomb'. For Cowper, the doctrinal use of the image has become a metaphor for a consciousness imprisoned in its own fear; but its theological source is still visible.

A rich man's flowering lawns traditionally serve the opposite purpose from these images, of symbolising, that is, the harmony between soul and body which denotes economic and spiritual security. The prosperous house, in established Christianity, is a common symbol of the social macrocosm. The quotations I have been using, however, all come from dissenting Christian sources in the eighteenth century. Scholars have established that the mortuary tradition which flourished in the eighteenth century, and whose popular theological texts were reprinted throughout the nineteenth century, was the product of the 'bourgeoisification' of dissenting Calvinism, rather than of established Protestant tradition. Sentimental Calvinism acts as an important social and theological determinant of the centrifugal, subjectivist tendency in Romantic aesthetics in the 'pre-Romantic' period.[10] Graveyard poetry, written largely by regular divines such as Young, is, as Eleanor Sickels pointed out in *The Gloomy Egoist*, actually as doctrinal as it is introspectionist: it is part of an individualist reaction against the tendencies of Deism, which led such people into a precarious alliance with Methodism. This theological movement blends, through the vehicle of growing antiquarianism, with the eighteenth-century interest in the religion of the past and the materials of the 'Gothic' romance.

And here was the whole world of the bygone Age of Faith being opened up by scholars and antiquaries; a world in which religious terror was by no means confined to a far-distant *dies irae*, but was a very present reality, compounded of strange asceticisms and secret ecclesiastical lusts, of ghost-lore, necromancy, and contracts with the devil. This world arose on the imagination, furthermore, against a background of those ruined castles and abbeys, those twilight churchyards and midnight charnels, already connected in life and in literature with religious musing and half-superstitious fears. What wonder that religious terror, dying out as a living, subjective force in most breasts, should flame anew in the vicarious terrorism of the 'Gothic' romance.[11]

This central image of the dark house, in other words, is not just a vague 'medievalising'; it carries, as I have been suggesting, a contemporary social and theological 'charge' for the audience.

Thus Hervey's *memento mori* rhetoric sets up a counterpoint between the daylight, secure, orderly 'house', and its counterpart, the dark, potentially imprisoning, guarantee of the spiritual. He gloats rhetorically over the tombs of the rich:

Did he not lay schemes for enlarging his fortune, and aggrandizing his family? Did he not purpose to join field to field? and add house to house, till his possessions were almost as vast as his desires?[12]

The eighteenth-century *cumulard* landlord, building up his estate by enclosure, is precisely the target of this biblical contrast between the man who builds on rock and the man who builds on sand. A firm foundation comes through acceptance of material insecurity in this symbolic equation between house and body. The orthodox consolation of a spiritual victory is induced through fear, anxiety and insecurity about the material basis of this 'fortress of the identity'. Property in this image, however momentarily, is associated with anxiety and uncertainty; this traditional, but still widely current image of the dark house stresses the tenancy, not the ownership, of the 'soul's dark cottage'.

The horror tradition draws strongly upon the metaphor of the isolated house. It is worth looking again at Henry Tilney's famous 'anti-Gothic' speech to Catherine Morland in *Northanger Abbey* in this context, because it establishes the counterpoint of the *heimlich*. Catherine's suspicions about life at the Abbey, whose historical associations are firmly suppressed, are dispelled by an appeal, not to domestic and moral values, but to the presence of the whole social system in microcosm:

'If I understand you rightly, you had formed a surmise of such horror as I have hardly words to – Dear Miss Morland, consider the dreadful nature of the suspicions you have entertained. What have you been judging from? Remember the country and the age in which we live. Remember that we are English, and that we are Christians. Consult your own understanding, your own sense of the probable, your own observation of what is passing around you – Does our education prepare us for such atrocities? Do our laws connive at them? Could they be perpetuated without being known, in a country like this, where social and literary intercourse is on such a footing; where every man is surrounded by a neighbourhood of voluntary spies and where roads and newspapers lay everything open? Dearest Miss Morland, what ideas have you been admitting?'

They had reached the end of the gallery; and with tears of shame she ran off to her own room.[13]

It takes Henry just the length of the gallery – potentially 'Gothic', it shrinks into a stage prop as he talks – to set everything back in proportion. Of course, Jane Austen is guying Henry's pomposity, as well as Catherine's adolescent romanticism, but it is significant that he should appeal to a whole middle ground of cultural institutions which mediate between the private and the public aspects of their lives. The Christianity which he refers to is obviously that of the established Church, comfortable and eminently socialised. And it is supported by a nexus of other social connexions: Education, the Law, the Newspapers, the roads and even, comically, the Neighbours. Northanger Abbey is a virtual pantechnicon, its walls open to the gaze of a whole society.

In the horror novel, the rhetorical strategies of the picturesque have the effect of removing the presence of all these mediating factors. The domestic space, in isolation, is neither comforting nor familiar; on the analogy of the visual picturesque, it has no scale, except indefiniteness, and yet description carries the same subdued but insistent humanising equation as the theological metaphor. Ann Radcliffe, for example, in *The Mysteries of Udolpho* employs this picturesque technique to describe Emily's first sight of the castle. The narrative halts, and we have a set piece, a moment in which, ostensibly, the human scale has vanished altogether:

'There,' said Montoni, speaking for the first time in several hours, 'is Udolpho.'

Emily gazed with melancholy awe upon the castle, which she understood to be Montoni's; for, though it was now lighted up by the setting sun, the Gothic greatness of its features, and its mouldering walls of dark grey stone, rendered it a gloomy and sublime object. As she gazed, the light died away on its walls, leaving a melancholy purple tint, which spread deeper and deeper as the thin vapour crept up the mountain, while the battlements above were still tipped with splendour. From these, too, the rays soon faded, and the whole edifice was invested with the solemn duskiness of evening. Silent, lonely and sublime, it seemed to stand the sovereign of the scene, and to frown defiance on all who dared invade its solitary reign.[14]

Emily and Montoni act as picturesque mediators, small figures seen in the bottom of the picture. The writer deliberately makes them out of scale, like a painter, so that the reader is overcome by the impression of sublime grandeur (see Plates 1 and 2). But there is a subdued human analogy too. Emily's awe and her attraction to her abductor make the castle into the very image of what she feels its owner to be: 'Silent', 'lonely' and 'frowning defiance'.

The opening of Maturin's *Melmoth the Wanderer* provides us with what has become the paradigm of the horror-plot: the journey from the capital (in this case, Dublin) to the provinces. John Melmoth, a student, is summoned by his dying uncle to his remote house in Wicklow. After the uncle has died, John is left alone in the darkening house. Maturin halts the narrative, while a servant is dispatched to get some candles:

> As Melmoth leaned against the window, whose dismantled frame, and pieced and shattered panes, shook with every gust of wind, his eye encountered nothing but that most cheerless of all prospects, a miser's garden – walls broken down, grass-grown walks whose grass was not even green, dwarfish, doddered, leafless trees, and a luxurious crop of nettles and weeds rearing their unlovely heads where there had once been flowers, all waving and bending in capricious and unsightly forms, as the wind sighed over them. It was the verdure of the church-yard, the garden of death. He turned for relief to the room, but no relief was there – the wainscotting dark with dirt, and in many places cracked and starting from the walls, – the rusty grate, so long unconscious of a fire, that nothing but a sullen smoke could be coaxed to issue from between its dingy bars, – the crazy chairs, their torn bottoms of rush drooping inwards, and the great leathern seat displaying the stuffing round its worn edges, while the nails, though they kept their places, had failed to keep the covering they once fastened, – the chimney-piece, which, tarnished more by time than by smoke, displayed for its garniture half a pair of snuffers, a tattered almanack of 1750, a time-keeper dumb for want of repair, and a rusty fowling-piece without a lock.[15]

The narrative gives way to motif and allegory. The scale of the garden of death is not a human one: nature has reclaimed it from human art. The picturesque analogy, the wandering 'eye', takes us to the house, and this effect is intensified by the use of a human projection in local metaphors: the grate is 'unconscious of a fire', the nails of the seat 'kept their places'; the timekeeper is 'dumb'. The impression of desolate human absence is conveyed by the projection of the human into the inanimate.

Emily Brontë's domestic picturesque in *Wuthering Heights* uses the same technique of removing the human scale, and then reimporting it via allegorised detail. The house is a bleak fortress, 'the narrow windows . . . deeply set in the wall and the corners defended with large jutting stones'. Lockwood's description of what he finds inside confounds his social expectations; and, quite rapidly, his sense of physical orientation:

> One step brought us into the family sitting-room, without any introductory lobby, or passage: they call it here 'the house' pre-eminently. It includes kitchen, and parlour, generally, but I believe at Wuthering Heights the kitchen is forced to retreat altogether into another quarter, at least I distinguished a chatter of tongues, and a clatter of culinary utensils, deep within; and I observed no signs of roasting, boiling, or baking, about the huge fireplace; nor any glint of copper saucepans and tin cullenders on its walls. One end, indeed, reflected splendidly both light and heat, from ranks of immense pewter dishes, interspersed with silver jugs and tankards, towering row after row, in a vast oak dresser, to the very roof. The latter had never been underdrawn, its entire anatomy laid bare to an enquiring eye, except where a frame of wood laden with oatcakes, and clusters of legs of beef, mutton, and ham, concealed it. Above the chimney were sundry villainous old guns, and a couple of horse-pistols, and, by way of ornament, three gaudily-painted cannisters disposed along its ledge. The floor was of smooth, white stone: the chairs, high-backed, primitive structures, painted green: one or two heavy black ones lurking in the shade. In an arch, under the dresser, reposed a huge, liver-coloured bitch pointer surrounded by a swarm of squealing puppies; and other dogs haunted other recesses.[16]

This is more like the nave of a Gothic Cathedral than a parlour. The fireplace is 'huge'; the ranks of dishes are 'immense' and 'towering'; the dresser is 'vast'. The rhetoric imitates the wandering of the eye, until we are lost in shadows and recesses. At the same time, the metaphor of the body is present in 'the anatomy' of the roof. And a spiritual menace is suggested in the dogs that 'haunt' other recesses.

Wuthering Heights is explicitly cast as hell in this novel, as the other well-lit, socialised house across the moor, Thrushcross Grange, is 'heaven' for the young Cathy and Heathcliff. Later, Nellie refers to Heathcliff's eyes in true mortuary style as 'the clouded windows of hell'. In his final desperation, Heathcliff gives orders for the side of his coffin to be let down, so that his dust may mingle with Cathy's. The famous final sentence toys, deliciously, with the idea of a profane resurrection:

> I lingered round them [the three headstones] under that benign sky; watched the moths fluttering among the heath and harebells; listened to the soft wind breathing through the grass; and wondered how anyone could ever imagine unquiet slumbers, for the sleepers in that quiet earth.[17]

This cadence is notoriously ambigious for readers; it sums up the poise, in the fluctuations of the novel's narrative, between its realism and its 'Gothic'. It is a very good example of Freud's theory of negation, summing up in its own structure the counterpoint between *heimlich* and *unheimlich*. And in this counterpoint, whether we read it as suppressed, or profanely affirmed, the substratum of doctrine becomes momentarily visible.

The visual equivalent of Emily Brontë's verbal ambiguity is contained in Bowler's bravely executed Pre-Raphaelite painting, 'The Doubt: Can These Dry Bones Live?' (1854) (Plate 3). Here the pensive widow leans over her husband's headstone in full autumn sunlight and stares down into his open grave, which reveals his skull and 'dry bones'. The headstone reads 'Sacred to the Memory of JOHN FAITHFUL', while a neighbouring slab parades as its inscription the single word of Christ: RESURGAM, 'I shall Arise'. On this slab lie the two halves of a burst horse-chestnut husk, symbolic of the body – what the seventeenth-century Anglican George Herbert describes as 'the shells of fledge souls left behind'. Amongst the graves, behind the doubtful widow and out of her sight, flutter the 'fledge souls' themselves in the form of two cabbage-white butterflies (a similar suggestion is perhaps present in Emily Brontë's 'moths') – the twin psyches of the Victorian domestic dream.

The obvious reading of this picture is that it represents the crisis in orthodox faith produced by the impact of Darwinism: the subtitle 'Can These Dry Bones Live?' with its allusion to Ezekiel, suggests the question: 'Is there a Resurrection *at all*?' and expects the answer 'No'. But there is more in the picture's symbolic details than this. The allegory and the narrative seem to work against each other: the hints to the viewer, which the young widow doesn't recognise, suggest perhaps that she is too literal in her expectations of the Resurrection; that Nature itself would ironically give testimony to the truth of the existence of the soul and the spiritual Resurrection, if she could only read the signs. In this sense, 'The Doubt' is, for the viewer, an assertion of Faith. To this extent, the allegorical level is intimately concerned with doctrine: it is about the *nature* of the Resurrection, rather than its denial.

These last three examples are all concerned, in one way or another, with anxieties about imprisonment, suffocation and burial alive; they inject a theological undertone into their painterly transformations of domestic environment, implictly, via metaphors of the body. Poe's 'Fall of the House of Usher', on the other hand, is a piece of nineteenth-century Gothic which draws explicitly upon an earlier tradition of mortuary writing. The house in question is an aristocratic lineage which is dying out. As the narrator explains, it is a socialised house, an estate, which has long begun to decay and turn in upon itself:

> It was this deficiency, I considered, while running over in thought the perfect keeping if the character of the premises with the accredited character of the people, and while speculating upon the possible influence which the one, in the long lapse of centuries, might have exercised upon the other – it was this deficiency, perhaps, of collateral issue, and the consequent undeviating transmission from sire to son, of the patrimony with the name, which had, at length, so identified the two as to merge the original title of the estate in the quaint and equivocal appellation of the 'House of Usher' – an appellation which seemed to include, in the minds of the peasantry who used it, both the family and the family mansion.[18]

The famous 'vacant and eye-like windows' mirrored in the tarn in the story's opening are the presence, or rather spiritual absence, of Roderick Usher himself, whose senses have become so refined that they are indistinguishable from his environment. Poe consciously modulates Christian doctrine into an attack on dualism. The story is built on a carefully controlled set of simultaneous tautologies and paradoxes around this theme. Roderick is so sensitive, his senses are so atrophied, that is to say, that he can perceive through the walls of his 'house'. His paintings are either of the most abstract images, or ironically pictures of an empty grave, done from the inside. Roderick's poem, 'The Haunted Palace' is an allegory, in the Spenserian mode, of his own condition of living death. His attempt to bury his sister, which results in a violent resurrection, is an attempt to impregnate the house, and this unspoken play on 'womb' and 'tomb' has given rise to a great deal of orthodox Freudian commentary. Poe's use of the picturesque technique is integrated into this theme.

> The room in which I found myself was very large and lofty. The windows were long, narrow, and pointed, and at so vast a distance from the black oaken floor as to be altogether inaccessible from within. Feeble gleams of encrimsoned light made their way through the trellised panes, and served to render sufficiently distinct the more prominent objects around; the eye, however, struggled in vain to reach the remoter angles of the chamber, or the recesses of the vaulted and fretted ceiling.[19]

This is the narrator talking, but he reflects in his language the same oscillation as Roderick between mind and body: the movement of the mind to expand – for the reader, perceptually to encompass 'remoteness' – is checked by the limits of the body: this picturesque 'eye' is not 'enquiring' but, horrifyingly, 'struggling'.

Poe frequently uses the domestic picturesque for symbolic purposes which have an inherently theological basis. In 'William Wilson', for example, the narrator Wilson's opening picture of the house ('a large, rambling, Elizabethan house, in a misty-looking village of England') looks like an inert stage set which merely gives 'atmosphere' to the tale. But as soon as he goes into detail, the effect becomes sharply symbolic:

> But the house! – how quaint an old building was this! – to me how veritably a place of enchantment! There was really no end to its windings – to its incomprehensible subdivisions. It was difficult, at any given time, to say with certainty upon which of its two stories one happened to be. From each room to every other there were sure to be found three or four steps either in ascent or descent. Then the lateral branches were innumerable – inconceivable – and so returning in upon themselves, that our most exact ideas in regard to the whole mansion were not very far different from those with which we pondered upon infinity.[20]

Rapidly, the human scale and point of view is disorientated and apparently removed: this is like a cross between Piranesi and a

Borges library. The heartiness of tone is probably drawn from the memoirs of early nineteenth-century travellers, the kind of thing of which Rose Macaulay made a survey in *The Pleasure of Ruins*. Here the fantasy is of infinity, of being out of the body, a sublime loss of corporeal identity. But there is a curious bathos in the mention of only 'two' stories. This is a deliberate irony inserted by Poe, for this is a doppelgänger story: Wilson, the narrator, believes himself to be the double of another, and his whole mental apparatus – projected here as innocent-looking background – is dominated by the binary. Again, the picturesque technique removes the human scale to 'infinity', only to have it reasserted again in 'two'.

Wilson's story is one of suppressed guilt, and this is a common extension of the theological theme hidden, or allegorised, in domestic picturesque. A good example of this association is the story by Charles Collins, still occasionally anthologised today in the omnibuses, called 'The Compensation House', which was originally one of a sequence commissioned by Dickens for *All the Year Round*. Dickens had purposely briefed his authors to include references to the railway in their stories, and Collin's opening hides the allegory of the dark house in a series of rambling details of a legal variety:

'There's not a looking glass in all the house, sir. It's some peculiar fancy of my master's. There isn't one in any single room in the house.'

It was a dark and gloomy-looking building, and had been purchased by this Company for an enlargement of their Goods Station. The value of the house had been referred to what was popularly called 'a compensation jury', and the house was called, in consequence, the Compensation House. It had become the Company's property; but its tenant still remained in possession pending the commencement of active building operations.[21]

The details are deliberately designed to throw the reader off the scent. 'Compensation' in this story is not literal, but theological and spiritual, and the left-over tenant, so frequently a theme in the horror tradition, lives on in his dark, mausoleum-like house:

It was square, cold, grey-looking, built of rough-hewn stone, and roofed with thin slabs of the same material. Its windows were few in number, and very small for the size of the building. In the great blank, grey broadside, there were only four windows. The entrance door was in the middle of the house; there was a window on either side of it, and there were two more in the single story above. The blinds were all closely drawn, and when the door was shut, the dreary building gave no sign of life or occupation.[22]

The tenant, Oswald Strange, has murdered his wife's lover. For ever afterwards, when Strange looks in a mirror, he sees reflected there, not his own face, but the face of his wife's lover; Strange had stolen up while the man had been shaving in a mirror, and cut his throat from behind. Literally wasting away for want of a self, he comes to the Compensation House; and it is here, on his deathbed, that he is finally able to see himself again. The picturesque evocation serves the theological metaphor here in a strictly orthodox fashion: the spiritual compensation of the tenant has been paid in his dark fear and self-loathing, and at last he can die with integrity of soul and body (lacking in the opening description of this dark house), estranged no longer, knowing he can be judged.

Dickens himself, as might be expected, is a good deal more subtle and practised in this kind of allegory. Collins's story is quite close to the doppelgänger, with its central convention of the mirror. Dickens's *Edwin Drood* is an explicit doppelgänger story, which explores this theme of guilt and the suppressed conscience in its central figure, John Jasper, the saintly organist, whose staring eyes and dark countenance betray the presence of another self. Dickens uses the environment and the architectural metaphor persistently throughout the novel to symbolise the idea of self-repression and split personality. The setting is Anglican; the gatehouse to the Cathedral, in which Jasper lives, is alive with subdued human correspondence. Again it is a form of picturesque which conveys the allegory to the reader:

They all three look towards an old stone gatehouse crossing the Close, with an arched thoroughfare passing beneath it. Through its latticed window a fire shines out upon the fast darkening scene, involving in shadow the pendent masses of ivy and creeper covering the building's front. As the deep Cathedral bell strikes the hour, a ripple of wind goes through these at their distance, like a ripple of the solemn sound that hums through tomb and tower, broken niche and defaced statue, in the pile close at hand.
    'Is Mr Jasper's nephew with him?' the Dean asks.
    'No, sir,' replies the Verger, 'but expected. There's his own

solitary shadow betwixt his two windows – the one looking this way, and the one looking down into the High Street – drawing his own curtains now.'[23]

As his two windows indicate, Jasper is a split personality, a Mr Facing-Both-Ways. Cloisterham is a repressive environment, living literally and parasitically on the remains of an older Catholic religious community. The picturesque ruins of 'broken niche and defaced statue' are symbolic of the smugness of Anglican tradition; at the same time, they are a subdued projection of the central figure of Jasper himself, whose 'niche' as organist is merely the conscious, suppressed part of his demonic personality. The environment is alive with profane resurrection, as the children in the alleyways of Cloisterham make mudpies out of the remains of Abbots and Friars. And the theological metaphor is strong again, in the following joky description of The Nun's House in the centre of Cloisterham, now rendered innocent of its historical associations by one Miss Twinkleton. The airy disclaimer taps a contemporary theological unease:

> Whether the nuns of yore, being of a submissive rather than a stiff-necked generation, habitually bent their contemplative heads to avoid collision with the beams in the many low ceilings of the many chambers of their House; whether they sat in its long low windows telling their beads for their mortification, instead of making necklaces of them for their adornment; whether they were ever walled up alive in odd angles and jutting gables of the building for having some ineradicable leaven of busy Mother Nature in them which has kept the fermenting world alive ever since; these may be matters to its haunting ghosts (if any) but constitute no item in Miss Twinkleton's half-yearly accounts.[24]

Miss Twinkleton, in siting her 'Academy' in this rented building, is actually repeating the historical associations of the environment: she is simply walling up her 'Young Ladies' for money. But the comic figure of the repressed Miss Twinkleton herself is a parody of the Gothic villian Jasper's schizoid personality, for she too is said to have 'two distinct and separate phases of being'. The satire acts in two directions at once: towards the mechanism of the Puritan conscience, and towards the dangers of a comfortable socialised religion, which seems to be losing its strength by 1870 in the context of the contemporary political activity from Rome and the Oxford Movement. The 'haunting ghosts' are in the audience here, and in the idea of a short-sighted materialism which forgets that the past is always returning into the present.

Wilkie Collins's tone on this question is very similar to Dickens. It represents the unease of a secularised religion, joking at the expense of an audience to whom orthodox doctrine was still of vital political importance. Collins's novels are full of dark houses like Blackwater Park, for example, in *The Woman in White*, a dark, Elizabethan mansion, contrasted with Limmeridge House, the light and socialised house of Henry Fairlie. Collins, in his anti-Jesuit novel, *The Black Robe*, shows to what lengths this kind of disclaimer can go. Like Dickens, he provides his reader with an elaborate piece of ostensible *anti-picturesque*, which disclaims all sensational or 'Gothic' description. This is 'The Retreat', an Oxford Movement seminary in North London:

> But the convert privileged to pass the gates left Protestant England outside, and found himself, as it were, in a new country. Inside The Retreat, the paternal care of the Church took possession of him; surrounded him with monastic simplicity in his neat little bedroom; and dazzled him with devotional splendour when his religious duties called him into the chapel. The perfect taste – so seldom found in the modern arrangement and decoration of convents and churches in southern countries – showed itself here, pressed into the service of religion, in every part of the house. The severest discipline had no sordid and hideous side to it in The Retreat. . . . A faint perfume of incense was perceptible in the corridors. The soothing and mysterious silence of the place was intensified rather than disturbed by soft footsteps, and gentle opening and closing of doors. Animal life was not even represented by a cat in the kitchen. And yet, pervaded by some inscrutable influence, the house was not dull. Heretics, with lively imaginations, might have not inappropriately likened it to an enchanted castle. In one word, the Catholic system here showed to perfection its masterly knowledge of the weakness of human nature, and its inexhaustible dexterity in adapting the means to the end.[25]

Is this *heimlich* or *unheimlich*? The wordly tone disclaims the theological menace of the picturesque ('Heretics with lively imaginations'), and yet the overriding impression is of a cross between an embassy and a tomb. This is a dark house in disguise, as the last theological crack about Jesuit equivocation (i.e. 'inexhaustible dexterity in adapting the means to the end') makes clear. The ancient threat is brought up to date.

Collins's allegory turns the traditional use of the picturesque inside out: the house reflects the external politics of its occupants, not their bodies. But there is a hint in the (disclaimed) 'enchantment' that the occupants are hypnotised by silence, and the gentle opening and closing of doors is a discreet rhythm which paralyses their judgement and their consciences. In Stevenson's *Dr Jekyll and Mr Hyde*, we have another version of urban picturesque which serves to indict a social community as much as it projects the theological allegory:

> Two doors from the corner, on the left hand going east, the line was broken by the entry of a court; and just at that point, a certain sinister block of building thrust forward its gable on the street. It was two stories high; showed no window, nothing but a door on the lower storey and a blind forehead of discoloured wall on the upper; and bore in every feature, the marks of prolonged and sordid negligence. The door, which was equipped with neither bell nor knocker, was blistered and distained. Tramps slouched into the recess and struck matches on the panels; children kept shop up on the steps; the schoolboy had tried his knife on the mouldings; and for close on a generation, no one had appeared to drive away these random visitors or to repair their ravages.[26]

The door is simultaneously humanised (the lack of windows is a lack of eyes in a 'blind forehead of discoloured wall') and converted into a dead natural object. It is a perfect emblem of the ravaged body, the dead site of the world's insults: yet sinister and aggressive, as if this dross might resurrect itself in a frightening, attenuated form of life. This is the door by which Hyde (his name is the opposite of 'seek') secretly comes and goes. The counterpoint of this, the *heimlich* house in the square nearby, belongs to Henry Jekyll:

> Round the corner from the by-street, there was a square of ancient, handsome houses, now for the most part decayed from their high estate and let in flats and chambers to all sorts and conditions of men; map-engravers, architects, shady lawyers,

and the agents of obscure enterprises. One house, however, second from the corner, was still occupied entire; and at the door of this, which wore a great air of wealth and comfort, though it was now plunged in darkness except for the fanlight, Mr Utterson stopped and knocked.[27]

In fact, this is the 'front' of the other picture; and it is hinted that the whole area is morally shady: the house is 'plunged in darkness', though inside it is a fantasy of country-house security. The narrative proceeds on the assumption that these two buildings, the span of an enormous gap, are unconnected. But this is the social fiction of the story's plot, allegorised in its environment; the one door and the other are connected together. Like Dickens's picture of Jasper in the gatehouse, the house symbolises the state of its owner. The hints above suggest a connection between the 'good' ('repressed') front of Jekyll, and his sinister (unrepressed) Hyde, though Stevenson, like his predecessors, hides the allegory in the narrative. In his first transformation, Hyde/Jekyll steals across the courtyard between the two buildings, feeling like 'a stranger in my own house'.

What these examples suggest, I think, is that what we loosely think of as a 'medieval' allegory survives to a large extent in the narrative form of nineteenth-century Gothic fantasy. But the point is not mindlessly to recall the past: quite the opposite, the presence of this hidden, allegorical structure taps a contemporary ability in the audience to read the signs of its presence. That ability derives from a deeply sown, deeply contested set of theological expectations in nineteenth-century culture, which exist for both reader and writer alike. The allegory may have internal psychological dimensions, or it may have a more externalised social dimension. It is often to be found in an intersection between the past and the present, in which apparently harmless traditional threats to Protestant belief are reactivated as a form of contemporary political menace.

Similar conjunctions between picturesque set piece and theological allegory are present in twentieth-century visual and verbal contexts, too. For some examples of striking visual uses of the motif, see Plates 4, 5 and 6. In Plate 4, the famous still from Franz Murnau's *Nosferatu*, the picturesque analogy between the motif of the 'vacant eye-like windows' and the emergent figure of Max Shreck as Count

Dracula hints strongly at an imprisonment in the dark house of the tomb/body. In Plate 5, an illustration by the artist Stephen Lawrence for a horror story in the pulp magazine *Famous Fantastic Mysteries* (1946), the exaggerated cross-section of thick roots suggests unmistakably to the viewer the claustrophobia of burial-alive and the failure of true (spiritual) resurrection. And in Plate 6, from *Psycho* (1960), Alfred Hitchcock exploits the traditional topographical tension between the figure of Norman Bates and the looming mass of his house. The plot of the film is based on the resurrection motif: Bates impersonates his dead mother, keeping her alive, while her skeleton sits in a chair down in the cellar of the house. The two markedly different styles of the film – decorative Gothic and naturalistic thriller – correspond to the different levels of explanation of its central fable. Hitchcock was brought up as a Catholic in the East End of London, and his films are steeped in theological unease. Reportedly devout all his life, his attitudes towards Catholicism are complex. If the following anecdote is to be believed, his views of the Church are pervaded by an anti-clericalism worthy of dissenting Protestantism:

> On one occasion in Switzerland recently he surprised his companion in the car by suddenly saying, 'That is the most frightening sight I have ever seen, and pointing to a little boy walking past with a priest who had his hand on his shoulder and was talking very seriously to him. Hitch leaned out of the car and called, 'Run, little boy, run for your life.'[28]

Mervyn Peake, on the other hand, absorbed his Protestantism during a childhood spent on a Chinese Missionary Station where his father was a surgeon. His *Titus Groan*, for example, shows its theological preoccupation from its opening sentences. The novel is a fantasy about a labyrinthine building, whose tower 'patched evenly with black ivy, arose like a mutilated finger from among the fists of knuckled masonry and pointed blasphemously at heaven'. The prose burgeons into set pieces at every point, as the novel circles round the problem of consciousness-in-the-body. The allegory is presented in the barest possible form:

> Around the lakeside was the castle's breath. Only the old stone lung remained. Not a footfall. Not a voice. Only wood and stone,

and doorway, bannister, corridor and alcove, room after room, hall after hall, province after province.

It was as though, at any moment some inanimate Thing must surely move; a door open upon its own, or a clock start whirling its hands: the stillness was too vast and charged to be content to remain in this titanic atrophy – the tension must surely find a vent – and burst suddenly, violently, like a reservoir of water from a smashed dam – and the shields fall from their rusty hooks, the mirrors crack, the boards lift and open and the very castle tremble, shake its walls like wings; yawn, split and crumble with a roar.

But nothing had happened. Each hall a mouth that gaped and could not close. The stone jaws prised and aching. The doors like eye-teeth missing from the bone! There was no sound and nothing human had happened.[29]

After such intense humanising of the environment, the last phrase strikes the reader as paradoxical. Yet it charts perfectly the idea of a failed resurrection, the restless manoeuvres of consciousness buried alive inside a vast, decaying body. The whole of Peake's narrative is subordinated to this form of allegory: it is a form of theological picturesque.

David Storey's powerful piece of Gothic, *Radcliffe*, transforms the insolubility of a relationship between self-conscious intellect and the life of the body into a historical fantasy. Set in a bleak Pennine valley, much of the action centres round a large, decaying mansion called 'The Place'. The house is the seat of the Radcliffe dynasties, an ancient family whose origins include both Puritan and Catholic sides of the split in the Civil War. The novel is set in the present, projecting this social and political fissure into the axis of the psychological. John Radcliffe, the last of the line, has returned to the house to become its caretaker. Dispossessed, he is a stranger in his own house. Storey's evocation of his memories of this house is another perfect piece of picturesque:

He still retained his childhood memory of The Place seen through a long avenue of elms, a late autumn sunlight reflected in its numerous windows, something dark and even frightening against a pale and luminous sky. There had been a vast moorland crowded with sheep and, beyond, a park across which were scattered great trees. The Place had seemed like an animal crouched at the summit of the hill. Scarcely that: something he could not describe. There was the black stonework, the smell of the damp stone, and the walls that had seemed so tall they must fall down. And somewhere, whether a statue or a carved relief, a large and fragmentary stone figure. It was as if he had sensed his father's own disappointment with such a deserted monument, as if there were scmething obscene in its desolation. As he sat in the train and tried to recollect this impression, he realised that in all his thinking about The Place the building had never developed for him beyond an abstraction: one which fitted exactly, however, into some central vortex of his mind.[30]

What is grafted skilfully into this allegory is the idea that a true relationship between mind and body once existed, before the historical split. The 'large and fragmentary stone figure' is a hint of the Ur-Radcliffe. John himself is destined to be a precursor only, but when his son Leonard is born, the 'fault' on which 'The Place' is built shows itself: the house is rocked by three huge seismic blows. Leonard cannot distinguish between this dark house and himself:

His habitation of The Place was like his habitation of his own brain, its cellular structure disposed around him as the endless ramifications of his thoughts. The identity of the building itself, its size and the scale of its architecture, its sense of duration, seemed to be that exact image he now possessed of his own mind. As he took on the identity of The Place, and became the building in the sense that all his feelings were invested in it, the aristocratic form of its dark shape became that essence which occupied every cell and atom of his brain.[31]

This corresponds to Poe's obsession in Usher with an aristocratic lineage, passed over by history; but Storey also links his motif on the other side of this 'fissure' to the history of radical Puritanism. It is Leonard's destiny to release, with shattering, apocalyptic force, the dream imprisoned in the stone. By his violent liaison with the working class giant Tolson, he stirs into life the *disjecta membra* of the Radcliffe superman, the Puritan Aristocrat, the impossible man who can, as Marvell said of Cromwell, both 'act and know'.

Storey's recall of the Gothic tradition is an interesting blend of robust naturalism and painterly surrealism. Angela Carter's *Heroes and Villains* appropriates the picturesque set piece for the purpose of deliberate anachronism. The language is a self-conscious pastiche of the nineteenth-century novel:

> This house was a gigantic memory of rotten stone, a compilation of innumerable forgotten styles now given some green unity by the devouring web of creeper, fur of moss and fungoid growth of rot. Wholly abandoned to decay, baroque stonework of the late Jacobean period, Gothic turrets murmurous with birds and pathetic elegance of Palladian pillared façades weathered indiscriminately together towards irreducible rubble. The forest perched upon the tumbled roofs in the shapes of yellow and purple weeds rooted in the gapped tiles, besides a few small trees and bushes. The windows gaped or sprouted internal foliage, as if the forest were as well already camped inside, there gathering strength for a green eruption which would one day burst the walls sky high back to nature.[32]

Like The Place, this picture symbolises a relationship between the present and the past, but Angela Carter's novel is set in the future, and her heroine, Marianne, the daughter of a professor of history has only seen photographs and engravings of these styles of architecture. There is a hint, in the final lines, of the natural bursting out of this rotting 'memory' of stone, of a violent resurrection.

The vitality of the house symbol here is inseparable from the idea of a violation of civilised life. Angela Carter is writing 'purer' Gothic than Emily Brontë in the above passage. The reader knows exactly where he is when he reads the dialogue between Marianne and her father, in which he asks her the meaning of the word 'cities', and she hazards a post-apocalyptic guess: 'Ruins?': in the landscape of nineteenth-century picturesque.

The function of this picturesque is the creative but disorientating use of anachronism. Living in a huge stone memory, are we pre- or post-civilisation? Marianne has to live in the house with the Barbarians, after her life with her father is destroyed. At the breakfast table she finds a child who is wearing a tunic of long-haired fur that makes her look vaguely like an ancient Briton. Marianne wonders 'if her clothing were proof of the speed at which the Barbarians were sinking backwards or evidence of their adaptation to new conditions'. The primal explosion – in the case of Marianne, a rape – which hovers in these ruins of the future, is sublimated, distanced, exoticised in a self-consciously anachronistic prose.

Another striking, more obviously theological, use of the picturesque in a recent novel is J. G. Farrell's *Troubles* (1970). The tone of this novel is persistently comic, but Farrell too appropriates the 'Gothic' mode for political and psychological anachronism. The novel is set in Ireland in 1919, when Major Brendan Archer returns from service at the front to claim his fiancée, Angela Spencer. The plot, however, is relatively perfunctory: the main character of the book is the gigantic, three-hundred-roomed Majestic Hotel at Kilnalough, in which Angela lies dying of leukaemia. The move away from the metropolis is a standard change of 'scale', and Farrell exploits all the traditional humanising of the picturesque as the reader catches his first glimpse of this building over the Major's shoulder:

> Not far away the two massive, weatherworn gateposts of the Majestic rose out of the impenetrable foliage that lined the sea side of the road. As they passed between them, (the gates themselves had vanished, leaving only the skeletons of the enormous iron hinges that had once held them) the Major took a closer look; each one was surmounted by a great stone ball on which a rain-polished stone crown was perched slightly askew, lending the gateposts a drunken, ridiculous air, like solemn men in paper hats. To the right of the drive stood what had once no doubt been a porter's lodge, now so thickly bearded in ivy that only the two dark oblongs of smashed windows revealed that this leafy mass was hollow. The thick congregation of deciduous trees . . . returned again as they reached the park over which loomed the dark mass of the hotel. The size of the place astonished the Major. As they approached he looked up at the great turreted wall hanging over them and tried to count the balconies and windows.[33]

This hotel is the living corpse of the Protestant Ascendancy in Ireland, already passed by in 1919, already a part of the sleepwalking of empire, as the satirical hint about the 'crowns' on the gateposts suggests. Throughout, Farrell weaves analogies between the troubles of Empire in India and South Africa, and the situation in Ireland. The book is an enormous rhetorical *figura*, a set piece. Isolated, embattled, decaying, inhabited only by cats and ancient lady guests who have 'stayed on', the Majestic is the perfect picturesque collision between the traditional Pauline metaphor and the Protestant culture which was built upon it. The owner of the hotel, Edward Spencer, is a Protestant landlord of the old school, whose prejudices against the Catholic Irish are composed of a familiar mixture of class and theology:

> the unhealthy smell of incense, the stupefying and bizarre dogmatic precepts, the enormous families generated by ignorance of a doctrine of 'the more souls the better' (no matter whether their corporeal envelopes went barefoot or not), the absurd squadron of saints buzzing overhead like chaps in the Flying Corps supposedly ever ready to lend a hand to the blokes on the ground (and each with his own speciality), the Pope with all his unhealthy finery, the services in a gibberish of Latin that no-one understood, least of all the ignorant, narrow-minded and hypocritical priests.[34]

Ironically, the theological crack about 'corporeal envelopes' here applies also to the Majestic and its owner; the motif represents the grotesque death of a materially 'fat' landowning class, founded on a set of other-wordly ideals. The inhabitants of the hotel, mainly old ladies and cats, form the soul of this vast body, imprisoned and rotting until the final moment of apocalyptic conflagration. The theological analogy is not lost on the inhabitants of Kilnalough, who gather to watch it burn:

> It was from these black windows that flaming, shrieking creatures suddenly began to leap – hundreds of them, seething out of the windows on to the gutters and leaping out into the darkness. Those not already ablaze exploded in mid-air or ignited like flares as they hurtled through the great heat towards the earth. Someone in the crowd remarked that it was like watching the fiery demons pouring out of the mouth and nose of a dying Protestant.[35]

This technique of picturesque allegory is not merely a 'visual' matter: terms like 'background' and 'setting' are only metaphorical when used about language, and the rhetoric of these set pieces is inseparable from a rich deposit of social and psychological expectations, which are in turn deeply associated with theological and political tradition. The *unheimlich*, the dark house, is predominantly in this tradition the bad face of nineteenth-century Protestantism: it is the representation in pseudo-visual form of a set of theological paradoxes which are reactivated by contemporary biblical reference points, and by the endless reprinting of popular works of theology throughout the nineteenth and early twentieth centuries. It is these sources which, intersecting with various forms of political and historical anxiety, determine the apparently anachronistic continuity and survival of this form of symbolism.

2

The Unwritten Tradition: Horror and the Rhetoric of Anti-Catholicism

As a mere glance at the *Punch* cartoons of the period will amply demonstrate (see Plates 7 and 8), Cardinal Newman and his colleagues Wiseman and Pusey are the most ritually maligned figures of the mid-nineteenth century in England. In 1850, the year of the so-called 'Papal Aggression', he gave a series of talks to a Catholic audience at the Birmingham Oratory, entitled 'Lectures on the Present Condition of Catholics in England'. These lectures, published in 1851, were so outspoken that they resulted in an extraordinary libel case with an ex-monk, a Protestant convert, called Dr Giacinthio Achilli. Newman, the convert in the opposite direction, lost the case to the tune of several thousand pounds the judge commenting that this character appeared to have deteriorated since he had gone over to Rome.

The main argument of these lectures is about the nature of the popular tradition of horror in England. As a convert, Newman was well placed to observe the pyschology of the Protestant readership and he makes some acute remarks about this; but the real interest of his argument lies in its broad analysis of the insidious process by which cultural stereotypes are transmitted:

> Tradition in its fulness is necessarily unwritten; it is the mode in which a society has felt or acted, during a certain period, and it cannot be circumscribed, any more than a man's countenance and manner can be conveyed to strangers in any set of propositions.[1]

The tradition of Established Protestantism, he describes as 'The keeper-in-ordinary of those national types and blocks from which Popery is ever to be printed off'. This tradition, with all the legal and constitutional implications of Erastianism is, in a sense, Newman

26

argues, far wider than just a literary tradition. It is prior to literacy. It is the very oxygen of the culture:

> this Tradition does not flow from the mouths of the half-dozen wise or philosophic, or learned men who can be summoned in its support, but is a tradition of nursery stories, school stories, public-house stories, club-house stories, drawing-room stories, platform stories, pulpit stories; – a tradition of newspapers, magazines, reviews, pamphlets, romances, novels, poems, and light literature of all kind, literature of the day; – a tradition of selection from the English classics, bits of poetry, passages of history, sermons, chance essays, extracts from books of travel, anonymous anecdotes, lectures on prophecy, statements and arguments of polemical writers made up into small octavos for class-books and into pretty miniatures for presents; a tradition floating in the air.[2]

Such a description democratises, at a single stroke, the expression of cultural anxiety. This is not a stratified, or hierarchised version of 'the popular' versus the 'literary': the novelist becomes one amongst a whole nation of witnesses. 'False Witness,' declares Newman, 'is the principle of propagation.'

Newman's concern is to promote in his lectures an apparent paradox: that a religion which has always upheld private judgement as the basis of its faith is more intolerant than one which traditionally allows no latitude at all in matters of belief. Thus the common factor in the Protestant tradition, the cement as it were, of this nebulous and divergent culture, is the assumption that individual testimony has a special value. Although he makes no mention of it by name, I am sure that, when he uses metaphors of wood-blocks, Newman has in mind one of the most popular books of the last four centuries, besides the Bible itself: Fox's *Book of Martyrs*. This lurid, endlessly reprinted, reillustrated, encyclopaedia of Protestant propaganda is a roll-call of the testimonies of 'ordinary', individual martyrs. Exiled in Geneva and Strasbourg during the reign of Mary Tudor, Fox collected the materials and wrote the book to which, for years afterwards, he added 'realistic' details. A version of it was still being published in Fleet Street in 1954 by the Protestant Truth Society. The literary method of the book was intended at the outset to be a direct expression of the religion upon which the English Constitution is

based. Even in the eighteenth century, when the pious could read it
at home in a sixpenny edition, it was still be seen, chained to the
pulpit alongside the Bible. Macaulay, for example, testifies to
having been intrigued, as a child, by a 'great black letter volume',
chained to the reading desk in Church, which he itched to look
into.[3]

This violently illustrated work, the source of shock and
disturbance to many a tender imagination, had an official, quasi-
legal status conferred upon it by its form of first-hand, living
testimony. But, as Newman indicates, it was only one amongst a
never-ending stream of such productions. Horror is endemic to
English Protestantism:

> we must have a cornucopia of mummery, blasphemy, and
> licentiousness – of knives and ropes, and faggots; and fetters, and
> pulleys, and racks, – if the Protestant Tradition is to be kept alive
> in the hearts of the population.[4]

Indeed, this was very near to home for Newman in 1850. During
the laying of the foundations, one end of the Birmingham Oratory
was observed to be of a different depth from the other. Despite
denials by Newman, rumours began to circulate in the press that
dungeons were being built on the Hagley Road. It took Newman
some time to convince the public that they were only store-rooms.
Such a degree of insecurity was by no means confined to the
ignorant. Dr Arnold at Rugby, bringing up a future generation of
eminent Victorians, is reputed to have said, 'I look upon a Roman
Catholic as an enemy in his uniform; I look upon a Tractarian as an
enemy disguised as a spy.' Lord John Russell, well on the way to
introducing the Ecclesiastical Titles Act, whereby all territorial titles
were denied to Roman Catholic Bishops, quoted Arnold's words to
Queen Victoria, in agreement with her that the real enemy was
already within the gates of the Established Church. The stereotype
of invasion by aliens operated at the lowest and highest levels.[5]

The rhetoric of what Newman refers to as this 'unwritten
tradition' reveals a fascinating spectrum of culturally determined
attitudes, which throws a good deal of light on the nature of the
literary tradition of horror. I propose to begin by exploring a simple
hypothesis: that the rise and currency of literary Gothic is strongly
related to the growth of the campaign for Catholic Emancipation
from the 1770s onward until the first stage ends temporarily with the

Emanicipation Act of 1829; but further, that continuance of the horror novel is equally, if not more strongly, related to the subsequent struggles, doctrinal and political, which flared up between Catholic and Protestant throughout the course of the nineteenth century and well into the twentieth.

The famous question about Ann Radcliffe's *Mysteries of Udolpho* is, what was behind the black veil? This incident, during which the author deliberately refuses to tell the reader what Emily saw, is alleged to have kept a whole generation on tenterhooks. Here is the passage in which Emily, after an enormous build-up, terrified but fascinated, succeeds in penetrating the mysterious chamber:

> Emily passed on with faltering steps; and having paused a moment at the door before she attempted to open it, she then hastily entered the chamber, and went towards the picture, which appeared to be enclosed in a frame of uncommon size, that hung in a dark part of the room. She paused again, and then with a timid hand lifted the veil; but instantly let it fall – perceiving that what it had concealed was no picture; and before she could leave the chamber she dropped senseless on the floor.[6]

The reader now has to wait for hundreds of pages for the explanation. When the author, as if by some gigantic, but forgivable, slip of memory returns eventually to this burning issue, it is apparently to confirm the suspicion that the reader has been harbouring all this time, that it is a corpse behind the veil, and a particularly nasty one at that:

> It may be remembered that in a chamber of Udolpho hung a black veil, whose singular situation had excited Emily's curiosity, and which afterwards disclosed an object that had overwhelmed her with horror; for, on lifting it, there appeared, instead of the picture she had expected, within a recess of the wall, a human figure, of ghastly paleness, stretched at its length, and dressed in the habiliments of the grave. What added to the horror of the spectacle, was that the face appeared partly decayed and disfigured by worms, which were visible on the features and hands.[7]

But even as the author confirms our worst fears, the voice of rationality asserts itself:

On such an object it will be readily believed that no person could endure to look twice. Emily, it may be recollected, had, after the first glance, let the veil drop, and her terror had prevented her from ever after provoking a renewal of such suffering as she had then experienced. Had she dared to look again, her delusion and her fears would have vanished together, and she would have perceived that the figure before her was not human, but formed of wax. The history of it is somewhat extraordinary, though not without example in the records of that fierce severity which monkish superstition has sometimes inflicted on mankind. . . . [8]

The traditional literary explanation of effects like this concerns Mrs Radcliffe's 'pre-Romanticism'; and it is quite true that she does envince a split or conflict between a romantic commitment to the emotions and the necessity of rational explanation, which gives rise to what has been labelled her convention of the 'explained supernatural'. What is not commented on is the sectarian role assigned to 'explanation' in the above passage. The veil is indeed a metaphor for the numinous mystery of experience, but the explanation of what lies behind it is not merely a matter of neutral 'fact' or 'rationality'. It is deliberately designed to titillate the conscience of the Protestant readership. The author suddenly turns into a Reformation historian, offering her fiction as testimony with which to score a point off Romish superstition.

This rhythm of climax and bathos, as readers cannot help but remark, is a distinct pattern in the novel. But it is not there simply because Mrs Radcliffe cannot make her mind up whether she is an eighteenth-century rationalist or a Romantic. It is also part of a reciprocation between her own rhetoric of suspicion and the popular arena of sectarian dispute. Mrs Radcliffe is an expert at the double art of manipulating the idea of 'reason' to produce threat, and whittling away at 'threat' to produce reason. The novel is ostensibly set in sixteenth-century France and Emily St Aubert is, nominally, a Catholic. But the setting and the character are fairly perfunctory. The novel's relevance is to a contemporary readership, and the intrepid Emily, with whom we are constantly invited to sympathise, is really a Lutheran mouthpiece. The emotional vocabulary Mrs Radcliffe uses is partly designed as a trigger for a fine range of sectarian distinctions in the reader. In the following passage, for example, the term 'Apprehension' represents the legitimate fear of Protestant rationality, while 'superstition' is self-evidently Romish. These signals are active in the fairly typical exchange between Emily and her Catholic servant, Annette:

> 'Oh Lord! they say the room is haunted, and has been so these many years.'
>
> 'It is by a ghost, then, who can draw bolts,' said Emily, endeavouring to laugh away her apprehensions, 'For I left the door open last night and found it fastened this morning.'
>
> Annette turned pale and said not a word.
>
> 'Do you know whether any of the servants fastened this door in the morning, before I rose?'
>
> 'No ma'am, that I will be bound, they did not; but I don't know; shall I go and ask, ma'amselle?' said Annette, moving hastily towards the corridor. . . .
>
> She hurried from the room without waiting Emily's reply, whose heart, lightened by the certainty that Morano was not arrived, allowed her to smile at the superstitious terror which had seized on Annette; for though she sometimes felt its influence herself, she could smile at it when apparent in other persons.[9]

All emotion is reified; it lives at a distance from the subject. And what Emily is afraid of is not 'the ghost' – she knows that Morano has not yet arrived – but of being, or rather *appearing*, superstitious. The narrative energy is a kind of shuttling between public reassurance (remember your Protestant upper-class heritage) and private admissions of insecurity (even Catholic servants are human).

Little is known about Ann Radcliffe's life. The fullest contemporary account is Talfourd's quaintly snobbish memoir affixed to her novel *Gaston de Blondeville*. She was descended from Dutch Protestant stock, the writer tells us with evident satisfaction; one of the De Witts of Holland was invited over under Charles I 'to execute a plan for draining the fens in Lincolnshire'. The Civil War interrupted the project, but he stayed on for the rest of his days in a mansion near Hull. Mrs Radcliffe was closely connected to the Protestant establishment: she was related, on her mother's side, to the Bishop of Gloucester and to Dr Halifax, George III's physician. Her journal reveals that in 1807, after she had finished writing novels, she visited Knole House and her response to the Holbein portraits there has none of the aesthetic haze of the picturesque, of Salvator Rosa or Claude. For her, the paintings are, quite clearly, windows on to the Protestant succession, objective correlatives to her own imaginative piety:

> Holbein's Erasmus, in the gallery, must be truth itself: the keen and quick, small eye; the humorous, though serious smile; the thin, finely-pointed yet bending nose; the thin-drawn lips and chin, are all exquisite. In a picture containing three portraits, that in the middle is of Luther. His bluff, blunt, strong habits of expression; his dauntless and persevering mind; his consciousness of the truth and importance of his cause, and his resolution to maintain it, are well expressed; strength and resolution in the chin. On his right is Melancthon, reasoning, acute, aimiable. On his left, Pomeranius; a somewhat sly and monkish countenance.[10]

Udolpho was published in 1794. The rhetoric of the novel taps a profound and widespread insecurity. Throughout the later eighteenth century, pressure for Catholic Emancipation had begun to grow. English Catholics, numbering about 60,000, were mainly the products of well-to-do aristocratic or upper-middle class families. George III had suggested to one wealthy Catholic landowner, Mr Weld of Lulworth, that he build his family chapel disguised as a Mausoleum in order to circumvent the law that proscribed Catholic assemblies within locked doors. But the atmosphere had changed completely with the Gordon riots of 1780, and, later, the Catholic aristocracy, fleeing from revolutionary France to their relatives in England, were viewed with suspicion. Across the Irish Sea pullulated three million Catholics, deprived, poor and of a militant disposition. The connection between Ireland and France was well known and must have felt, to successive English Governments throughout the later eighteenth century, like an open, undefended flank. By 1792, Wolfe Tone was openly working as the agent of the Catholics and campaigning for the franchise. A deputation of Irish Catholics had been received by the King in 1793 and Pitt had compelled the Irish Parliament to accept the franchise. 1795 saw the founding of the Orange Order; Maynooth College was founded in the same year, in an attempt to sever the connection between the Irish priesthood and the Continent.[11]

Udolpho contains epigraphs and allusions drawn from the darker side of Shakespeare, in particular *Macbeth*; but the connection between images of Satanic evil and gloom and 'fiends that palter with us in a double sense' is not, as Mrs Radcliffe no doubt knew, merely a matter of romantic sensibility. The famous Shakespearian pun on 'equivocation' derives partly from the contemporary trial of the Jesuit Father Garnett, and Shakespeare himself was alluding to a contemporary Protestant insecurity. For Ann Radcliffe, the 'sly and monkish countenance' is there throughout history; and never more so than in the present, despite the fact that in her England the monastic orders were prohibited. Her masterpiece *The Italian* was published in 1797, the year before French troops landed at Killala Bay; significantly, its action approaches the present – it is brought forward to 1764. Though a Dominican, and not a Jesuit, her villain Schedoni is an equivocator. Like Milton's devils, who resemble nothing so much as Catholic theologians 'in wandering mazes lost', he is said to thrive on acts of labyrinthine speculation; but his author, ironically through the testimony of his fellow-monks, denies him true learning.

For Ann Radcliffe, the imaginative act is characteristically legalistic; it is a rooting out of the truth. The reader sometimes appears to be overhearing legal proceedings rather than reading a novel. Take the following example, where Vivaldi the hero listens to his servant's account of someone else's account of what happens inside the monastery. As it proceeds, the narrative sinks into a maze of testimony:

> One of the fathers, who had crossed the aisle, on his way to the cloisters, upon the first alarm of Ansaldo's disorder, remembered that a person, such as was described, had passed him hastily. He had seen a tall figure, muffled up in the habit of a white friar, gliding swiftly along the aisle, towards the door which opened into the outer court of the convent; but he was himself too much engaged to notice the stranger particularly. . . .
>
> 'In white, was he?' said Vivaldi; 'if he had been in black, I should have thought this must have been the monk, my tormentor.'
>
> 'Why, you know, Signor, that occurred to me before,' observed Paulo, 'and a man might easily change his dress, if that were all.'[12]

Ann Radcliffe's novels are full of discarded clothes, some of them bloodstained, and this image of appearance and reality is a rich one for the Protestant reader. The monk is essentially in disguise. It is worth remembering that at the time when this novel was written, Catholic priests were forbidden to wear their robes. There is an ancient comic tradition, stemming from Boccaccio and Shakespeare, about what goes on under the clothes of monks and priests, which is revived by Lewis's *The Monk*; but, for Ann Radcliffe, the habit of the monk is a symbol of deviousness and secrecy, which has a directly theological meaning.

Charles Maturin in *Melmoth the Wanderer* (1820) takes up this image and develops it into the full-blown theatrical metaphor, which it already was, latently, for Mrs Radcliffe. The tale of the Spaniard Monçada in that novel is a rhetorical *tour de force* which describes in energetic detail the fashion in which the Director of the ex-Jesuit monastery (the Order has been banned) in sixteenth-century Madrid angles for the soul – and thereby, the inheritance – of a thirteen-year-old son of the family, through the power of the Confessional. Here is one of the first of his interviews:

> 'Embrace, my dear child, the monastic life; this will accomplish the views of all who love you, ensure your own salvation, and fulfil the will of God, who is calling you at this moment by the voices of your affectionate parents, and the supplications of the minister of heaven, who is now kneeling before you.' And he sunk on his knees before me.
>
> This prostration, so unexpected, so revolting, and so like the monastic habit of artificial humiliation, completely annihilated the effect of his language. I retreated from his arms, which were extended towards me. 'My father, *I cannot*, – I will never become a monk.' 'Wretch! and you refuse, then, to listen to the call of your conscience, the adjuration of your parents, and the voice of God?!' The fury with which he uttered these words – the change from a ministering angel to an infuriated and menacing demon, had an effect just contrary to what he expected. I said calmly, 'My conscience does not reproach me, – I have never disobeyed its calls.'[13]

Appropriately, it is the issue of conscience which sparks off the rebellion, for the child is a Lutheran puppet here in the author's hands. The externalising of conscience into institutions like the confessional, leaves the individual Catholic 'free'. Like the Android of modern science fiction, he *looks* human enough; but he is completely cold, unscrupulous and devoid of any real feelings. He is a shape-changer:

> As I spoke thus, the Director changed the whole character of his figure, his attitude, and his language; from the extreme of supplication or of terror, he passed in a moment, with the facility of an actor, to a rigid and breathless sternness. His figure rose from the ground before me like that of the Prophet Samuel before the astonished eyes of Saul. He dropt the dramatist, and was the Monk in a moment.[14]

Shakespeare had long ago in *Measure for Measure* associated the theatrical possibilities of the cowl with the theme of Civil Obedience; his 'fantastical Duke of dark corners' invades his own kingdom disguised as a friar, and through the abuse of the confessional indulges in some far-reaching and disturbingly immoral manipulations of his own citizens. But Maturin's analysis of artifice here, like Mrs Radcliffe's revelation of Schedoni's 'artificial candour' in *The Italian*, is an earnest exposure of the psychology of the invader. Maturin was a Dublin-born Protestant of Huguenot descent. He did a spell as a curate in Galway and he was aware at first hand of the primitive, chillingly alien nature of the Catholic West of Ireland; this journey away from light and civilisation to a barren province, so much a motif of the horror novel and film, is recorded in *Melmoth*. His sensibility remains throughout his life that of an embattled and passionate Calvinist. In 1824 Maturin joined the pamphleteering fray, his novels culminating in a series of polemical sermons in Dublin, which he afterwards published under the title of *Five Sermons on the Errors of the Roman Catholic Church*.

The 1820s were as turbulent as the 1790s. Pamphleteering for and against the cause of Catholic Emancipation erupted again, exacerbated by the threat of invasion from Europe through Ireland. The tone of these pamphlets is totally uninhibited. Cobbett, Jeffrey and Thomas Moore, for example, produced a variety of attacks on the Reformation; while Blanco White and Pugin, among others, gave 'loaded' accounts of their Catholic education.

The literature of anti-Monasticism is voluminous throughout the nineteenth century. It takes all forms; but a recurrent stereotype is the fictionalised biography of the convert. The Emancipation Act of 1829 makes little difference to this steady stream of outrageous revelations. One very famous example is *The Awful Disclosures of Maria Monk* (1839) which seeks to convey the horror to the American people of the Quebec nunneries. Doubtless 'ghosted', it conveys a sensational stream of fantasies (murder, infanticide, illicit sexual relations) to the reader, improbably illustrated by a series of rather sweet little engravings; yet it also has a considerable amount of detail about the actual places in which these things are reputed to have happened. Maturin and Ann Radcliffe feed directly into an ongoing tradition of popular 'horror' of this kind.

But the tradition is not confined to the written word, as Newman pointed out. Victorian England also had a special kind of mountebank, particularly after Tractarianism had got under way. B. J. Armstrong's *Norfolk Diaries* give several accounts of these touring 'lecturers' during the period of the Tractarian upheavals. Armstrong, Vicar of Dereham and a Tractarian himself, is acutely sensitive to such matters and notes them down at every opportunity. On 7 July 1856 he was holidaying in Yarmouth:

> To Yarmouth with my wife and family for a fortnight. The town placarded with announcements. A foreigner, professing himself to be a Count, is to give frightful details about the Jesuits, nunneries, the Inquisition, etc. The lecture embraces details which compel this modest 'Count' to decline the company of ladies on that occasion: 'Females not admitted.'[15]

The previous year, Armstrong had journeyed into Norwich especially to hear a 'lecture' by Alessandro Gravazzi, a lapsed monk. He describes Gravazzi's performance as a cross between a mountebank and a tragedian.

These popular fairground performances pander to an earnest and deep-seated cultural suspicion, and such a tradition is a confluence of different factors. The Protestant suspicion of Rome already has an ancient theatrical metaphor at its heart (the Greek word for actor being hypocrite) which encapsulates, to the English Protestant mind, the essential duplicity of Catholicism. Gladstone's pamphlet of 1871, *The Vatican Decrees and Civil Obedience*, for example, contains a characteristically casual use of this metaphor, this time linked explicitly to the theme of Civil Obedience:

> It is certainly a political misfortune that, during the last thirty years, a Church so tainted in its views of civil obedience, and so

unduly capable of changing its front and language after Emancipation from what it had been before, like an actor who has to perform several characters in one piece, should have acquired an extension of its hold upon the highest classes of this country. The conquests have been chiefly, as might have been expected, among women; but the number of male converts, or captives (as I might prefer to call them), has not been inconsiderable.[16]

Gladstone's evangelical childhood rears up, the suspicion fuelled, no doubt, by his recent consultations with the zealous old Catholic, Dr Döllinger, in Munich. The language of this best-selling pamphlet is, at certain points, the popular medium of cultural suspicion that lies ready to hand in both fiction and the press. In fact, the point that Gladstone is actually making is a sociological observation of a milder kind than it appears to be: he is saying that the *proportion* of Catholic marriages among the aristocracy has increased, rather than that the actual numbers of conversions to the Catholic faith amongst the population as a whole have increased. As he remarks sourly, 'if the Pope does not control more souls, he controls more acres'.

Gladstone's language in this piece exhibits simultaneously two quite different pressures: the need to *worry*, rationally and moderately, and the urge to whip up the reader's instincts, and to revive all the old pre-Emancipation fears of invasion and fifth-columnism. One can feel these pressures at work in the following piece of coat-trailing, in which the Un-Dead make their appearance, apparently, as part of the apparatus of *realpolitik*:

I am not now going to pretend that either foreign foe or domestic treason can, at the bidding of the Court of Rome, disturb these peaceful shores. But though such fears may be visionary, it is more visionary still to suppose for one moment that the claims of Gregory VII, of Innocent III, and of Boniface VIII, have been disinterred, in the nineteenth century, like hideous mummies picked out of Egyptian sarcophagi, in the interests of archaeology, or without a definite and practical aim. As rational beings, we must rest assured that only with a very clearly conceived and foregone purpose have these astonishing reassertions been paraded before the world.[17]

At this point, it is worth coming back for a moment to the theological paradox, to Protestants, of an externalised conscience. The guarantees of human identity disappear in the image of an alien being, cloaked in an array of ever-changing roles. There are, for example, no conscious, no *internal* checks on spiritual pride. The self of a Catholic, to the Protestant imagination, is not approachable; it does not exist in the body, but elsewhere. Maturin is an eloquent witness to this absence of conscious guarantees. The Romish idolator has given up his conscious identity in a form of 'inebriation':

> The secret of this ecstatic swoon might be traced to an apothecary's shop, or purchased at a cheaper rate. The inhabitants of the north of Europe procure this state of exaltation by the use of liquid fire – the Turks by opium – the Dervises by dancing – and Christian monks by spiritual pride operating on the exhaustion of a macerated frame. It is all intoxication, with this difference only, that the intoxication of men of this world produces always *self*-complacency – that of men of the other world, a complacency whose supposed source is derived from God.[18]

But there's the rub; it is not derived from God. The agents, or dupes, of Anti-Christ are essentially, by definition, of this world, too. One of the standard plots of the horror novel involves the incarceration of the heir or heiress by the agents of Anti-Christ. One of the ways of recognising Anti-Christ is his need for money (see Plates 9 and 10).

Those who have been 'taken over' in this way, are purely material: mere bodies, operated by remote control from the Vatican. To appeal to the better nature of these Androids is like trying to find out the time from a clock without innards. Here is a modern historian's picture of the nineteenth-century process of 'relaxation':

> How well one knows the face of certain converts to Catholicism – that smooth exhausted look, burnt-out and yet at rest, as of a motorist who, after many mishaps and mounting insurance premiums, has at last decided to drive himself no more, and having found a chauffeur with excellent references, resigns himself to safer travel in a cushioned back seat.[19]

No doubt readers can find their own candidates; but this composite sounds to me like nothing more than a blur between the cartoon image of Newman and a death mask of Oscar Wilde. Hugh Trevor-Roper's studied anachronism makes it sound as if David

Low had been assigned to the *Punch* staff of 1850. To be sure, this is not meant to sound 'Gothic' – in fact, part of the point he is making is that Jesuits are 'passive idealists' and should not be feared as an active threat; but the description hovers between spiritual plutocrat and corpse (as the phrase 'at rest' implies) and elsewhere in this essay Trevor-Roper alludes to the phrase *perinde ac cadaver*. This is from the deathbed command of Ignatius Loyola, that 'Every member of the Order shall be, in the hands of his superiors, even as a corpse'. Despite his urbanity of tone, Trevor-Roper associates the Jesuits with Plato and, in the history of modern Europe, Hitler: such figures represent the dangers of a renunciation of Protestant individualism. We are not that far away from Mrs Radcliffe among the Holbeins.

Maturin was popular in France. His novel was translated almost instantly into French and it inspired both Balzac and Baudelaire. In England its literary reputation did not survive the reviewers. Despite his connections with Romanticism, Maturin is only a name to conjure with amongst 'Gothic' devotees. But the plot of *Melmoth* was recycled into Victorian culture via Eugene Sue's popular French novel *The Wandering Jew*. This extraordinary novel takes up the motif of the wandering Jew and grafts it on to a rabble-rousing tale about the regaining of France by the Huguenots. The plot is back-dated to the 1830s in order to remind the French audience of the anti-Catholic riots and church-sackings of those years. By the time the novel was published in the 1840s the Jesuits had been allowed back into France and Sue was writing anti-Jesuit propaganda. *The Wandering Jew* had all the apparatus of the English Gothic novel but from the 'other side', as it were; the Huguenots are a band of determined outsiders invading France from various remote parts of the earth to which they have long ago been exiled: they are destined to win back their inheritance. The English horror novel, on the other hand, fantasises characteristically from the point of view of legal and constitutional Establishment.

The French Gallican articles of 1682 do not imply the same connection between Church and State as the English constitution of 1688.[20] In one scene of Eugene Sue's novel we have a mirror-image of the traditional English fear of invasion. The secretary Rodin is reading out in code to his Jesuit master reports of their various infiltrations of national sovereignty throughout Europe. The globe is dotted with red flags. Amongst them, we find the following item:

'Thompson of Liverpool, has at length succeeded in procuring for Justin the place of agent or manager to Lord Stewart, a rich Irish Catholic, whose head grows daily weaker.'

'Let the fact be once verified, and Thompson shall have a premium of fifty louis. Make a note of it for Duplessis. Proceed.'[21]

This makes a joke out of the Irish–French connection; from a perspective of French politics it is merely one amongst the legion daily incursions of the ever-expanding Jesuit empire. But for an English audience in the late Victorian period, the joke was a serious matter: the allegiance of even aristocratic Catholics – especially Irish ones – to the English Crown appeared profoundly suspect. Eugene Sue was read avidly from the English point of view.

Sheridan Le Fanu is another Dublin Huguenot whose father was a Dean in the Irish Church. Le Fanu's career has more or less the same timespan as that of Dickens and indeed he did write for *All the Year Round*. This covers roughly the two major flare-ups of the Victorian period: the Papal Aggression, so-called, of 1850 and the 'Syllabus Errorum' of 1871, which gave rise to Gladstone's pamphlet. Le Fanu was a classics graduate from Trinity College, Dublin, who was called to the Irish Bar, but became a literary man and a Tory propagandist instead. Eventually, he bought the *Dublin Magazine* where he published his stories. He was very much in touch with London literary culture, despite his isolated Dublin life: he was the close friend of Charles Lever and was thought of as the rival of Wilkie Collins.

His tone is not as zealous as that of Maturin or Mrs Radcliffe. Le Fanu often writes with a kind of black and grotesque humour. But he takes a similar freedom with history, often posing as an antiquarian and writing with ironic footnotes and digressions, in the manner of the earlier novelists. The tone is elegiac, sometimes nostalgic for a more rugged, primitive, undemocratic age. Towards the end of his life Le Fanu collected his early stories, including a first version of his masterpiece *Uncle Silas*, and presented them as the manuscript papers of one Father Francis Purcell, a Catholic priest from the South of Ireland, 'a curious and industrious collector of old local traditions'. But he feels obliged to add a historical rider to the fiction, in case his more vigilant Protestant readers should feel uneasy:

To such as may think the composing of such productions as these inconsistent with the character and habits of a country priest, it is necessary to observe, that there did exist a race of priests – those of the old school, a race now nearly extinct – whose education abroad tended to produce in them tastes more literary than have yet been evinced by the *alumni* of Maynooth.[22]

The jibe at the present race of country bumpkins, from one whose ancestors fought in the army of William III, is a heartfelt one. But just in case it backfires, he immediately assumes the poker face of the antiquarian:

> It is perhaps necessary to add that the superstition illustrated by the following story, namely, that the corpse last buried is obliged, during his juniority of interrment, to supply his brother tenants of the churchyard in which he lies, with fresh water to allay the burning thirst of purgatory, is prevalent throughout the south of Ireland.[23]

Le Fanu is having it both ways here. The English founded Maynooth in order to sever the connection between Irish priests and revolutionary Europe. Doubtless the earlier priests were a more cultured group of people; in the later nineteenth century, the indigenous Irish priest would be, as likely as not, the son of a publican or a farmer returning to an ambience he was familiar with. But Le Fanu is being both perverse and snobbish: the Tory anarchist in him looks back over the shoulder, as it were, of his priest to an eighteenth-century Ireland in which life, including its horrors, was painted in primary colours. This habit of 'pastoral' backdating is an important one for Gothic fiction: it is not just an idea of 'medievalising'; it is the *tic* of cultivating views of the past, a specially adapted form of the historical romance, often for the purpose of political irony. The fictional Father Purcell is made to call up the decay of the Catholic Aristocracy and the passions aroused by 'great exertions and self-devotion and sacrifices in the cause of a lost country and a despised religion'. Through his persona, Le Fanu makes explicit the *political* associations of the picturesque:

> It is this feeling which has thrown the magic veil of romance over every roofless castle and ruined turret throughout our country; it is this feeling that, so long as a tower remains above the level of the soil, so long as one scion of a prostrate and impoverished

family survives, will never suffer Ireland to yield to the stranger more than the 'mouth-honour' which fear compels. I who have conversed *viva voce et in propria persona* with those whose recollections could run back so far as times previous to the confiscations which followed the Revolution of 1699 – whose memory could repeople halls long roofless and desolate, and point out the places where greatness once had been, may feel all this more strongly, and with a more vivid interest, than can those whose sympathies are awakened by the feebler influence of what may be called the *picturesque* effects of ruin and decay.[24]

This parody of Catholic nationalism however is an elaborately transparent hoax, for the device patently allows the Protestant writer to *introduce* those roofless towers, once again, and reanimate those ruined walls. For a few moments, the threat can live again, out there 'beyond the Pale'. Posing as editor, Le Fanu finally caps this passage with a 'historical' footnote on the phrase 'mouth-honour':

This passage serves (*mirabile dictu*) to corroborate a statement of Mr O'Connell's, which occurs in his evidence given before the House of Commons, wherein he affirms that the principles of the Irish priesthood '*are* democratic and were those of Jacobinism' – *See digest of the evidence upon the state of Ireland, given before the House of Commons.*[25]

O'Connell and Bishop Doyle gave vital evidence on the question of Civil Obedience in 1825, evidence which paved the way for the Emancipation Act of 1829. This story was first published in the 1830s, just after Emancipation. I quote, however, from the edition of 1880; Le Fanu obviously felt that the Purcell device would still work some fifty years later. He or his publishers must have known that this bringing of fictional evidence to corroborate a lingering historical suspicion would still be effective. 'Mouth-honour' might be translated without too much violence as 'equivocation'; and Gladstone in *Vatican Decrees and Civil Obedience* is harking back to this very enquiry and wondering, as we have seen, about the trustworthiness of the Catholic Church since then. What is certain, I think, in Le Fanu's case, is that the fictional pose of a benign and tolerant antiquarianism has a set of ironic cultural nuances which take it far beyond the merely 'literary'. Le Fanu's self-consciousness may look more progressive than the earlier zeal of a Maturin or an

Ann Radcliffe, but this, in a sense, makes him all the more credible as a purveyor of the traditional threat.

These quotations come from a short story called 'The Last Heir of Castle Connor'. In *Uncle Silas* (1864), Le Fanu translated the heiress-plot of the story into the present and set his three-volume novel in Derbyshire. The threatening secret creed here is Swedenborgianism rather than Jesuitism. But the marvellous figure of Madame de la Rougierre, agent of the mysterious Uncle Silas, draws directly on all the old Protestant suspicion about French morals and the lack of inner guarantees. Here is how Maud, the sensitive heiress reacts to her:

> I did not know well what to make of this woman, whom I feared with a vein of superstitious dread. I hated being alone with her after dusk in the schoolroom. She would sometimes sit for half an hour at a time, with her wide mouth drawn down at the corners, and a scowl, looking down into the fire. If she saw me looking at her, she would change all this on the instant, affect a sort of languor, and lean her head upon her hand, and ultimately have recourse to her Bible. But I fancied she did not read, but pursued her own dark ruminations, for I observed that the open book might often lie for half an hour or more under her eyes and yet the leaf never turned.
>
> I should have been glad to be assured that she prayed when on her knees, or read when that book was before her; I should have felt that she was more canny and human. As it was, those external pieties made a suspicion of a hollow contrast with realities that helped to scare me; yet it was but a suspicion – I could not be certain.[26]

The novel feeds off, and expresses, the insecurity of a Protestant society which was proscribing superstition, but had already begun to sense the weakness of the connection between Church and State which allowed it to do so. The Eccelesiastical Commission of 1871 bravely pronounced Roman Catholic burial rites superstitious and Armstrong thinks of them as illegal. But the basis of Establishment was already faltering from within. With the publication of *Essays and Reviews*, the Gorham judgment and the suspicion about ritual and mutual spying that went on at parish level in the church itself, it had begun to seem as if the bulwark of Erastianism was giving way. Meanwhile the paranoia about Catholicism had reached a new height and to some the threat of invasion seemed imminent. As Disraeli said in the House of Commons in 1868: 'High Church Ritualists and the Irish followers of the Pope have long been in secret combination and are now in open confederacy.'

In Le Fanu's novel, Maud's suspicions of the Frenchwoman are amply confirmed, when she takes her to the churchyard:

The crows nests hung untenanted in the trees; the birds were foraging far away from their roosts. The very cattle had forsaken the place. It was solitude itself.

Madame drew a long breath and smiled.

'Come down, come down, cheaile – come down to the churchyard.'

As we descended the slope which shut out the surrounding world, and the scene grew more sad and lonely, Madame's spirits seemed to rise.

'See 'ow many gravestones – one, *two* hundred. Don't you love the dead, cheaile? I will teach you to love them. You shall see me die here today, for half an hour, and be among them. That is what I love.'

We were by this time at the little brook's side, and the low churchyard wall with a stile, reached by a couple of stepping stones, across the stream, immediately at the other side.

'Come, now!' cried Madame, raising her face, as if to sniff the air; 'we are close to them. You will like them soon as I. You shall see five of them. Ah, ça ira, ça ira. Come, cross quickly! I am Madame la Morgue – Mrs Deadhouse! Ça ira, I will present you my friends, Monsieur Cadavre, and Monsieur Squelette. Come, come leetle mortal, let us play. Ouaah!' And she uttered a horrid yell from her enormous mouth, and pushing her wig and bonnet back, so as to show her great bald head.[27]

Maud finds out three years later that Madame Rougierre was only *acting* at this moment; our heiress gains, literally, another point of view in which, as soon as she has left her, she becomes 'cold and businesslike' in an instant. She is not a metaphysical being, but the agent of Uncle Silas who is after Maud's money. But for the child at the time the vision is a terrifyingly real one; the complication of play-acting is already there for the Protestant reader in the theological conception of ultimate hypocrisy which informs this image of the walking dead. 'Madame' is a spiritual Bawd. She is purely material, the body personified. And in the novel this vision of the medieval Dance of Death is prophetic: ironically she herself is to die by mistake at the hands of her master.

The antidote to this invader, this walking corpse with 'a mouth like a gaping reptile' is Cousin Monica, Lady Knollys, a sensible High-Church Protestant, who finds Maud too gloomy and fearful of death; too susceptible, as she jokes significantly of becoming either 'a Nun on the one hand, or a Puritan on the other'. Lady Knollys is a mouthpiece for Anglican anxiety, threatened by Catholicism on the one hand, and Dissent on the other. It is into her mouth that Le Fanu puts the crucial piece of Pauline consolation. 'Oh Death, King of Terrors!' shudders Maud at the thought of her father and mother in the vault 'damp and dark and solitary under the storm'. But Cousin Monica gently corrects the theology of this heretical tendency:

> 'We are such materialists, we can't help feeling so. We forget how well it is for us that our present bodies are not to last always. They are constructed for a time and place of trouble – plainly mere temporary machines that wear out, constantly exhibiting failure and decay, and with such tremendous capacity for pain. The body lies alone, and so it ought, for it is plainly its good Creator's will; it is only the tabernacle, not the person, who is clothed upon after death, Saint Paul says, "with a house which is from Heaven". So Maud, darling, although the thought will trouble us again and again, there is nothing in it; and the poor mortal body is only the cold ruin of a habitation which they have forsaken before we do. . .'.[28]

Some sixty years previously, Coleridge who spent pages in the Appendix to his *Lectures on Church and State* proving philosophically that the Pope was Anti-Christ, reacted in truly horrified fashion to some lines of Wordsworth, for similar reasons. The rhetoric of the 'Immortality Ode' he finds either unrealistic, or heretical:

> 'To whom the grave
> Is but a lonely bed without the sense or sight
> Of day or the warm light,
> A place of thought where we in waiting lie.'

Surely it cannot be that this wonder-rousing apostrophe is but a comment on the little poem, 'We are Seven?' that the whole meaning of the passage is reducible to the assertion that a *child*, who bye the bye at six years old would have been better instructed in most Christian families, has no other notion of death than that of lying in a dark, cold place? And still, I hope, not as in a *place of thought*! not the frightful notion of lying *awake* in his grave![29]

As Ernest Jones pointed out in *Nightmare*, the ancient notion of burial is to ensure the palpable corruption of the body. The corruptible body is an innocent body and the soul should, as Yeats put it, 'louder sing for every tatter in its mortal dress'. Hence the paradox deriving from the Protestant reading of St Paul, that the struggling suffering ruin which we inhabit is, in fact, the guarantee of our salvation.

Uncle Silas, living on in his timeless, weed-choked ruin Bartram-Haugh, is the very image of an attenuated survival that contravenes the proper ravages of the body:

> He rose, tall and slight, a little stooped, all in black, with an ample black velvet tunic, which was rather a gown than a coat, with loose sleeves, showing his snowy shirt some way up the arm, and a pair of wrist buttons, then quite out of fashion, which glimmered aristocratically with diamonds.
>
> I know I can't convey in words an idea of this apparition, drawn as it seemed in black and white, venerable, bloodless, fiery eyed, with its singular look of power, and an expression so bewildering – was it derision, or anguish, or cruelty, or patience?[30]

The suggestion of the Vampire is light, but the figure is a prototype of Count Dracula. The lightness of touch is typical of the way Le Fanu, very much like Mrs Radcliffe, introduces a social explanation at almost every point of what we might be tempted to think is supernatural. Silas needs money, Maud's money, in order to carry on. Like Montoni, he is either Satanic or a cheap crook, dependent on what light you see him in. But since the Prince of Darkness is also king of the material world, this counterpoint is not ultimately a counterpoint at all.

The rhetorical climax of *Uncle Silas* shows how Le Fanu can change between one form of threat, and another, in apparently seamless fashion. Madame de la Rougierre, grotesque Madame of the Deadhouse, is murdered in mistake for Maud by Dudley, Uncle Silas's thug of a son. The horror is inseparable from the idea of violent rape, as Maud, crouching beneath the bed, watches innocently, while Dudley tests his 'instrument':

> Imagine a hammer, one end of which had been beaten out into a longish tapering spike, with a handle something longer than usual. He drew stealthily to the window, and seemed to examine this hurriedly, and tested its strength with a twist or two of his hand. And then he adjusted it very carefully in his grasp, and made two or three little experimental pricks with it in the air.[31]

The phallic violation which follows apparently exorcises forever the threat of the walking dead:

> He stole, in a groping way, which seemed strange to me, who could distinguish objects in this light, to the side of my bed, the exact position of which he evidently knew; he stooped over it. Madame was breathing in the deep respiration of heavy sleep. Suddenly but softly he laid, as it seemed to me, his left hand over her face, and nearly at the same instant there came a crunching blow; an unnatural shriek, beginning small and swelling for two or three seconds into a yell as are imagined in haunted houses, accompanied by a convulsive sound, as of the motion of running, and the arm drumming on the bed; and then another blow – and with a horrid gasp he recoiled a step or two, and stood perfectly still. I heard a horrible tremor quivering through the joints and curtains of the bedstead – the convulsions of the murdered woman. It was a dreadful sound, like the shaking of a tree and rustling of leaves. Then once more he stepped to the side of the bed, and I heard another of those horrid blows – and silence – and another – and more silence – and the diabolical surgery was ended.[32]

This apparently disclaims the metaphysical ('a yell as are imagined in haunted houses'); and the 'surgery', though diabolical, hints at some consolatory possibility in the horrific image. But the doctrinal threat is renewed in another direction, in the striking coda to the incident. There has, it appears, been another watcher all along:

> There was a little tapping at the door
> 'Who's that?' whispered Dudley, hoarsely.
> 'A friend,' answered a sweet voice.

> And a key was introduced, the door quickly unlocked, and
> Uncle Silas entered. I saw that frail, tall, white figure, the
> venerable silver locks that resembled those upon the head of John
> Wesley. . . .[33]

This has the effect of grafting a new form of threat on to the
apparently naturalistic climax. We realise that 'diabolical' does have
a force here; and that Uncle Silas's black dress and pale melancholia
have another meaning too. Ambiguously, at this moment, he
becomes the very symbol of hypocritical Dissent.

This novel is almost wholly ambiguous, skating between
theological extremes, swapping one frame of reference for another.
In doing so, it conjures up by implication the problems of an
established Church, trying to steer its way, threatened by
superstition from more than one direction; and these murky
anxieties in the mind of its innocent narrator give ample room for a
suspicion in the reader's mind that was doubtless already there –
that Anglican Protestantism is established by consensus only, not
by any 'natural' connection with the State.

Sensitivity over matters of ritual in the 1890s was as great, if not
greater than in the 1850s and 1870s. The Colenso Affair had not
exactly strengthened the constitutional links between Church and
State. In 1888, the Bishop of Lincoln was observed by two of his
parishioners to be facing eastward while performing a service in the
Cathedral and was reported to the Archbishop of Canterbury. He
was tried for this and other illegal practices at Lambeth Palace.
During the trial the judge, Archbishop Benson, was convinced that
several members of the public in the gallery were, in fact, Catholic
priests disguised in plain clothes. The judgment was eagerly
awaited in all quarters because it would draw up certain lines in
matters of ritual and show where the Church stood. Of course, it did
nothing of the kind, because the charge was dealt with in a
piecemeal fashion and Bishop King of Lincoln was found guilty of
some illegal practices and not of others.[34]

This kind of spying was by no means uncommon in the later
nineteenth century. B. J. Armstrong had trouble from the vigilant
Protestant Church Association earlier in the century: he records
being heckled from the pews by a member of his congregation
whom he suspected was an agent but who turned out to be an
ordinary drunk. It was becoming obvious that the basis of the
Anglican creed in law demanded a clear doctrinal justification which

was, increasingly throughout the last decade of the century, not forthcoming. Here is how one pro-Catholic propagandist put it in 1900:

Such doctrines are definite, historical, or philosophical propositions, and they require a philosophic foundation no less definite than themselves. This foundation none of the three theories of authority possible within the limits of the Anglican or any Protestant Church, is any longer competent to supply.[35]

The three theories referred to here are: (a) the witness of individual testimony, (b) the authority of the primitive Church, and (c) the consensus of Christian believers.

One doctrine which assumes a central importance in any debate about religious faith is the interpretation of the Eucharist; this is one of the doctrines referred to above as lacking philosophic foundation outside itself. The Roman doctrine is that the sacramental elements are actually the Body and Blood of Christ; that the Redeemer, who died on the cross for each individual sinner, enters under the form of these elements into each sinner's body. Traditionally this is a crucial test of an individual's civil allegiance. Since the time of the Marian martyrs who died at the hands, so the mythology of Fox's *Book of Martyrs* runs, of a brutal and illegitimate *de facto* regime, this particular doctrine has had a direct connection with the question of civil obedience. The characteristic pattern of question and response is summarised from Fox's testimonies by a modern writer as follows:

But this grace was something that had actually happened to them, not something to be argued about. Consequently, every attempt of the representatives of authority to argue the question of the real presence with the man before them got nowhere, and, failing to convince him of his error by the ordinary processes of their dialectic, they could only demand his instant submission as a subject of the queen in her capacity as head of the civil state.[36]

Fox and his companions, in exile in Geneva and Strasbourg, set out to compile a book that would prove, from first-hand testimonies of countless ordinary individuals, the truth of the opposing mythology: that the elect nation accepted by grace the symbolic presence of Christ. He records, for example, the case in 1555 of one

George Marsh of Chester, who, when pressed in theological
language by his Catholic inquisitors on the question of the body and
blood of Christ in the sacraments, requested them not to ask such
hard unprofitable questions 'whereby to bring my body into danger
of death and to suck my blood'. This Parthian shaft is calculated to
ring true, theologically and politically, to a Protestant reader; it
really *is* his blood, not Christ's. The 'vampires' here are the
authorities, backed by a heretical doctrine.

The Protestant *reductio ad absurdum* of the Roman doctrine of
transubstantiation often retains this charge of 'vampirism'.
Maturin's yell of derision and horror in 1824 is startlingly close,
rhetorically speaking, to George Marsh of Chester, as he reduces the
Last Supper, for the benefit of the Catholics in his audience, to an
orgy of cannibalism and auto-ingestion.

> Thus I demand if the Roman Catholics do not believe the sacrifice
> of the Mass was offered, and transubstantiation took place, at the
> Last Supper Christ ate with his disciples? They do – then if so,
> Christ held his own body in his hand, and ate and drank his own
> body on that night; and his disciples also ate and drank that body
> which was then *alive* . . .[37]

The horrified stress on the last word, which takes this fascinated
vision far beyond mere cannibalism, gives away the anxiety
concealed in the rhetorical frame of Protestant rationality. The
political tradition, initiated by Foxe, is latent in this image of the
ultimate violation and invasion of the individual soul.

Bram Stoker is another Dublin Protestant who was born in 1845 in
Clontarf, overlooking the site of the Danish invasion. He actually
wrote for the same paper of which Le Fanu was at one time the
editor, the weekly *Warder*, though their careers do not appear to
have overlapped. Stoker was educated at a private day school by a
Reverend Woods, and his family was pious but also full of a macabre
sense of humour. Stoker graduated in General Science from Trinity
College, Dublin. After he left university, he joined the Irish Civil
Service and became an official in Dublin Castle, the Inspector of
Petty Sessions. Much to his family's consternation, he fell in love
with the theatre, and more particularly, with the charismatic figure
of Henry Irving. Abruptly, he resigned his secure career in the Civil
Service and became Irving's acting manager at the Lyceum. Irving's
acting style had a good deal to do with horror; and eventually, he

had a great deal to do with the figure of the tall, becloaked Transylvanian.

Stoker's *Dracula* is an extended play on various senses of 'blood'; an imaginative inversion of the Roman Doctrine of the Eucharist, grafted on to the more familiar invasion-projection. Its marvellous opening pages take the familiar journey away from rationality and the security of London, as Jonathan Harker (named after a stage hand at the Lyceum) penetrates deeper and deeper into the untouched peasant culture of Catholic Eastern Europe. Arminius Vambery, the Hungarian professor who visited the Beefsteak Rooms at the Lyceum and supplied Stoker with some of the detail for the book, was no mere neutral anthropologist; he had travelled in disguise in the Far East and was recognised for taking an active part in the defence of British interests in Asia. He had advocated taking a leaf out of the Russians' book in diplomatic matters; for which 'advice' on treating Eastern problems, he was decorated with the Royal Victorian Order and received by the Prince of Wales in Pesth in 1888.[38] Stoker was well aware of what it felt like to enter a superstitious peasant culture from his experience of the West of Ireland; he had, like Le Fanu, written demotic stories about the peasantry which Gladstone had read and was enthusiastic about. The *frisson* of the following passage is often lost on the modern reader, but in 1897, the source of insecurity was still raw in the audience:

> She then rose and dried her eyes, and taking a crucifix from her neck offered it to me. I did not know what to do, for, as an English Churchman, I have been taught to regard such things as in some measure idolatrous, and yet it seemed so ungracious to refuse an old lady meaning so well and in such a state of mind. She saw, I suppose the doubt in my face, for she put the rosary round my neck, and said, 'For your mother's sake', and went out of the room. I am writing up this part of the diary whilst I am waiting for the coach, which is, of course, late; and the crucifix is still round my neck. Whether it is the old lady's fear, or the many ghostly traditions of this place, or the crucifix itself, I do not know, but I am not feeling nearly as easy in my mind as usual.[39]

Harker is a fall-guy, an unvigilant Protestant who is a born victim. His sense of duty forces him to continue on to the Count's castle, but from this moment he has been tainted by superstition.

'Blood' in this novel is a grotesque pun, which brings together several different mythic associations. The sense of national identity is defined by blood, which passes into the ground and fertilises the soil of the homeland. This is the myth of Nationality (*Blut und Boden*) which was understood and believed in by many Victorians. The aggressive, nationalistic rhetoric of the period is full of references to this myth. As late as 1914, in his famous enlistment sonnet, Rupert Brooke used a passive version of the idea. The soldier in that poem, through his blood-sacrifice, actually claims the spot where he dies for England. Count Dracula explains to Harker that the blood of Attila the Hun runs in his veins. Transylvania is, as he puts it, the 'whirlpool' of European races, a kind of genetic Bermuda Triangle; a vortex, where Nationality is achieved only by the perpetual violent annexation of one 'blood' by another. The fantasy, presented as history, is of an Absolute Imperialism:

> Ah, young sir, the Szekelys – and the Dracula as their heart's blood, their brains, and their swords – can boast a record that mushroom growths like the Hapsburgs and the Romanoffs can never reach. The warlike days are over. Blood is too precious a thing in these days of dishonourable peace; and the glories of the great races are as of a tale that is told.[40]

But not so: Dracula is out to annexe further territory. For he takes over the microcosmic space of the individual soul through sucking the blood from the body. He travels in the blood-soaked soil of his own empire, and the fear of invasion exploited by the novel takes a sudden leap as we actually see him setting foot on English soil in the shape of a large dog. The method of entry is ingenious. Dracula is able to slip into the empty graves of suicides and mariners killed at sea, supposedly buried at the top of the cliffs in the Whitby cemetery. Stoker includes a parody of the materialist idea of the Resurrection of the Body, through the mouth of an old local Yorkshireman, Mr Swales. In conversation with Lucy one day in the graveyard, he satirically envisages the fallen mariners making a rush to Whitby to collect their tombstones on the last day before proceeding on up to Gabriel, the tombstones being needed as proof of identity. The conversation is worth quoting at length, for in context it appears so inconsequential that one may easily not see its ironic relevance to the book's main theme:

'But,' I said, 'surely you are not quite correct, for you start on the assumption that all the poor people, or their spirits, will have to take their tombstones with them on the day of Judgement. Do you think that will be really necessary?'

'Well, what else be they tombstones for? Answer me that, miss!'

'To please their relatives, I suppose.' 'To please their relatives, you suppose.' This he said with intense scorn. 'How will it pleasure their relatives to know that lies is wrote over them, and that everybody in the place knows that they be lies?' He pointed to a stone at our feet which had been laid down as a slab, on which the seat was rested, close to the edge of the cliff. 'Read the lies on that thruff-stean,' he said. The letters were upside down to me from where I sat, but Lucy was more opposite to them, so she leant over and read:-

'Sacred to the memory of George Canon, who died, in the hope of a glorious resurrection, on July 29, 1873, falling from the rocks at Kettleness. The tomb was erected by his sorrowing mother to her dearly beloved son. He was the only son of his mother, and she was a widow.' – Really, Mr Swales, I don't see anything very funny in that!' She spoke her comment very gravely and somewhat severely.

'Ye don't see aught funny! Ha! Ha! But that's because ye don't gawm the sorrowin' mother was a hell-cat that hated him because he was acrewk'd – a regular lamiter he was – an' he hated her so that he committed suicide in order that she mightn't get an insurance she put on his life. He blew nigh the top of his head off with an old musket that they had for scarin' the crows with. 'Twarnt for crows then, for it brought the clegs and dowps to him. That's the way he fell off the rocks. And as to hope of a glorious resurrection, I've often heard him say masel' that he hoped he'd go to hell, for his mother was so pious that she'd be sure to go to heaven, an' he didn't want to addle where she was. Now isn't that stean at any rate' – he hammered it with his stick as he spoke – 'a pack of lies? and won't it make Gabriel keckle when Geordie comes pantin' up the grees with the tombstean balanced on his hump, and asks it to be took as evidence!'[41]

This diatribe parodies simultaneously the materialist idea of the Resurrection of the Body and the social vanity of the hypocritical relatives who have fallen into such idolatry; but also it digs, in its reference to the idea of 'evidence', at the accompanying corruption of legalism. Lucy and Mina are close to their own fate here, for these weak hypocrites have allowed the Anti-Christ to invade and come among us, annexing the blood of individuals for his ever-growing empire of the Un-Dead.

If Dracula's profane quotation from Deuteronomy, 'the blood is the life', is an inversion of the Protestant Eucharist the sub-plot of the novel parodies Dracula. The lunatic Renfield tries to imitate his Satanic Master's annexations by absorbing the lives of various animals. The image is again of material ingestion, but a parodic version; you get the spider to eat the fly, and then the bird to eat the spider, and the cat to eat the bird, then you eat the cat, thus absorbing all these lives into yourself and growing proportionately more powerful and long-living. The 'empirical scientist' Dr Seward, observing Renfield under objective conditions, does not fail to relate his behaviour to the Catholic doctrine of the Eucharist:

> After a few minutes, however, I could see that he did not take note of anything around him, and so ventured to draw nearer to him – the more so as my men had now crossed the wall and were closing him in. I heard him say:-
>
> 'I am here to do your bidding, Master. I am your slave, and You will reward me, for I shall be faithful. I have worshipped You long and afar off. Now that You are near, I await your commands, and You will not pass me by, will You, dear Master, in your distribution of good things?'
>
> He *is* a selfish old beggar anyhow. He thinks of the loaves and the fishes even when he believes he is in a Real Presence.[42]

Dr Seward is obviously, from his final comment, a good Protestant, but he doesn't realise, at this point, how relevant his little joke is. In fact, the jibe is central to the book's elaborate attack on facile scepticism, purblind belief in 'progress' and scientific materialism. Seward is one of the people in the book who have to learn that empirical science – this new religion of Good Works – can't explain everything and it is necessary finally to fall back on true faith; not the materialistic imperialism of idolatry, which is a kind of mirror-image of the truth, but that final, true irrational yielding of scepticism before the immaterial truths of existence. The figure of Van Helsing, far from being a scientist, is that of a vigilant Priest, a mirror-image of Dracula (his eyebrows meet in the middle too) who fights him with white magic, and persuades the rest of the novel's cast to help him.

Van Helsing's extraordinary allegory of 'King Laugh' takes us back to the *danse macabre* again, and its Protestant associations; it takes us all the way back to Cyril Tourneur and the 'consolation' of the lipless grin, which the Anglo-Catholic Eliot, perhaps more in the fashion of a Victorian Protestant than he knew, praised for its other-wordliness. Van Helsing finds himself suddenly laughing at the funeral of Lucy Westenra; but his laughter, as he explains, does not stem from ordinary motives. It is partly, of course, because of the irony of the situation: Van Helsing alone knows that, since she is Un-Dead, the 'funeral' is no better than mumbo-jumbo. But he elaborates beyond that:

> Keep it always with you that laughter who knock at your door and say, 'May I come in?' is not the true laughter. No! he is a king, and he come when and how he like. He ask no person; he choose no time of suitability, he say, 'I am here'. Behold, in example I bleed my heart out for that so sweet young girl; I give my blood for her, though I am old and worn. . . . And yet I can laugh at her very grave – laugh when the clay from the spade of the sexton drop upon her coffin and say, 'Thud! thud!' to my heart, till it send back the blood from my cheek . . . even at such a moment King Laugh he come to me and shout and bellow in my ear, 'Here I am! here I am!' till the blood come dance back and bring some of the sunshine that he carry with him to my cheek. Oh, friend John, it is a strange world, a sad world, a world full of miseries and woes and troubles; and yet when King Laugh come he make them all dance to the tune he play. Bleeding hearts, and dry bones of the churchyard, and tears that burn as they fall – all dance together to the music that he make with that smileless mouth of him. And believe me, friend John, that he is good to come, and kind. Ah, we men and women are like ropes drawn tight with strain that pull us different ways. Then tears come; and, like the rain on the ropes, they brace us up, until perhaps the strain become too great and we break. But King Laugh he come like the sunshine, and he ease off the strain again; and we bear to go in with our labour, what it may be.[43]

This is a rich passage and, despite its grotesque demotic, it is at the heart of the book. It adapts the Dance of Death among other things, to a theory of the Unconscious (Stoker was very interested in Charcot, Freud's teacher in Paris); but the theory, so far as it can be discerned, is a kind of repressive tolerance *par excellence*. Nevertheless, the comfort derived from the mirthless laugh is a traditional one. Dracula, we note, has to ask us in over the threshold; or he has to be invited in. This is the image of a sudden possession. It is the same as Cousin Monica's comfort at the rotting of the body in the grave. The soul is allowed to go free if the body rots. But the Un-Dead have no lipless grin; for them the Resurrection is not symbolic, but hideously literal. The grotesque playing on 'blood' in the passage shows what radically different contexts Stoker brings together in his language: the sexual convention of romantic love ('bleeding hearts'); the Roman doctrines of the Eucharist and the Resurrection; and the scientific knowledge that the heart is only a pump, and that blood is transfusable from one body to another.

One of his brothers, William, was a surgeon, and the story goes that when Ellen Terry cut her finger in the rehearsal of a play; it became poisoned and William was called in to lance it. He did so; but had to leave before seeing the process through. Miss Terry almost died after the lancing but eventually recovered. Bram Stoker was watching closely and taking it all in.

One meaning of this farrago of imagery literalises and undercuts another. A blush is at once more, and less, than a suffusion of blood to the cheeks. The pallid woman is the sexually active, sexually exciting one, but she is a moral threat. The blushing, yielding woman demands, according to the chivalric code of bleeding hearts, manly protection which includes liberal donations from the veins. Eventually the fascination with the beautiful but bloodless ('selfish') woman was to take Stoker over completely in his last novel, *The Lair of the White Worm*, which he wrote on his deathbed. His biographer-nephew attributes this obsession with La Belle Dame sans Merci to the last throes of tertiary syphilis, which seems to be the point behind the euphemism 'Exhaustion' on the death certificate.[44]

The nominal hero of *Dracula* is called Arthur; and, with some help from Americans, about whom Stoker was very enthusiastic (they have the same 'blood, religion and social ideas', he wrote in an early essay, and 'our manifold interests are not only vast, but almost vital'), Arthur manages finally to assert, simultaneously, his phallic manliness and his national identity:

Arthur placed the point over the heart, and as I looked I could see its dint in the white flesh. Then he struck with all his might.

The Thing in the coffin writhed; and a hideous, blood-curdling screech came from the opened red lips. The body shook and quivered and twisted in wild contortions; the sharp white teeth champed together till the lips were cut, and the mouth was smeared with a crimson foam. But Arthur never faltered. He looked like a figure of Thor as his untrembling arm rose and fell, driving deeper and deeper the mercy-bearing stake, whilst the blood from the pierced heart welled and spurted up round it. His face was set, and high duty seemed to shine through it; the sight of it gave us courage so that our voices seemed to ring through the little vault.[45]

The pornographic thrill of rape is unmistakable; blood also equals sperm. In a few thrusting phallic strokes, he turns the white woman into the red. Stoker is quite unique in the kinds of association he manages to bring together in one description. In the fantasy system of the book, Arthur's orgasm here denotes *un*selfishness; it would have been selfish to have shrunk from violating the merely material body of his wife. Faith, like Science, can penetrate mere appearance, and the Thing only resembles Lucy. Now she can rot in peace and her spiritual body will rise on Judgement Day.

Far from allaying, the early twentieth century renews the same conflicts over major doctrines. The Eucharistic Congress of 1908, for example, had to be abandoned, on the order of Asquith, as 'provocative to Protestant sentiment'.[46] The Commission on Doctrine in the Church of England, set up in 1922, did not report until 1938. As late as 1922 there was a heresy case over the doctrine of the Resurrection of the Body. The Vicar of Camberwell brought formal proceedings against the Reverend H. D. Major of Ripon Hall, Oxford, concerning a sermon which the latter had given on the Resurrection. The case was referred to the Bishop of Oxford who was required to institute proceedings. The Bishop of Oxford referred it to three Professors of Theology, who eventually pronounced no heresy to have taken place. Interestingly, it is the accuser in this case, perhaps under the influence of F. D. Maurice, who has a more materialistic interpretation of the doctrine than the accused: the offending phrase in the sermon appears to have been: 'the survival of death by a personality which has shed its physical integument for ever', which, it is claimed, is contrary to both Holy Scripture and the Ancient Creeds of the Province of Canterbury.

The discussion papers are lengthy and impossible to summarise here, but one thing is striking: the arguments presented on both sides are only versions of the ancient conflict between Protestant and Catholic theologians, except that the rift between symbolic and literal interpretations reveals the historical insecurity within Anglicanism itself. Locke replied to Bishop Stillingfleet in 1699 in exactly the same terms as the modern Professors of Theology. Locke, just like Le Fanu's Cousin Monica, went back to his Corinthians, and tried to establish that St Paul said nothing about 'the Body', only 'the Dead'. The Greek, claimed Locke, has no mention of 'Body', or indeed 'Flesh'; and so the removal of a literal interpretation of the phrase in the *Book of Common Prayer* is justified.[47]

There are similar ambiguities over 'of' or 'from' the Dead. It appears as if the phrase *'per carnem'*, for example, was inserted into various Public Creeds in the fourth century AD, including the Athanasian Creed, which the Tractarians revived; but the Apostles Creed, upon which the Book of Common Prayer is based, has no such Romish literalism. The 'modern' Protestant argument explains the early Church Fathers on political grounds; they had to show the converts they made that something was added to what Plato and Pythagoras had said on the matter, and to what the Gnostics were urging. That 'something' was the Body or Flesh of the individual. But various eighteenth-century controversies on the subject are essentially making the same point exactly.[48]

But the twentieth century also sees the continuance of a tradition of suspicion. The old fear of a link between heresy and the threat to national identity is renewed. One of the most famous figures in this field is Dr George Coulton of Cambridge. This redoubtable controversialist is not just an eccentric; his famous exposure of the Jesuit historian Father Gasquet has the respect and approval in the next generation of Professor Trevor-Roper, who quotes it as a precedent for his own attacks on Father Christopher Devlin, sj.[49]

In 1944 Coulton wrote his autobiography. In that book he tells the reader how he saw Satan one day during his childhood while on the roof of his father's house in King's Lynn in Norfolk. The rhetoric of personal testimony is heavily filtered through evangelical Protestantism:

> This window being in the slope of the roof, one could creep out over the sill and sit in a sort of pocket, perfectly secure, and puffed up with superiority over ordinary folk creeping like insects below. From the back of the room itself nothing could be seen but this broad, flat chimney of time-stained grey brick, with flickering cloud shadows in chequered weather. One day, however, these shadows assumed special significance. I was alone, very possibly with a bad conscience, but certainly I had a hallucination, optically clear and distinct, though psychologically far more vague. A black shadow passing slowly over this chimney curtain seemed like an exact silhouette portrait of Satan as depicted in *Pilgrim's Progress* and other similar sources.[50]

Fortunately, he concludes, the Devil was after someone else at the time; as soon as he realised this he was not so afraid. Throughout his long life Dr Coulton, fuelled no doubt by this experience, issued a stream of pamphlets directed at the Catholic hierarchy over questions of historical interpretation. He defends H. P. Lea's four-volume *History of the Inquisition* from the attacks of Catholic historians with fire and sword. His crusade is explicitly linked with the defence of the liberty of the individual, within the context of modern European politics. It is the old argument about Catholicism. For example, when the poet Alfred Noyes was finally converted in 1927 to Catholicism, Coulton commented in a pamphlet called *Sectarian History*:

> His religion makes him citizen of another State very different from Britain, which maintains to the present day its immemorial claim to be a *societas perfecta*, with full jurisdiction and immense rights of punishment over its citizens.[51]

The date of this is interesting. Coulton was an old man. He had been educated at St Omer in Second Empire France, an experience which was one of a thread of experiences which convinced him that Catholicism was inherently connected with the rise of Fascism in Europe:

I was at school at St Omer in France, at a French Lycée. I was a boarder there under the Second Empire, the most clerical and strongly Roman Catholic Government that France has had in the lifetime of anybody living at the present time. The last thing I saw at St Omer in 1867 was a boy being run off to the school prison for having played the Marseillaise on the school piano. That was the freedom of France under Catholicism. In 1914, again, I was under commission to go and make certain researches among the Socialists in Belgium. They assured me with one accord that it was practically impossible in Belgium to be Socialist and a Roman Catholic. Again in 1921 or 1922 I was in Italy during that election which first put the Fascists quite beyond contest at the head of the Government. I went to one of the election meetings in the public square. When I came back I remarked to my host that, in spite of the extraordinarily inflammatory and partisan speech of the speaker, among all the hundreds whom I saw there, not only nobody had the boldness to heckle the speaker, but I could not trace even an open sign of disapproval on one of their faces. . . . Lastly, a few weeks ago I was in Roman Catholic Austria. There was an extremely intelligent youth there of about 25 or 26 with whom I was anxious to talk politics, and who was anxious to discuss politics with me. In order to do so we rowed out in a little boat into the middle of the lake by moonlight; and there, a quarter of a mile from the shore, he felt able to talk freely with me.[52]

This passage comes from a pamphlet called *The Reformation and British Liberty*, reprinted in 1936, whose title speaks for itself. The political ranting about the dangers of collectivism and passivity revive the old Protestant fears about what C. G. Jung refers to as 'participation mystique'; and the element which links, rhetorically and spiritually, his early vision of the Devil and his lifelong exposure of Catholicism is the language of a passionate witnessing. The heir to this reformation pamphleteering tradition is George Orwell, whose writings, the later ones some of the most horrific and disturbing exposures of the totalitarian mentality, depend for their effectiveness on a similar rhetorical strategy of passionate testimony. In the sketch Orwell left behind for *Nineteen Eighty-Four*, one finds the telling note 'Position of RCs'.[53]

Dr Coulton did not write horror stories in a formal, literary sense, though it seems clear from his rhetorical gift and sensibility that he could well have done so. That task was accomplished for his generation by a Protestant scholar and medievalist of a different character and temperament, M. R. James. The Provost of both Eton and King's College, Cambridge, James was a scholar of extreme piety and immense reputation. There is no taint of evangelicism about his beliefs: the son of the Rector of Livermere in Suffolk, James grew up in the shadow of an Abbey and appears to have developed antiquarian interests from a remarkably early age. The story goes that, having fallen ill as a small boy, he was asked what he wanted; he called for a Dutch Bible he had seen at the home of one of his father's friends and was completely comforted when it was brought to him. James's High-Church background accounts for a strain of anti-Puritanism; but his attitudes towards Catholicism are much more uneasy and complicated. He did, moreover, edit several important works: among them the Apocrypha and the Apocalypse, and he may be said to have contributed in a major fashion to modern Biblical scholarship – the kind of scholarship, in fact, which lies behind the 1922 heresy case I have quoted.

There is no evidence, as far as I know, as to what James thought of Stoker. The reticent Dr James would no doubt have been disgusted by the sexuality of *Dracula*, whatever he thought of its theology. But we do know from the few (for the most part, determinedly trivial) letters that he wrote to the widow of his best friend, that Sheridan Le Fanu was his favourite author. He even did some work on Le Fanu's anonymous contributions to Dickens's *All the Year Round*, using his scholar's nose for attribution; and he was childishly proud of himself for having spotted that Conan Doyle had cribbed the plot of one of his stories from Le Fanu.

James lived in the very heart of the Protestant Establishment; and from what one can gather from the memoirs and the long *Times* obituary, the two sides of his character sum up perfectly the connection I have been trying to establish between the apparently secure daylight centre of Anglican culture and its concomitant twilight of political and theological unease.

His scholarly work is a painstaking, detailed form of problem-solving. He is responsible for the cataloguing of manuscripts in Lambeth Palace Library, and he wrote the official history of the Citadel of the Established Church. His fussy, apparently timid, retiring persona (he parodies himself in one of the stories as 'henlike') seems totally abstracted from anything around him. In his introduction to *Ghost Stories of an Antiquary*, he is careful to present his stories as an unpretentious form of amusement. Ironically, though, we glimpse the scholar using his authority to disclaim the seriousness of his antiquarian narrators:

> As for the fragments of ostensible erudition which are scattered about my pages, hardly anything in them is not pure invention. . . .[54]

which is an effective way of making it seem pretentious on the readers' part to read 'deep meanings' into these trifles of pure fictional doodling. But the fact is that these horror-projections are very strongly patterned in cultural terms. As inventions, they are not in the least 'pure': on the contrary, they project fantasy on to history in patterns of anxiety that are recurrent.

James secretly cultivated the subterranean network of meanings that this work had for his own life and his complicated personality. Take, for example, the frequently anthologised story, 'Oh, Whistle, and I'll Come to You, My Lad'. The tale involves the trip to the crumbling coast of Essex of a sceptical Cambridge Professor called Parkins, a parody of James himself, described as a man 'somewhat henlike in his ways'. Indeed, James often used to stay in Aldeburgh after the First World War, and the whole thing is obviously a joke about himself. At the Globe Hotel, Parkins finds a Colonel Wilson:

> The most conspicuous figure was, perhaps, that of an *ancien militaire*, secretary of a London club, and possessed of a voice of incredible strength, and of views of a pronouncedly Protestant type. These were apt to find utterance after his attendance upon the ministrations of the Vicar, an estimable man with inclinations towards a picturesque ritual, which he gallantly kept down as far as he could out of deference to East Anglian tradition.[55]

Professor Parkins has been requested by a colleague, Mr Disney, to have a look round the site, now on the beach for the sea has encroached so far, of the Templar's preceptory, with a view to the possible mounting of an excavation the following year. Parkins does so and finds a whistle inscribed with the words *Quis est iste qui venit*. On the way back to the hotel, he sees someone who seems to be following him and, as in the case of Dr Coulton, the sight instantly recalls Bunyan: 'Now I saw in my dream that Christian had gone but a very little way when he saw a foul fiend coming over the field to meet him.' The indirectness of these hints is typical of James's fictional method. In an idle moment after he has reached the hotel Professor Parkins blows the whistle; instantly a wind attacks the inn and that night Parkins suffers a disturbing dream. He tells Colonel Wilson about it, who goes off into one of his anti-Tractarian rants:

> the Colonel grunted and opined that, in Parkins's place he should himself be careful about using a thing that had belonged to a set of Papists, of whom, speaking generally, it might be affirmed that you never knew what they might not have been up to. From this topic he diverged to the enormities of the Vicar, who had given notice on the previous Sunday that Friday would be the Feast of Thomas the Apostle, and that there would be service at eleven o'clock in the church. This and other similar proceedings, constituted in the Colonel's view a strong presumption that the Vicar was a concealed Papist, if not a Jesuit; and Parkins, who could not very readily follow the Colonel in this region, did not disagree with him.[56]

The Colonel's opinions are absurd, of course, but he is beginning to be a comfort; because there is now something in Parkins's room which keeps on disrupting the clothes of the empty bed. Here is the climax of the story.

> Now it began to move, in a stooping posture, and all at once the spectator realised, with some horror and some relief, that it must be blind, for it seemed to feel about it with its muffled arms in a groping and random fashion. Turning half-way from him, it became suddenly conscious of the bed he had just left, and darted towards it, and bent over and felt the pillows in a way which made Parkins shudder as he had never in his life thought it possible. In a very few moments it seemed to know that the bed was empty and then, moving forward into the area of light facing the window, it showed for the first time what manner of thing it was.
>
> Parkins, who very much dislikes being questioned about it, did once describe something of it in my hearing, and I gathered what he chiefly remembers about it is a horrible, an intensely horrible, face *of crumpled linen*.[57]

Parkins is rescued by the Colonel, who suddenly enters: the Thing turns instantly back into a crumple of bedclothes and the Colonel **takes charge** of the whistle, 'which he cast as far into the sea as a very brawny arm could send it'. The final paragraph laces the 'message' for the Protestant audience with disclaimers and innuendos:

> The Colonel, who remembered a not very dissimilar occurrence in India, was of opinion that if Parkins had closed with it it could really have done very little, and that its one power was that of frightening. The whole thing, he said, served to confirm his opinion of the Church of Rome.
>
> There is really nothing more to tell, but, as you may imagine, the Professor's views on certain points are less clear cut than they used to be. His nerves, too, have suffered: he cannot even now see a surplice hanging on a door quite unmoved, and the spectacle of a scarecrow in a field on a winter afternoon has cost him more than one sleepless night.[58]

This ending is highly tentative and ambiguous but it is scepticism towards superstition that is being shaken. The Colonel has come out of the whole thing, as a man of action and defender of the faith, rather well. Even after the First World War, the donning of a surplice was a sign to a vigilant Protestant congregation that you were probably a Ritualist. On the other hand, as Cousin Monica could have told Parkins, the scarecrow is an image of the body to be rejoiced at.

This story is quite typical of James's stories as a whole in terms of its method; they move through a tissue of testimonies, often impersonally recorded but for which the author appears to disclaim all authority, to a nasty epiphany. Moreover, that epiphany is often a version of the Resurrection motif: it occurs repeatedly in connection with grave-robbing and the desecration of tombs. Grave-robbers in the nineteenth century were known almost universally, in a widespread form of humour, as 'resurrection men'. James's story, 'A Warning To the Curious', combines the idea of an unholy Resurrection with the notion of invasion. The story takes place again on the Suffolk coastline, perhaps the fastest-eroding beaches in England. The setting, with the Martello tower built to repel Napoleon, the dykes and the bleak beach, is traditionally 'picturesque'; but although the narrator alludes to *Great Expectations* for 'atmosphere', the landscape is not merely 'picturesque': it is also the crumbling edge of an island that faces a hostile Europe. The local Vicar explains to the protagonist Long about the local superstition: that there has always been a belief in those parts in the three 'holy' crowns. The old people, he says, say they were buried in different places near the coast to keep off the 'Danes or the French or the Germans'.

The story was published after the War in 1925. One of the crowns, according to the Vicar's report of the 'superstition' is still doing its work. A local family, he explains, the Agers, have traditionally been its guardians:

> These Agers – its a very old name in these parts, but I can't find that they were ever people of quality or big owners – these Agers say, or said, that their branch of the family were the guardians of the last crown. A certain old Nathaniel Ager was the first one I knew – I was born and brought up quite near here – and he, I believe, camped out at the place during the whole of the war of 1870. William, his son, did the same, I know, during the South African war. And young William, his son, who has died only fairly recently, took lodgings at the cottage nearest the spot, and I've no doubt hastened his end, for he was a consumptive, by exposure and night watching. . . . So the last of the holy crowns, if it's there, has no guardian now.'[59]

A kind of Spiritual Home Guard, you might say. The business about the name is a familiar form of symbolism: 'Ager' in Latin, as James the scholar well knows, means field, an allegorical allusion that Le Fanu also used. In *Uncle Silas*, the Anglican Rector is called Dr Clay, and his Curate is named Fairfield. This story implies that the Agers *are* the soil of the country (we are close, in a subdued way, to Stoker's sense of *Blut und Boden* here) and James frequently implies, through building the story on a 'legend' which comes nastily true, that the peasant is the backbone, the soil, the true inheritor, of the nation, which we forget at our peril.

The rhyme of the Agers is a kind of resurrection ditty:

> Nathaniel Ager is my name and English is my nation,
> Seaburgh is my dwelling-place and Christ is my Salvation,
> When I am dead and in my Grave, and all my bones are rotton,
> I hope the Lord will think on me when I am quite forgotton.[60]

A character called Paxton, however, takes it into his head to rob the barrow out on the shore and obtain the crown. But then, because of some strange happenings, he becomes guilty and persuades Long

and another friend to help him restore it. Again James uses the idea
of clothes in his description of what they see:

> We were a couple a yards from the hill when Long suddenly said
> to him: 'I say, you've left your coat there. That won't do. See?'
> And I certainly did see it – the long dark overcoat lying where the
> tunnel had been. Paxton had not stopped however: he only shook
> his head, and held up the coat on his arm. And when we joined
> him, he said, without any excitement, but as if nothing mattered
> any more: 'That wasn't my coat.'[61]

Paxton knows the score and is inconsolable: 'I've got to pay for that
miserable sacrilege still,' he says, 'I know what you're going to say.
The Church might help. Yes, but it's the body that has to
suffer. . . .'

It's worth asking *why* exactly, because the rest of the horror of the
story depends on this knowledge that Paxton has. Help from the
Church would presumably be a tautology, since Anglican doctrine
holds the Resurrection to be spiritual. But Paxton has become
through his sacrilege an invader – he is, spiritually, a Dane, a
Frenchman or a German, and William Ager, martyred for the Land
during the First World War, has been 'released' in order to destroy
him. Paxton has restored the crown, and in doing so perhaps has
saved his soul, but he is technically – physically, that is – an
un-Saxon, already an invader, a mere material body to be destroyed.
The others find him, true to his prediction, on the beach in the old
gun battery near the Martello tower:

> You don't need to be told that he was dead. His tracks showed
> that he had run along the side of the battery, had turned sharp
> round the corner of it, and, small doubt of it, must have dashed
> straight into the arms of someone who was waiting there. His
> mouth was full of sand and stones, and his teeth and jaws were
> broken to bits. I only glanced once at his face.[62]

This idea of the 'deadly embrace' is the recurrent epiphany in many
of the stories. The Thing, as for example in *The Treasure of Abbot
Thomas*, which looks at first sight like a sack or a coat or an article of
bedclothes, suddenly reaches out, grips the victim and suffocates
him. The nominal crime is often, as here, desecration. But it is
interesting to see how far James is prepared to go; for, in order to

show that Providence finally belongs to the People, he himself is prepared to use a vision that is theologically idolatrous. Crimes of desecration are committed by vulgar modern materialists: dealers and the like. The revenge of Providence is an acting-out in horrified fantasy of the Materialist doctrine of the Resurrection, burial alive, suffocation in the tomb, the mirror-image of the materialists' own actual condition.

But here the fictional method has a crucial significance. We, as readers, never *see* this happening, we are only allowed to follow footprints, the clues, and listen to the accounts of participants. The images are always seen by someone else 'out of the tail of the eye' – from the mortal side, as it were. The imprint of the spiritual through the material is like the momentary bulge of a face in random folds of cloth. Providence declares itself only *post eventum*, working itself out in signs, signatures, footprints and the testimony of individuals.

One final example will suffice. Crimes of desecration are frequently committed by materialists, foreigners and upstarts. People who regard themselves as sceptics. As might be expected, James is not overfond of Cromwell. 'The Un-Common Prayer-Book' is the story of a revenge, planned for Cromwell in the event of his desecration of their chapel by an aristocratic Royalist family, which happens instead in the twentieth century to the first desecrator who comes along. The prayer book in the chapel at Brockstone Court is dated 1653, 'seven years before the Restoration, five years before Cromwell's death, and when the use of the book, let alone the printing of it' as the narrator tells us, 'was penal'. The prayer book opens itself at a single page on St Mark's Day, which turns out to have been Cromwell's birthday (the scholar helps the antiquarian this time) at the 'very savage' Psalm 109. Mr Davidson, the scholarly protagonist begins to see the light:

> That, coupled with the painted ceiling, seemed to explain a good deal. The figure of old Lady Sadleir became more substantial to his imagination, as of one in whom love for Church and King had gradually given way to intense hate of the power that had silenced the one and slaughtered the other. What curious evil service was that which she and a few like her had been wont to celebrate year by year in that remote valley.[63]

But the prayer book is stolen by a rascally Jewish dealer, who takes it to his office and puts it in his safe. Typically, the climax of the story is witnessed by Commissioner Watkins through a locked plate-glass door, as the Jew takes his loot out of the safe to gloat over it:

> And then, sir, I see what looked to be like a great roll of old shabby white flannel, about four to five feet high, fall for'ards out of the inside of the safe right against Mr Potwitch's shoulder as he was stooping over; and Mr Potwitch, he raised himself up as it were, resting his hands on the package, and gave an exclamation. And I can't hardly expect you should take what I says, but as true as I stand here I see this roll had a kind of face in the upper end of it, sir. . . . Yes sir, it fell right over on to Mr Potwitch's shoulder, and this face hid in his neck – yes, sir, about where the injury was – more like a ferret going for a rabbit than anythink else.[64]

The modern Jewish upstart, in his gold-rimmed spectacles and neat beard, gets what was originally meant for Cromwell, and we are meant to feel a certain Providential appropriateness in this end; and the image itself is once again a version of the Un-Dead, an idolatrous Resurrection, used here by Providence for its own devious, but ultimately satisfying purposes.

A writer's alignment in matters of religion throughout the nineteenth century was more evident to his audience than it is now – be he novelist, historian, journalist, political satirist or mere autobiographer. When we talk about 'contracts' between writer and reader, the metaphor is sometimes misleading, for the culture is a babel of contracts established, as Newman's ethereal metaphor suggests, prior to the individual act of writing. Signs are expected to be read, consciously and sometimes unconsciously, and this is part of the indirection, the joke and sometimes the sophistication of this kind of fiction. Horror fiction is a specialised form of the historical romance, perhaps, but it does not merely toy with 'history', it inserts itself directly into a propaganda war, and our model of interpretation needs broadening to include certain essential continuities in the politics of belief.

The politics, however marginal they may appear, go on reactivating themselves. A few years ago a colleague of mine had a leaflet thrust into his hand on the main street of Cambridge. It was called *God's Reasons Against the Pope's Visit to Britain* and it contained many of the doctrinal implications that I have been discussing above. But the paragraph which is perhaps most pertinent is the following:

13. *Invasion.* The Roman Catholic Church is ecclesiastical Fascism. It brought both Hitler and Mussolini to power. It caused the American Civil War and the assassination of Abraham Lincoln. Having caused two world wars and failed to achieve her aims, she is now successfully invading us through commerce and politics by the Common Market, the patron saint of which is the 'Virgin Mary' (heathen Queen of Heaven). The RC control of Eire almost lost us the last war, but we were saved through Protestant North Ireland. But now the Roman Catholics control our press, radio and television, and are dominant in aforetime Protestant city councils, and have dominance in the Foreign Office, great influence in Parliament through well known individuals.

The richness of horror fiction testifies to the complexity of the cultural changes which have taken place in the last two hundred years. But the continuity of its rhetoric, its narrative methods, and its symbolism also reveals that the ground-conditions for fantasy-projection of this kind have not passed away in the least.

3
Criminals and Christians: the Paradox of the Internalised Conscience

Apart from its obvious class and sexual dimensions, the clash between Richardson's Pamela and Mr B is a conflict between two entirely different ways of seeing the world. In the course of repudiating his increasingly urgent advances, Pamela delivers a homily to him on his lack of fear of 'God Almighty, in whose presence we all stand, in every action of our lives'. The would-be seducer, though still careless, grows slightly uneasy in the exchange that follows, an exchange that reveals plainly the conflict between an internalised and an externalised morality:

> He took my hand in a kind of good-humoured mockery, and said, 'Well urged, my pretty preacher! When my Lincolnshire chaplain dies, I'll put thee on a gown and cassock, and thou'lt make a good figure in his place.' – 'I wish', said I, a little vexed at his jeer, 'your honour's conscience would be your preacher, and then you would need no other chaplain' – 'Well, well, Pamela,' he said he, 'no more of this unfashionable jargon.'[1]

The Anglican jeer falls flat; and the reader has a sudden glimpse of the schematic opposition between the assumptions of two different kinds of Protestant Christianity. The 'established' Mr B buys, or rather rents, his conscience in the form of a chaplain. His landed status mediates his inner life for him. Pamela, on the other hand, lives in a world of God-fearing self-scrutiny, in which not only every action, but also every intention, is recorded in the presence of a God who looks on unceasingly.

Now the standard account of the relation between Puritanism and the novel suggests that Pamela's world is the more secure of the two. It is, so the familiar argument runs, her new, bourgeois conscience, the characteristic expression of which is the novel itself, which will survive to define the 'real' in human relations. The most famous and persuasive version of this is Ian Watt's *The Rise of the Novel* which stresses the connection between Puritan individualism and the epistemology of realism. The breadth of this analysis is impressive; and yet I feel it is this very breadth which causes Professor Watt to uncover in passing material which may have connections of quite another, or even an opposite kind, from those he imputes to it. For example, his remarks about the relation between the Calvinist habit of self-scrutiny and the prevalence of autobiographical confession throw up some interesting counter-possibilities:

> This 'internationalization of conscience' is everywhere manifested in Calvinism. In New England, it has been said, 'almost every literate Puritan kept some sort of journal'; and, in England, *Grace Abounding* is the great monument of a way of life which Bunyan shared with the other members of his sect, the Baptists, who were, with one or two minor additions and subtractions, orthodox Calvinists. In later generations the introspective habit remained even where religious conviction weakened, and there resulted the three greatest autobiographical confessions of the modern period, those of Pepys, Rousseau, and Boswell, all of whom were brought up under the Calvinist discipline; their fascination with self-analysis, and indeed their extreme egocentricity, are character traits which they shared both with later Calvinism in general and with Defoe's heroes.[2]

Now it is striking that, of the books he quotes here, three should be not only great, of their kind, but also, something he doesn't mention, very disturbing. Bunyan, Boswell and Rousseau are all in their different ways preoccupied, even obsessed, by their own horrors and agonies of mind and body. The later books of Rousseau's *Confessions* are the most spectacular and detailed expressions of what used to be called 'persecution mania' one could ever wish for. Boswell's repeated contractions of syphilis and his subsequent egocentric wrestlings with guilt form a bizarre mental drama. And Bunyan's *Grace Abounding* is an extraordinary catalogue of the author's horror and self-loathing, before his final vocation and admission into God's elect.

But Ian Watt's picture of the novel form is of a developing organism in competition with other organisms. The novel wins this

evolutionary struggle. And the suggestiveness of his account of
Calvinism and self-expression is used only to show what is *not*
'novelistic' about confessional autobiography. Thus Defoe's
Robinson Crusoe 'initiates that aspect of the novel's treatment of
experience which rivals the confessional autobiography and
outdoes other literary forms in bringing us close to the inward moral
being of the individual' (p. 83). Secularisation is the key factor in
determining this (economic) victory:

> It would seem, then, that Defoe's importance in the history of the
> novel is directly connected with the way his narrative structure
> embodied the struggle between Puritanism and the tendency to
> secularisation which was rooted in material progress. At the same
> time it is also apparent that the secular and economic viewpoint is
> the dominant partner, and that it is this which explains why it is
> Defoe, rather than Bunyan, who is usually considered to be the
> first key figure in the rise of the novel.[3]

Now there is a strong connection between Protestantism and
economic realism, as many writers have shown; and that connection
is undoubtedly reflected in the novel, both formally and
thematically; but it is not exclusive of other relationships, at the
same time, with fiction. For the structure of Protestant belief, and in
particular its elaborately introspective premises, neither weakens
nor decays as easily as Ian Watt perhaps implies. And when one
thinks of the survival of the confessional autobiography throughout
the nineteenth century, and its overlapping contact with certain
non-realistic forms of novel, together with the general complexity of
the rhetoric of self-description within the Protestant context, this
model of 'form' seems inadequate.

Yet it is a view of novel history which is still widely accepted.
Here, for example, is the writer of a recent study of the relations
between dissent and the nineteenth-century novel, using exactly
this set of assumptions as a yardstick:

> To put it briefly and roughly, Defoe wrote a sort of programme for
> the English novel. The Puritan background, the diary-keeping
> habit, the practice of daily self-scrutiny before God, provided
> him, as it were, with some of the novel's most recognisable
> features, particularly its sense of what would be continuingly
> important to it: the everyday, the domestic circumstance; the

quotidian process, the diurnal round (what happened next); and the ordinary life of ordinary people (the hero as *petit bourgeois* rather than as Aristotelian prince). And underpinning this ordinariness was the Puritan liberalism, this faith in democratic rule and in the priesthood of all believers, the rights of every man to follow his conscience in politics and religion.[4]

To be sure, Valentine Cunningham is arguing that this 'programme' was *not* carried out; but the idea of 'following your conscience' here is a kind of sociological cliché. It is merely an external description of a process which, viewed from the angle of its (necessary) internalisation, is a recurrent source of horror.

For there is a sense in which Bunyan is as important to the nineteenth- and twentieth-century novel as Defoe. The mechanism of self-scrutiny which both have in common, but to startlingly different degrees, is as intimately connected with the Gothic tradition as it is with any form of realism. Max Weber spoke of Calvinism as creating in the individual 'an unprecedented sense of inner isolation'; and the imaginative shape of this isolation is the result of a set of introspective manoeuvres which are a vital centre of the theology of the Reformation.

Bunyan's narrative is a repository of the mental shapes and postures (their exemplary nature reveals their underlying structure more clearly) which Calvin was insisting on when he declared: 'To Know God is to be struck with horror and amazement, for then and only then does one realise his [i.e. one's] own character.' These mental structures inform many of the narratives of nineteenth- and twentieth-century horror fiction, transmitted to their authors not simply by 'literary' means, but socially, as conditioning orthodoxy. In this context, the 'everyday, domestic circumstance, the quotidian process' leads not to 'ordinariness', but in the opposite direction – away from *any* common measure of social reality into the landscapes of the mind. A broader look at this particular relation between literary form and social structure yields, I believe, a pattern which can explain what writers as far apart socially as Baptist and Huguenot, and as distant geographically as Scottish and American, have in common.

Marcuse's essay on Luther and Calvin shows how there is a 'double morality' at the heart of Protestantism. Luther's denial of works creates a distinction between the inner man who is free and the outer who is bound. There is a mental space which gives the illusion of freedom, which Marcuse expresses in a neat donkey-and-carrot kind of paradox:

> The 'inner' *a priori* freedom makes man completely helpless, while seeming to elevate him to the highest honour; it logically precedes all his action and thought, but he can never catch his freedom up and take possession of it.[5]

With the denial of works, freedom no longer belongs to the realm of the body. The *reductio ad absurdum* of this is Luther's argument to the Christian slaves who had been bought by the Turks: they must not rebel, said Luther, because their bodies only had been bought, and indeed as Christians, they were duty-bound in conscience not to remove the property of other men. The idea of a double function is endemic in Lutheran thought:

> The separation of office and person is only an expression for the autonomization (*Verselbständigung*) and reification of authority freed from its bearer. The authority system of the existing order assumes the form of a set of relationships freed from the actual social relationships of which it is a function; it becomes eternal ordained by God, a second 'nature' against which there is no appeal. 'When we are born God dresses and adorns us as another person, he makes you a child, me a father, the one a lord, the other a servant, this one a prince, that one a citizen, and so on.'[6]

That realm of freedom is also illusory for other, more subtly psychological reasons. For Luther, the denial of the efficacy of works in purchasing grace creates a whole new shape for the mind, a shape which is strongly paradoxical. Justification by faith is prior to behaviour in the world. The logic of this is that the moral law is external to the individual; it is in the world. Therefore the individual, if just, has no need of the moral law, for man is justified by faith alone. At this point, Luther himself has sown the seeds of Antinomianism:

> It is clear, then, that a Christian has all that he needs in faith and needs no works to justify him; and if he has no need of works, he has no need of the law; and if he has no need of the law, surely he is free from the law. It is true that 'the law is not laid down for the just'. (1 Tim. 1:9)[7]

The implications of this famous passage are potentially revolutionary and anarchic; and it is this one half of the Lutheran logic which Antinomianism adopts, which is the primary reason why it is feared and suppressed again and again.

But there is one catch in all this heady freedom of the individual, namely, the little phrase 'if just'. What, then, we might ask, *is* the role of the moral law? Luther has already allowed for this. The moral law is a starting-point for the scrutiny of the self. It is a place in which to hang the mirror:

> Here we must point out that the entire Scripture of God is divided into two parts: commandments and promises. Although the commandments teach things that are good, the things taught are not done as soon as they are taught, for the commandments show us what we ought to do but do not give us the power to do it. They are intended to teach man to know himself, that through them he may recognise his inability to do good and may despair of his own ability.[8]

Two things spring up instantly here: the idea of self-scrutiny, and the idea of despair. The journey inwards has begun, the journey that shrinks and darkens the inner realm of freedom, even as it appears to preserve it. The mind must monitor *itself* through the mechanism of conscience, and this is the point at which the dialectic of the split self has sprung into being, for both Luther and Calvin insist upon the Pauline paradox of despair as the test of faith.

William James in *The Varieties of Religious Experience* has a lengthy discussion of the relation between non-conformism and the divided self. His view seems to be that the logic of Luther's position rests upon a profound form of psychological observation:

> It is needless to remind you once more of the admirable congruity of Protestant theology with the structure of the mind as shown in such experiences. In the extreme of melancholy the self that consciously *is* can do absolutely nothing. It is completely bankrupt and without resource, and no works it can accomplish will avail.[9]

The point that needs to be made here is that the mechanism of the Protestant model is also an effective means of *inducing* this view of the mind. As Marcuse remarks, 'somewhere on the road from

Luther to Calvin, the concept of *libertas Christiana* becomes a
negative one'. I think 'admirable congruity' in the quotation above is
meant descriptively; but the confident 'sympathetic' paraphrase
James gives of the logic of Luther's commentary on 'Galatians'
reveals only part of that logic:

> That is, the more literally lost you are, the more literally you are
> the very being whom Christ's sacrifice has already saved.[10]

What exactly is involved in 'literally' here? Is there some way in
which our despair, our feelings of isolation and self-disgust, might
only be 'metaphorical'? Is Calvin being 'literal' when he gleefully
proclaims, 'Surely, there is no one who is not sunken in infinite
filth'?

The answers clearly depend on us. But there are some interesting
implications for language here. For 'literalness', of course, breeds
metaphor. Calvin's distinction in the *Institutes* between self-
deceiving optimism and sincere self-scrutiny (that is, despair) looks
as if it is getting more literal, but all it actually does is swop one
metaphor for another:

> Hence it appears how deep and dark the abyss is into which
> hypocrisy plunges the minds of men, when they indulge so
> securely as, without hesitation, to oppose their flattery to the
> judgement of God, as if they were relieving him from his office as
> judge. Very different is the anxiety which fills the breasts of
> believers, who sincerely examine themselves. Every mind,
> therefore, would first begin to hesitate and at length to despair,
> while each determined for itself with how great a load of debt it
> was still oppressed, and how far it was from coming up to the
> enjoined condition. Thus, then, faith would be oppressed and
> extinguished.[11]

The idea of being buried alive in your mind at the very height of
happiness and confidence, though terrifying, is only a 'metaphor'
for self-deception. The language of finance, however, in which the
sincere deal with themselves, supplies the most objective-seeming
metaphor of all for mental process: the account book. James in the
quotation above has unconsciously adopted the same metaphor
when talking of the 'bankrupt self'. The idea of debit and credit is

somehow more 'real': the 'weight of debt' seems literally to drag down the mind.

One can see how, in some of Bunyan's self-description, the power of this kind of metaphor prevents the language from shading over into psychopathology:

> By these words I was sustained, yet not without exceeding conflicts, for the space of seven or eight weeks; for my peace would be in it, and out, sometimes twenty times a day; comfort now, and trouble presently; peace now, and before I could go a furlong, as full of fear and guilt as ever heart could hold: and this was not only now and then, but my whole seven weeks experience; for this about the *sufficiency of Grace*, and *that* of Esau's parting with his birthright, would be like a pair of scales within my mind: sometimes one end would be uppermost, and sometimes again the other; according to which would be my peace and trouble.[12]

The effect here is of the invasion or possession of 'the mind' by one or other of two conditions. But the idea of the scales prevents this 'possession' from being patternless or superstitious: it tends to give the whole thing a kind of objective, 'rational' feeling of weighing and balancing. In fact, strictly speaking the scales imply another level of mental operation altogether, in which the conflict is monitored; but this implication lies dormant in the complexity of this simple-seeming form of retrospective narrative. Joan Webber has shown how there is a second Bunyan, concealed in the self-expressive 'I' who monitors his former self, leading his reader through the labyrinth of conflict to the present state. Bunyan pretends, rhetorically, not to be looking on at himself; yet this is the implicit strength of his language. The conflict between his 'selves', as it develops, becomes more explicitly a form of double possession: he longs for them both to come upon him at once and fight it out:

> Well, about two or three days after, so they did indeed; they bolted both upon me at a time, and did work and struggle strangely in me for a while; at last, that about Esau's birthright began to wax weak, and withdraw, and vanish; and this about the sufficiency of Grace prevailed with peace and joy. And I was in a muse about this thing.[13]

The art of this is not to let the 'I' appear at all unstable, so that the outcome of this wrestling match is exemplary. This conflict between the self-as-Esau, the hairy man who forfeited his birthright, and the 'justified' self, is very close to Stevenson's Hyde and Jekyll. And one can see from the final narrative of Stevenson's novel 'Henry Jekyll's Full Statement of the Case' how Stevenson has not only recalled the motif, but also how he has brought out the psychopathological implications of confessional narrative:

> The pleasures which I made haste to seek in my disguise were, as I have said, undignified; I would scarce use a harder term. But in the hands of Edward Hyde, they soon began to turn towards the monstrous. When I would come back from these excursions, I was often plunged into a kind of wonder at my vicarious depravity. This familiar that I called out of my own soul, and sent forth alone to do his good pleasure, was a being inherently malign and villainous: his every act and thought centred on self; drinking pleasure with bestial avidity from any degree of torture to another; relentless like a man of stone. Henry Jekyll stood at times aghast before the acts of Edward Hyde; but the situation was apart from ordinary laws, and insidiously relaxed the grasp of conscience. It was Hyde after all, and Hyde alone, that was guilty. Jekyll was no worse; he woke again to his good qualities seemingly unimpaired; he would even make haste, where it was possible, to undo the evil done by Hyde. And thus his conscience slumbered.[14]

'*His*' conscience, but not '*mine*'. For here Stevenson is beginning to bring out the instability of 'I'. Half-way through the passage 'Henry Jekyll' begins to talk about himself in the third person. The mind is fragmented, and this fragmentation is represented in the formal strategy of an ambiguous point of view. 'Henry Jekyll' by trying to undo Hyde's deeds is falling into 'works', and in doing that he enters Calvin's labyrinth. For the narrative point of view is that of a *waking*, not a slumbering, conscience (hence the irony of 'It was Hyde after all, and Hyde alone, that was guilty'). By taking Bunyan's conflict to its logical conclusion, Stevenson reveals its horrors and its contradictions: the waking conscience is *perpetually* reflexive, spawning, in the fashion of mirrors, a potentially infinite multitude of hidden witnesses. The differences between the complexity of Stevenson's actual rhetoric here and the cinematic attempt to render this section of the narrative in the Hollywood version are instructive. The mirror image is there, but not as a reflexive medium: Spencer Tracy looks in the mirror and we look over his shoulder. He sees himself changing back and forth (a triumph of make-up, and a new technique of 'fading' shots) and we see essentially what he sees. He is either one or the other, but there is no 'third' self, as there is in the irony created by the fragmented point of view of Stevenson's original.

In this passage it remains an 'implication', part of the logic of the point of view. But Stevenson goes on to make it fully explicit. The rhetorical climax of this confession, and indeed of the whole novel, is an extraordinary babble of voices. It begins as a third-person essayist might, and ends by recalling that all this is expressive of a 'self':

> The powers of Hyde seemed to have grown with the sickliness of Jekyll. And certainly the hate that now divided them was equal on each side. With Jekyll, it was a thing of vital instinct. He had now seen the full deformity of that creature that shared with him some of the phenomena of consciousness, and was co-heir with him to death: and beyond these links of community, which in themselves made the most poignant part of his distress, he thought of Hyde, for all his energy of life, as of something not only hellish but inorganic. This was the shocking thing; that the slime of the pit seemed to utter cries and voices; that the amorphous dust gesticulated and sinned; that what was dead, and had no shape, should usurp the offices of life. And this again, that that insurgent horror was knit to him, closer than a wife, closer than an eye; lay caged in his flesh, where he heard it mutter and felt it struggle to be born; and at every hour of weakness, and in the confidence of slumber, prevailed against him and deposed him out of life. The hatred of Hyde for Jekyll was of a different order. His terror of the gallows drove him continually to commit temporary suicide, and return to his subordinate station of a part instead of a person; but he loathed the necessity, he loathed the despondency into which Jekyll was now fallen, and he resented the dislike with which he himself was regarded. Hence the ape-like tricks that he would play me, scrawling in my own hand blasphemies on the pages of my books, burning the letters and destroying the portrait of my father.[15]

I think the entry of 'me' towards the end of this passage is a shock to most readers; it recalls the 'self' that has been supposedly speaking all along; but the *frisson* derives from the fact that it has been subverted and cannot be restored properly without some form of 'outside' view.

Now it is quite true that Defoe presents the 'hypostasis of the economic motive'. But the artifice of this presentation is visible, if we consider what a selection Crusoe's book-keeping conscience is from the whole set of implications present in the logic of internalisation. Defoe 'literalises' the metaphor of the account book, by rigorously and crudely abstracting only part of its structure of implication. He presents for the reader of Crusoe's journal what is in fact also a mirror of *mind* as a mirror only of the world:

Evil	Good
I am cast upon a horrible desert island; void of all hope of recovery.	But I am alive; and not drowned, as all my ship's company was.
I am singled out and separated, as it were, from all the world to be miserable.	But I am singled out too from all the ship's crew, to be spared from death; and he that miraculously saved me from death, can deliver me from this condition.
I am divided from mankind, a solitaire; one banished from human society.	But I am not starved, and perishing on a barren place, affording no sustenance.[16]

No wonder Watt argues that Defoe was not a Calvinist. This is a selection from the whole set of manoeuvres involved in the most rigorous action of the conscience. The two columns are a 'literal' representation of a hidden metaphor, which works upon the reader. We are apparently compelled to collude in Crusoe's 'sanity' by the act of reading itself – our eyes in the act of reading are forced to move from left to right, and so 'Good' has the last word. But supposing we refuse. As an experiment, let the reader try reversing the columns, leaving only the 'buts' where they are (and, in strict Calvinism, the titles of the columns). They are eminently reversible, and yet the process of 'rationally' weighing and balancing is now inseparably associated with fear, isolation, insecurity and despair.

For credit, argue Luther and Calvin, as soon as committed to the account book of the conscience, implies debit; it is the *rigour* with which this activity of book-keeping is carried out, not the activity itself, which keeps alive the final but unenvisageable possibility of spiritual profit in this world of mounting debt. Joyce's short story 'Grace', punning on the name for the period given to a debtor and God's grace, parodies the hypocrisy of a closed account. No doubt its satire would have been theologically pleasing to the fathers of the Reformation.

Compare this example of the metaphor from the context of the nineteenth-century novel. Wilkie Collins, like Dickens, is very close to the Gothic tradition and his neglected masterpiece *No Name*, though not a horror novel, uses the structure and pace of the melodramatic thriller to gain its effects. Collins's villain, Captain Wragge, employs the significantly named Magdalen, heroine and would-be heiress, as an actress, undertaking to 'manage' her performances. In doing so, of course, he cheats her; and Collins gives the reader a very interesting page from his account book:

Financial Statement	*Third Week in January*
Place Visited	Performances
Newark	Two

Net Receipts	Net Receipts
In black and white	Actually Realized
£25	£32.10s.

Apparent Division of Profits	Actual Division of Profits
Miss V £12.10s	Miss V £12.10s
Self £12.10s	Self £20.00

Private Surplus on the Week
or say
Self-presented Testimonial
£7.10s

Audited	Passed Correct
H. Wragge	H. Wragge[17]

Collins's joke restores some of its true complexity to this favourite metaphor of the Protestant conscience. H. Wragge is auditing H. Wragge, to see that he doesn't cheat him, but in the final line we are invited to perceive a third H. Wragge, the one, that is, who passes his own auditing as correct. The account book, posing as real, functions here merely as a mirror of mind; unlike Crusoe's, which purports to represent the external structure of Providence. The ambiguity of Collins's image, which takes for granted the psychopathology of a desocialised conscience and expects the reader to see the joke, is an emblem of the moral ambiguity of Wragge's character in the novel. Wragge is a criminal; but he is also 'sympathetic'. We cannot tell whether he possesses scruples which he doesn't ever reveal, or whether he is a book-keeping robot whose distrust extends automatically to his own cheating. Collins, like Dickens, whom we shall examine later, confounds a simple view of the historical process of secularisation by taking the metaphor back to its first paradoxical principles. Captain Wragge, consummate liar and criminal fraud, is a version of the most rigorous form of Christian self-scrutiny.

Formally, autobiographical confession is a complex medium; and the origins of this complexity are extra-literary. The converted Christian looks back at himself across the gulf of a total change of personality. This can give rise to the most artful forms of rhetoric. Kenneth Burke has written brilliantly, for example, about the Latin of Augustine's *Confessions*, which is a plethora of puns on the verb to turn, *vertere*, from which the term 'conversion', of course, itself derives. Thus *pervertere, convertere*, meaning to turn away from or towards God.[18] And this 'turning', this concept of direction, is organised retrospectively, so that the behaviour of the 'I' can be seen by the reader to have been governed, through all its freedoms and spontaneities of choice, by the final causation of God's Providence, proven by the narrative itself. Bunyan may appear to have eradicated any formal sophistication in *Grace Abounding*, but his narrative is organised according to this same underlying pattern of exemplary retrospection; his 'I', too, is a dramatic fiction.[19]

The *Adelphi* of William Cowper is a very interesting eighteenth-century example of the genre, because it is also very close in certain respects to the narrative strategies of horror fiction. Cowper was of good Anglican family and was converted to evangelical Protestantism late in his life. His account of his insanity is therefore written from the point of view of one who has been 'saved' by God's

Providence. Cowper records in minute detail his progress through the labyrinth of self-scrutiny, and he presents with extraordinary freshness the impact of horror and self-loathing upon a timid and sensitive disposition.

After an almost perpetual studenthood in the Inns of Court, Cowper's family secured him a post as clerk of the House of Lords. This unfortunately entailed the reading out of legal documents to the assembled company, a task to which he felt himself totally unequal. The job was changed; but he was still required, before he could take office, to be examined publically on his knowledge of the law. This was an ordeal greater, if anything, than the first. After months of futile swotting, the fateful morning arrived on which Cowper, rigid with fear, was due to be taken to Westminster. At this point, we plunge into a world of horror. In a state of almost Dostoievskian excitement, Cowper rushes forth from his apartment to kill himself. The whole tenor of his use of 'I' in the following passage reveals strongly the sense of looking on, as his mind is helplessly 'possessed' by rapidly fluctuating intentions:

> Before I had walked half a mile in the fields a thought struck me that I might yet spare my life; that I had nothing to do but to sell what I had in the Funds (which might be done in an hour), to go on board a ship, and transport myself to France. There, when every other way of maintenance should fail, I promised myself a comfortable asylum in some monastery, an acquisition easily made by changing my religion. Not a little pleased with this new expedient, I returned to my chambers to pack up all that I could at so short a notice. But while I was looking over my portmanteau my mind changed again, and self-murder was recommended to me once more in all its advantages. Not knowing where to poison myself, for I was liable to continual interruption in my chambers from my laundress and her husband, I laid aside that intention and resolved upon drowning. For this purpose I immediately took coach and ordered the man to drive to Tower Wharf, intending to throw myself into the river from the Custom House quay.[20]

But when he arrives, he finds the tide low and 'a porter or two seated on some goods there, as if placed on purpose to prevent me'. The narrative is rich in tone. It is horrific; but it also has the structure of grace, as, one after another, Cowper's manic attempts to destroy himself fail. He rushes back to his chambers and tries to hang himself with his garter from the bed, but the bed breaks, then from the door which strangulates him, but doesn't break his neck. And this solemn bathos is intentional, because it is the very anti-climax, repeated through successive failures to poison, drown, hang and finally to stab himself again and again through the heart with a stocking-needle, which demonstrates the working of God's Providence.

But Cowper is now possessed by new guilt for his attempts, and goes through fresh torments of a greater kind. The coincidence, in the rhetoric of the following passage, between paranoiac delusion and the workings of the desocialised conscience is striking:

> I never went into the street but I thought the people stared and laughed at me and held me in contempt, and could hardly persuade myself but the voice of my conscience was loud enough for everybody to hear it. They who knew me seemed to avoid me, and if they spoke to me they seemed to do it in scorn. I bought a ballad of a hawker who was singing it in the street because I thought it was written upon me. I either dined alone at the tavern, whither I went in the dark, or at the chop-house, when I always took care to hide myself in the darkest corner of the room. I slept generally an hour in the evening upon the bed, but it was only to be terrified in dreams, and when I awakened again it was some time before I could walk steadily. And through the passage into the dining room I reeled and staggered like a drunken man. The eyes of men I could not bear, but to think that the eye of God was upon me (which I was now well assured of) gave me the most intolerable anguish. If for a moment either a book or a companion stole away my attention from myself, a flash from Hell seemed to be thrown into my mind immediately, and I said within myself, 'What are these things to me who am damned?'[21]

The final step on the inward journey remains to be taken. Cowper is persuaded at last, like Bunyan, that he has committed the sin against the Holy Ghost, the unpardonable sin, and the dialectic of self-assertion and self-loathing expresses itself in an identification with Satan:

> Another time while I was musing, I seemed to myself to pronounce those words from Milton, 'Evil be thou my Good.' I

verily thought that I had adopted that hellish sentiment, it seemed to come so directly from my heart.[22]

Even though the heroic possibilities of this image are firmly suppressed by the irony of Providence, Cowper is within a hair's breadth here of acting the part of a Gothic hero. The rhetoric of Bunyan, who also suspected that he had committed the sin against the Holy Ghost, contains the same possibility of suppressed heroism:

What, thought I, must it be no sin but this? Must it needs be the *great transgression*? Psalm 19:13. Must *that* wicked one touch my soul? 1 John 5:18. Oh, what stings did I find in all these sentences! What, thought I, is there but *one* sin that is unpardonable? But *one* sin that layeth the Soul without the reach of God's mercy? And must I be guilty of *that*? Must it needs be that? Is there but *one* sin, amongst *so many* millions of sins, for which there is no forgiveness; and must I commit *this*?[23]

Compare the opening of Poe's *doppelgänger* story 'William Wilson', in which such potentialities are fully exploited:

I would not, if I could, here or today, embody a record of my later years of unspeakable misery, and unpardonable crime. This epoch – these later years – took unto themselves a sudden elevation in turpitude, whose origin alone it is my present purpose to assign. Men usually grow base by degrees. From me, in an instant, all virtue dropped bodily as a mantle. From comparatively trivial wickedness I passed, with the stride of a giant, into more than the enormities of an Elah-Gabalus. What chance – what one event brought this evil thing to pass, bear with me while I relate. Death approaches; and the shadow which foreruns him has thrown a softening influence over my spirit. I long, in passing through the dim valley, for the sympathy – I had nearly said the pity – of my fellow men. I would fain have them believe that I have been, in some measure, the slave of circumstances beyond human control. I would wish them to seek out for me, in the details I am about to give, some little oasis of *fatality* amid a wilderness of error. I would have them allow – what they cannot refrain from allowing – that, although temptation may have erewhile existed as great, man was never *thus*, at least, tempted before – certainly never *thus* fell.[24]

Technically, this is a close pastiche of autobiographical confession, but Poe has tilted the perspective slightly, so that the ambiguities of tone inherent in the dialectic of Christian self-scrutiny become explicit. The story is a rich satire upon the logic of conscience. Wilson's hyperboles, kept up by a brilliant *tour de force* throughout the story, trip over themselves as the boastful identification with Satan modulates, within the same passage, into the confession of a conscience so guilty that it pre-empts all the behaviour of the self. Wilson, who boasts of his wickedness toward his fellow men throughout the story, ironically never manages to commit a crime of any sort, because a second character, mysteriously possessed of the same name, always steps in at the last minute and prevents him. Wilson is pursued by Wilson throughout his life, who relentlessly exposes him. Just at the point, for example, when he is about to triumph by cheating at cards, Wilson the narrator hears the other Wilson enter the room and deliver a speech which, to his horror, reveals all to his companions:

> 'Gentlemen', he said, in a low, distinct, and never-to-be forgotten *whisper* which thrilled to the very marrow of my bones. 'Gentlemen, I make no apology for this behaviour because in thus behaving, I am but fulfilling a duty. You are, beyond doubt, uninformed of the true character of the person who has tonight won at *écarté* a large sum of money from Lord Glendinning. I will therefore put you upon an expeditious and decisive plan of obtaining this very necessary information. Please to examine, at your leisure, the inner linings of the cuff of his left sleeve, and the several little packages which may be found in the somewhat capacious pockets of his embroidered morning wrapper.'[25]

Poe inhabits the conceit so powerfully in this passage that farce and horror are inextricably fused. Wilson's pride and guilt are given such a precise equivalence, self-assertion is made so exactly correspondent to self-loathing, that his identity is totally subverted. Yet he remains the perfect Christian, whose mental processes are entered into the account book with an absolute rigour, as they happen. From one point of view, the fact that he is talking about himself in the third person is totally pathological; but we are not allowed to rest in an 'explanation' because of the way in which Poe unremittingly exploits the congruence between the language of theology and the language of psychological description.

Poe, keeping his face straight to the end, brings off the climax of the story in a welter of ambiguities. Wilson the narrator kills Wilson in the cloakroom at a ball: or so it seems:

> But what human language can adequately portray *that* astonishment, *that* horror which possessed me at the spectacle then presented to view? The brief moment in which I averted my eyes had been sufficient to produce, apparently, a material change in the arrangements at the upper or farther end of the room. A large mirror – so at first it seemed to me in my confusion – now stood where none had been perceptible before; and as I stepped up to it in extremity of terror, mine own image, but with features all pale and dabbled in blood, advanced to meet me with feeble and tottering gait.[26]

It looks as if the author has blown the gaff on his conceit at last, and Wilson has acknowledged his own conscience. But instead, by an impeccable piece of logic, the second Wilson, although it appears the reverse, becomes the first:

> Thus it appeared, I say, but was not. It was my antagonist – it was Wilson, who then stood before me in the agonies of his dissolution. His mask and cloak lay, where he had thrown them, upon the floor. Not a thread in all his raiment – not a line in all the marked and singular lineaments of his face which was not, even in the most absolute identity, *mine own*!
>
> It was Wilson; but he spoke no longer in a whisper, and I could have fancied that I myself was speaking when he said:
>
> 'You have conquered and I yield. Yet henceforward art thou also dead – dead to the World, to Heaven and to Hope! In me didst thou exist – and, in my death, see by this image, which is thine own, how utterly thou has murdered thyself.'[27]

In Freudian terms, the structure of the conceit is quite similar to Stevenson's Jekyll and Hyde. The ego becomes id by killing the superego. But the confessional narrative also maintains the irony – that this 'freedom' is the ultimate expression of guilt. The ambiguity of tone in the opening paragraph is sealed by the ending and the reader is trapped helplessly in the labyrinth of Wilson's mind. A non-paradoxical external description of the conceit is no longer possible.

R. D. Laing in *The Divided Self* quotes Freud's famous case of the small boy, who discovered, when his mother was out, how to make himself vanish by crouching down in front of a full-length mirror. This 'mirror-game' is used as an analogy by Laing:

> Now, whether the threat from the real other arises out of the contingency of the fact that the other may at any time go away or die or not reciprocate one's feelings for him, or whether the other represents more directly a threat in the form of implosion or penetration, the schizoid person seeks in the boy's way of being a mirror to himself, to turn his self, a quasi duality with an overall unity, into two selves i.e. into an actual duality. In this little boy of the 'two selves', his own actual self outside the mirror was the one which one could imagine would most readily be identified with his mother. This *identification of the self with the phantasy of the person by whom one is seen* may contribute decisively to the characteristics of the observing self. As stated above, this observing self often kills and withers anything that is under its scrutiny. The individual has now a persecuting observer in the very core of his being.[28]

Throughout most of his book, and this is what makes it so generally interesting, Laing is not examining clinical cases of schizophrenia; he is charting the features of what he calls the 'schizoid position', the mental disposition which may become psychotic, but which exists as a possibility in our daily behaviour. It would be interesting to know what class and religious backgrounds his subjects have; for the point I want to make here is that this very disposition is at the heart of the Protestant, and in particular the dissenting Protestant, model of the mind. But, furthermore, that Poe, who was adopted at a very early age by a Scottish tobacco merchant of strict disposition, and who was sent to the English Protestant school referred to in the story, is mounting an imaginative exposure, by means of a pastiche which 'adjusts' the confessional mode, of the logic of these premises.

One of the characteristic means of representing the workings of Grace in the mind is the Echo. This metaphor again stems, in its Christian as opposed to its Greek form, from the logic of internalisation. There is no way that, sunk in the filth of its mortal condition, the mind can perceive directly the workings of God's Grace. But if one listens hard, the echo of one's own thoughts, subtly altered, comes back like a sonar beam. Thus Poe's whispering *alter ego* is also true to another aspect of the psychology of the good Christian. Of course, the metaphor is by no means confined to the Puritan context. The poems of George Herbert, for example, frequently use the echo technique. Here the sophisticated Herbert uses all his poetic skill to establish the fact that God completes his rhymes. The formal structure of the poem is providentially governed; it is a model of the mind, which, in sincerely examining itself, is turning all the time towards God. The poem thus extinguishes itself in an echo:

> There is in love a sweetness readie-penn'd
> Copie out only this . . .

The formal playfulness, the artful subordination of art to truth is typically Anglican; but the structure of 'methought I heard a voice' is common to all types of Christianity. Indeed, confessional narrative, from Augustine's *Sume, lege* onwards, might be described without exaggeration as a tissue of auditory phenomena.

Of course, Puritanism gets nearer than any other form of Christianity to *directly* experiencing the voice of God. Bunyan, for example, uses Scripture as a kind of interior drama, whose authenticity is so great that he thinks it is *outside* him:

> Now, about a week or fortnight after this, I was much followed by this Scripture; *Simon, Simon, behold Satan* hath desired to have you, Luke, 22:31. And sometimes it would sound so loud within me, yea, and as it were, call so strongly after me, that once, above all the rest, I turned my head over my shoulder, thinking verily that some man had, behind me, called to me; being at a great distance, methought, he called so loud: It came, as I have thought since, to have stirred me up to prayer and watchfulness: It came to acquaint me, that a cloud and storm was coming down upon me; but I understood it not.[29]

Note the providential tailpiece here; the prolepsis ('to *have* stirred me up to prayer') precisely represents a double-focus of rationalising observer and ignorant participant. Bunyan, too, hears the echo in a way that is crude compared to Herbert, but in terms of *structure*, identical:

> But the next day at evening, being under many fears, I went to seek the Lord; and as I prayed, I cried, and my Soul cried to him in these words, and with strong cries; O Lord, I beseech thee, shew me, that thou hast loved me with an everlasting love, Jer. 31:3. I had no sooner said it, but with sweetness it returned upon me as an echo, or sounding again, *I have loved thee with an ever lasting love.* Now I went to bed in quiet; also when I awakened the next morning, it was fresh upon my Soul; and I believed it.[30]

Here, there is no formal pattern of art to 'prove' the echo by rhyme; but the structure is again prior, as it were, to its expression. The image derives from the logic of a mind turned obsessively towards itself; the inner ear strains, and finds, in the very materials that the self provides (the use of Scripture, of course, being God's word in the first place, gives this a hidden circularity) the 'trace' of God's guiding presence. No intervention has directly taken place.

A good example of the use of this pattern in the horror context is the fragmentary 'I' narrative, *Memoirs of Carwin the Biloquist* by the American 'Gothic' writer Charles Brockden Brown. Brown was from a Pennsylvania Quaker family, and though his biographers tend to stress his attraction to free-thinking Godwinism,[31] it is clear from this narrative that he was well-acquainted with logic of the internalised conscience. As Joan Webber points out, Quakerism was particularly prone to 'voices' and she quotes the Journal of George Fox the founding father of Quakerism:

> Fox hears voices commanding him to do things whose purpose he does not even understand – for example, to walk barefoot on the snow to the town at hand (whose name he does not know) and cry through the street 'Woe to the bloody city of Lichfield'. After obeying, he devises an explanation having to do with ancient persecution of Christians in Lichfield. The founder of the Quakers, he represents an extreme openness to visions and voices (direct communication with God), compared to which Bunyan's experiences seem almost ordinary.[32]

Brown tilts this logic into a conceit, in which his hero, Carwin, attempts to *control his own* echoes and therefore deceive others.

Having discovered a peculiar echo in a glen, to which he guiltily steals away from his strict and pious Pennsylvania father, Carwin develops his notion of biloquism:

> In leaving my chamber I was obliged to use the utmost caution to avoid arousing my brother, whose temper disposed him to thwart me in the least of my gratifications. My purpose was surely laudable, and yet on leaving the house and returning to it, I was obliged to use the vigilance and circumspection of a thief.
>
> One night I left my bed with this view. I posted first to my vocal glen, and thence scrambling up a neighbouring steep which overlooked a wide extent of this romantic country, gave myself up to contemplation, and the perusal of Milton's *Comus*.
>
> My reflections were naturally suggested by the singularity of this echo. To hear my own voice speak at a distance would have been formerly regarded as prodigious. To hear, too, that voice, not uttered by another, by whom it might easily be mimicked, but by myself! I cannot now recollect the transition which led me to the notion of sounds, similar to these, but produced by other means than reverberation. Could I not so dispose my organs as to make my voice appear at a distance.[33]

This is a rich interaction between the structure of the internalised conscience, the theology of which is strikingly expressed in Milton's *Comus*, and the ironic psychopathogical perspective of the 'Gothic'. The activity is itself a 'gratification' and is therefore productive of guilt. The guilty mind cannot discern true from false echoes, hence the authentic note of paranoia in 'not uttered by another, by whom it might easily be mimicked'. The logical step therefore is to control the echo. The image of 'biloquism' is very close to the whispering 'other' of Poe, except that it is the other way round: here, the biloquial other is the free play of desire, and the self is the repressed conscience. Hence Carwin soon contrives a scheme to use his new-found powers to gain his own ends. His father will not let him go and stay with his aunt in Philadelphia. His father is pious, but also 'a confident believer in supernatural tokens' and has heard the voice of his dead wife twice in the past, whispering at his pillow:

> I frequently asked myself whether a scheme favourable to my views might not be built upon these foundations. Suppose (thought I) my mother should be made to enjoin upon him compliance with my wishes?

This idea bred in me a temporary consternation. To imitate the voice of the dead, to counterfeit a commission from heaven, bore the aspect of presumption and impiety. It seemed an offence which could not fail to draw after it the vengeance of the deity.[34]

In the end, Carwin overcomes his guilt, and steals into his father's room to execute his project. He approaches the bed, hands outstretched like a somnambulist, and there is a tremendous flash of lightning.

The flash was accompanied with a burst of thunder, whose vehemence was stunning. I always entertained a dread of thunder and now recoiled, overborne with terror. Never have I witnessed so luminous a gleam and so tremendous a shock, yet my father's slumber appeared not to be disturbed by it.

I stood irresolute and trembling; to prosecute my purpose in this state of mind was impossible. I resolved for the present to relinquish it, and turn with a view of exploring my way out of the chamber. Just then a light seen through the window, caught my eye. It was at first weak but speedily increased: no second thought was necessary to inform me that the barn, situated at a small distance from the house, and newly stored with hay, was in flames, in consequence of being struck by the lightning.[35]

Here is the structure of Providence, employed for the reverse purpose from the orthodox Christian one; to protect the victim from the echo. The structure of this incident, the joke which informs it, owes a good deal to the author's awareness of the machinery of the inner light as potentially psychopathological. The tone of this fragment, which Brown left unfinished, is very close to Poe's monomaniacally self-obsessed narrators, and in a similar fashion the reliance on the confessional mode allows the author to assimilate the events to consciousness rather than action.

Brown himself, in his youth particularly, was no stranger to melancholic introspection. He was apt to leave the city and go off for months into Pennyslvania, lodging with his family and walking the Pennsylvania countryside. In the winter of 1797 one of his friends wrote, apparently in desperation at this solitary habit, 'Charles! Are you dead?', but Brown did not reply until the New Year, and then it was in the following vein:

I think upon the life of last winter with self-loathing almost insupportable. I sometimes wish they were buried in oblivion, but even a wish of this kind is a token of my intellectual infirmity. Alas! my friend, few consolations of a self-approving mind have fallen to my lot. I have been raised to a sublimer pitch of speculation only to draw melancholy from the survey of the contrast between what I am and what I ought to be. I am sometimes apt to think that few human beings have drunk so deeply of the cup of self-abhorrence as I have. There is no misery equal to that which flows from this source. I have been for some years in the full fruition of it. Whether it will end but with my life I know not.[36]

No doubt there is a certain amount of romantic posturing in this, but Brown, who married in 1804 the daughter of a Presbyterian clergyman, was not only open to the new ideas of free-thinking Europe; he was also turning the logic of the internalised conscience inside out in his imaginative work.

Interestingly, when one reads the journal of Fox the writing does not appear psychologically rich, except possibly in the extraordinary incident, in which the voice tells him to take off his shoes:

I was commanded by the Lord, of a sudden, to untie my shoes and put them off. I stood still for it was winter, and the word of the Lord was like a fire in me, so I put off my shoes and was commanded to give them to the shepherds, and was to charge them to let no one have them except they paid for them. The poor shepherds trembled and were astonished.

Then I walked on about a mile till I came to the town, and as soon as I was got within the town the word of the Lord came to me again, to cry 'Woe unto the bloody city of Lichfield!' So I went up and down the streets, crying with a loud voice, 'Woe to the bloody city of Lichfield!' It being market-day, I went into the market place, and to and fro in the several parts of it, and made stands, crying as before, 'Woe to the bloody city of Lichfield!' And no one laid hands on me; but as I went thus crying through the streets, there seemed to me to be a channel of blood running down the streets, and the market place appeared like a pool of blood.

And so at last some Friends and friendly people came to me and said, 'Alack, George, where are thy shoes?' I told them it was no matter.[37]

Here the 'I' is looking at itself from the inside, and including the
social perspective too, so confident is Fox that what appears bizarre
and even mad is governed by an inner justification; there is no gap at
all between the mind and God, and other voices have told Fox that
he is 'written in the book of the Lamb since before the beginning of
the world'. The theological pattern of Quakerism underwent some
changes in the eighteenth century which brought it nearer to
Calvinism. W. R. Inge summarises these changes in a manner which
brings out the paradox for the mind:

> The Quakers, under the guidance of Fox, escaped the snare of
> Bibliolatry, but in the eighteenth century, when the real mystical
> foundation of their faith was obscured, they were in danger of
> being merged in the general body of Evangelicalism. They
> accepted, under the influence of Barclay, the Calvinistic doctrine
> of man's total depravity, and this obliged them to make the Inner
> Light itself external, since their theory forbade them to find
> anything in the human mind itself.[38]

Inner certainty, particularly when coupled with a predestinarian
emphasis, tends to breed a paradox in the use of 'I' which some
writers have exploited imaginatively. Luther, as I remarked above,
sows the seeds of Antinomianism when explaining 'justification'.
Technically, the term means: 'one who maintains that the moral law
is not binding upon Christians under the law of grace'. Historically,
this doctrine is revolutionary and anarchistic. Gertrude Huehns in
Antinomianism in English History has assembled some interesting
material which shows, among other things, that Luther made
desperate attempts throughout his life 'to prove and disprove the
antinomian implications of his restatement of the Christian
doctrine'.

Antinomianism tends to diminish the reality of sin, and it was
fiercely suppressed both in the early Reformation period and later in
England when for a few years it began to spread in Cromwell's
model army. It is almost universally associated with a monstrous
degree of individual licence:

> Much more devastating was the criticism levelled at their view of
> individual morality and conduct. Their theory that perfection was
> obtainable in this life, was perverted into a general charter
> granted by them for licentiousness of all kinds. It has to be

admitted, as a matter of justice, that it did not take much ingenuity to read into some of their works the abhorred conclusion that an abundance of sinning would lead to an abounding of grace.[39]

The doctrine flared up again in eighteenth-century Scotland with the controversy over *The Marrow Of Divinity*;[40] and it was by no means felt to be dead in the early nineteenth century, as two of Browning's Gothic monologues show. 'Johannes Agricola in Meditation' and 'Porphyria's Lover', which he first published in 1839 under the title of 'Madhouse Cells I and II', again exploit the psychopathology of the internalised 'I' for Gothic effects. John Agricola was the founder of the Antinomians, and his monologue sounds the true organ-note for Browning of absolute egotism. In this way, history is converted by the Gothic poet to a psychopathological drama. Browning is explicitly interested, in the tissue of ironies with which the poem opens, in bringing out the paradox of an absolutely internalised identification with God:

> There's heaven above, and night by night
>   I look right through its gorgeous roof;
> No suns and moons though e'er so bright
>   Avail to stop me; splendour-proof
>   I keep the broods of stars aloof:
> For I intend to get to God,
>   For 'tis to God I speed so fast,
> For in God's breast, my own abode,
>   Those shoals of dazzling glory, passed,
>   I lay my spirit down at last.
> I lie where I have always lain,
>   God smiles as he has always smiled.[41]

This is a brilliant set of jokes, based presumably on Agricola's own rather witty statement that he will be content to be a sinner, so long as God remains God. Browning shows, in a series of paradoxes, which yet remain theologically impeccable that there is no reality in the universe except Johannes. This is space travel in the realms of the infinite ego: 'I look right through its gorgeous roof' contains the possibility that Johannes is looking *down*, and as the verse unfolds, the sense grows that he can be in two or more places and times at once. Johannes *is* God, in effect, for he has never left him. The spatial and temporal jokes are worthy of Milton's war in heaven, from which they, doubtless, partly derive: but here they are transferred into a single head, which contracts to a mote possessed by God, or dialectically expands to identify with the universe. Time is an illusion, like space. He keeps the stars 'aloof', and Browning twists his rhyme away from actually saying 'aloft'; but the subject–object relationship is perpetually reversing itself in the rhetoric, so we have the illusion that it is God, not Johannes, talking; for creator and creature are tied by an inexorable logic, testified to by the patterns of Johannes's own mind and speech. As the poem proceeds to the vision of a boundless criminality, Browning turns the satirical screw of his rhetoric to tip it over into farce: Johannes is beginning to rave:

> And having thus created me,
>   Thus rooted me, he bade me grow,
>   Guiltless for ever, like a tree
>   That buds and blooms, nor seeks to know
>   The law by which it prospers so;
> But sure that thought and word and deed
>   All go to swell his love for me,
>   Me, made because that love had need
>   Of something irreversibly
>   Pledged solely its content to be.
> Yes, yes, a tree which must ascend,
>   No poison gourd foredoomed to stoop!
> I have God's warrant, could I blend
>   All hideous sins, as in a cup,
>   To drink the mingled venoms up;
> Secure my nature will convert
>   The draught to blossoming gladness fast.[42]

Browning is often said to be a poor stylist; but here the most awkward sentence ('Me, made because that love . . .') is an enactment of the logic of internalisation; the self-description mimes the paradox, or the tautology, of God's love needing something to need it: God is dependent on Johannes, the great 'me' of creation; that is to say, of course, God is dependent upon himself. The collision is perfect, once again, between the most rigorous form of Christian self-scrutiny, and the psychopathology of what the Victorians thought of as 'the criminal mind'. Ironically, when the

Lutheran mechanism of conscience is removed, God becomes Johannes in the third person.

The companion piece, 'Prophyria's Lover', is a justly famous piece of nineteenth-century Gothic. This poem also hovers between farce and horror, as we realise that the confessional 'I' unwinds an existence so alienated that he is at certain points not there at all. Again, it is the momentary tortuousness of the style which deletes 'I' as a subject:

> . . . she rose, and from her form
> Withdrew the dripping cloak and shawl
> And laid her soiled gloves by, untied
> Her hat, and let the damp hair fall,
> And last, she sat down by my side
> And called me. When no voice replied . . .[43]

In fact, the heavy presence of the 'I' is as guaranteed by this device, as it would be in a cinematic version in which we look out of his eyes through the camera itself, because 'no voice' *is* a reference to himself, but in a kind of intermediate third person. The strangling is again described in a grotesquely alienated fashion ('I found / A thing to do'); but the tonal ambiguity of the poem's final lines reveals that, however hard the internalised conscience is repressed by the ego, it returns in a faint echo to haunt the mind:

> The smiling rosy little head,
> So glad it has its utmost will,
> That all it scorned at once is fled,
> And I, its love, am gained instead!
> Porphyria's love: she guessed now how
> Her darling one wish would be heard.
> And thus we sit together now,
> And all night long we have not stirred,
> And yet God has not said a word![44]

The tone is a fascinating exposure of a mental dialectic here: it appears to be denying guilt, and it forms a fitting climax to an apparently secularised study of the murderer's psychopathology. But the paradox that makes the tone so odd is that the expectation that God *will* say something is simultaneously present in the denial.

The poem is, as in the case of the Poe story, a confession of guilt; and yet also a lack of acknowledgement of it. For the 'I' of this poem, no less than Johannes, has exercised the rights of creator over his worshipping creature Porphyria: erotic love and religious obsession mutually feed each other. The structure of manoeuvre is the same in both poems, though their tone and subject matter throw a different stress on the central issue.

But perhaps the most famous example of a horror story which employs the premises of Antinomianism and the doctrines of extreme Calvinism is James Hogg's *The Private Memoirs and Confessions of a Justified Sinner*. Hogg knew the eighteenth-century case of his namesake James Hog and Thomas Boston of Carnock who had revived Antinomianism in a dialogue called *The Marrow of Modern Divinity*. In that dialogue there is a character called Antinomista, whose sayings are caricatured in the novel. It seems likely that Hogg, who came from the Episcopalian side of the Scottish hills, was opposed to the Renaissance of dogmatic Calvinism in Scotland in the early nineteenth century. He also, as Louis Simpson first pointed out, had to hand the contemporary case of the murderer Nichol Muschet who was hanged in the Grass Market in Edinburgh in 1817 and whose confession was published in 1818. Muschet ascribes his murders to the work of one Burnbank. Even while he hacks a poor woman to death, Muschet portrays himself as the victim of Burnbank. And it becomes clear from his confession that he himself is very close to Antinomianism:

> What shall I say of God's free grace and mercy! . . . What matter of admiration is it that ever a holy and just God should have cast his eye in mercy upon me, the chief of sinners, who have made it my business to delight myself in the works of darkness, most part of my short life! But very oft of the rudest pieces of clay, that most excellent potter makes vessels of honour, the more to manifest his singular power and art.[45]

The connection between the projected other self and the doctrine of election is present in Muschet's narrative, as surely as it is in Browning's 'fictional' Johannes, but it is not made, obviously enough, by Muschet. Hogg, however, performs the richest of satires on the whole tradition, again tilting into psychopathology the rhetoric of extreme Protestantism. The irony of the following passage, for example, uses the idea of free will against the speaker,

Wringhim. The preaching of Blanchard the moderate whom Wringhim, with the help of his friend Gil-Martin, will destroy, throws Wringhim into a fit of pious indignation:

> He was actually holding it forth, as a fact, that 'it was every man's own blame if he was not saved'! What horrible misconstruction! And then he was alleging, and trying to prove from nature and reason that no man ever was guilty of a sinful action who might not have declined it had he so chosen! 'Wretched controvertist!' thought I to myself an hundred times, 'Shall not the sword of the Lord be moved from its place of peace for such presumptuous, absurd testimonies as these!'[46]

The interesting thing here, which might have been responsible for the misunderstandings of nineteenth-century commentators on the novel, is that the satire uses the orthodox notion of conscience for ironic purposes. The consciences of Andrew Laing and the rest were so safe they thought Hogg was attacking his own beliefs. The novel is an ironic testimony to the power of conscience; many people in the novel see Gil-Martin, Wringhim's 'double'. He is their 'double' too, and the testimonies in the novel are a tissue of superstition, for Gil-Martin has the qualities of a shape changer, catering to the inner state of whoever perceives him. The dry old rascally lawyer, for example, doesn't turn a hair when addressed by Gil-Martin. But the central drama takes place within the psyche of Wringhim, who has the misfortune, ironically, to *fail* in repressing his conscience, and has to be brought back from the brink of self-doubt to egotistical fanaticism by the Devil: consider the irony of the following passage, for example:

> I *had* a desire to slay him, it is true, and such a desire too as a thirsty man has to drink; but at the same time, this longing desire was mingled with a certain terror, as if I had dreaded that the drink for which I longed was mixed with deadly poison. My mind was so much weakened, or rather softened about this time, that my faith began a little to give way, and I doubted most presumptuously of the least tangible of all Christian tenets, namely, of the *infallibility of the elect*. I hardly comprehended the great work I had begun, and doubted of *my own* infallibility, or that of any created being. But I was brought over again by the unwearied diligence of my friend to repent of my backsliding, and view once more the superiority of the Almighty's counsels and in its fullest latitude.[47]

'Most presumptuously' is very amusing here, for it sums up the complex double-focus in the satire. Hogg, who by his own confession loved to read nothing more than theology, inverts the traditional Protestant premise that self-doubt is necessary to true faith, which probably seemed rational to him anyway, and makes it into a form of 'backsliding' into reasonable behaviour, which is not to be indulged at all costs. The confessional mode serves the purpose of Hogg's satire beautifully, for Wringhim is confessing his *guilt*, of course.

In this state, Hogg treats us to a description of his psychopathology, as nightmarish as anything of its kind I have read which even makes the Devil doubtful:

> Immediately after this I was seized with a strange distemper, which neither my friends nor physicians could comprehend, and it confined me to my chamber for many days; but I knew, myself, that I was bewitched, and suspected my father's reputed concubine of the deed. I told my fears to my reverend protector, who hesitated concerning them, but I knew by his words and looks that he was conscious I was right. I generally conceived myself to be two people. When I lay in bed, I deemed there two of us in it; when I sat up I always beheld another person, and always in the same position from the place where I sat or stood, which was about three paces off me towards my left side. It mattered now how many or few were present: this my second self was sure to be present in his place, and this occasioned a confusion in all my words and ideas that utterly astounded my friends, who all declared that, instead of being deranged in my intellect, they had never heard my conversation manifest so much energy or sublimity of conception; but, for all that, over the singular delusion that I was two persons my reasoning faculties had no power. The most perverse part of it was that I rarely conceived *myself* to be any of the two persons. I thought for the most part that my companion was one of them and my brother the other; and I found that, to be obliged to speak and answer in the character of another man, was a most awkward business at the long run.[48]

This is a rich mixture of satire and horror; if his 'friends' are also Antinomians, then his ravings appear energetic and sublime, and we have a form of satirical inversion quite close to Swift. But it is clearly nineteenth-century; the fragmentation of self has gone so far in the last part of the confession, that, according to the theological structure of internalisation, the familiar third onlooker has been produced. What Hogg seems to be doing is using the orthodox structure of conscience against extreme Calvinism; but in doing so, he reveals the psychopathology implied in taking that orthodoxy to its 'logical' conclusion.

Laing also discusses in *The Divided Self* what he calls 'plate-glass feelings':

> The heightened sense of being always seen, or at any rate of being always potentially seeable, may be principally referable to the body, but the preoccupation with being seeable may be condensed with the idea of the mental self being penetrable, and vulnerable, as when the individual feels that one can look right through him into his 'mind' or 'soul'. Such 'plate-glass' feelings are usually spoken about in terms of metaphor or simile, but in psychotic conditions the gaze or scrutiny of the other can be experienced as an actual penetration into the core of the 'inner' self.[49]

This is, in fact, a motif in primitive Christianity which we can all recognise, if we let 'the other' equal God. Whether it is a metaphor or not, I suspect, depends on all sorts of different things – on how mediated the religion is by social structure (we can imagine Pamela or Clarissa feeling this way, but not Mr B) and as always, the disposition of the individual. Bunyan, for example, is comforted by this feeling; he talks of this kind of experience like a primitive painter might, and one might take this as the simplest version of the idea:

> At which time my understanding was so enlightened, that I was as though I had seen the Lord Jesus look down from Heaven, through the Tiles, upon me, and direct these words unto me. This sent me mourning home, it broke my heart, and filled me full of joy, and laid me low as the dust.[50]

Browning's Johannes parodies this kind of anthropomorphic other, because there is no difference for him in being underneath and above: all eternity lies open to his gaze and the dome of heaven is such that the plate-glass floor is also, so to speak, the plate-glass roof.

One of the most eloquent adaptations of this idea I can think of in the horror genre is in the following passage from Stevenson's story *Markheim*. Here we have brought together the potentially psychotic condition and the traditional Christian motif of being perpetually watched: Markheim has killed an antique dealer (a coarse materialist and parasite) and Stephen describes his reaction to what he has done in a very complicated and specific fashion:

> On that first story, the doors stood ajar, three of them like three ambushes, shaking his nerves like the throats of cannon. He could never again, he felt, be sufficiently immured and fortified from men's observing eyes; he longed to be home, girt in by walls, buried among bedclothes, and invisible to all but God. And at that thought he wondered a little, recollecting tales of other murderers and the fear they were said to entertain of heavenly avengers. It was not so, at least, with him. He feared the laws of nature, lest, in their callous and immutable procedure, they should preserve some damning evidence of his crime. He feared tenfold more, with a slavish, superstitious terror, some scission in the continuity of man's experience, some wilful illegality of nature. He played a game of skill, depending on the rules, calculating consequence from cause; and what if nature, as the defeated tyrant overthrew the chess-board, should break the mould of their succession? The like had befallen Napoleon (so writers said) when the winter changed the time of its appearance. The like might befall Markheim: the solid walls might become transparent and reveal his doings like those of bees in a glass hive.[51]

His plate-glass feelings, Markheim insists, are *social*: they are directed towards the world of men. The logic is somewhat similar to the narrator of 'Porphyria's Lover'; for Markheim is paradoxically so *used* to being watched by God that he feels secure: his conscience is internalised to such a degree that he fears only human, legal judgement. This is the *ostensible* structure of his thinking; but, although he appears to be a late nineteenth-century materialist, a Spencerian in his attitude towards 'the laws of nature', he is really, as Stevenson makes explicit, only a superstitious savage who is transferring and displacing his guilt from one part of his mind to another. The (inappropriate) reference to Napoleon's Russian campaign shows that the egotism which informs these speculations is approaching that of Agricola, or Wringhim. He feels 'justified': and Stevenson makes quite explicit the split between the two ways of regarding himself. God, for Markheim, is part of his innermost psyche, and he only just dimly suspects that he operates 'indirectly' in the social world of men. Perhaps there will be some sort of an 'accident', he thinks, which will lead to his discovery:

> These things he feared; and, in a sense, these things might be called the hands of God reached forth against sin. But about God Himself he was at ease: his act was doubtless exceptional, but so were his excuses, which God knew; it was there, and not among men, that he felt sure of justice.
>
> When he had got safe into the drawing-room, and shut the door behind him, he was aware of a respite from alarms. The room was quite dismantled, uncarpeted besides, and strewn with packing cases and incongruous furniture; several great pier glasses, in which he beheld himself at various angles, like an actor on a stage.[52]

It is at this point, when the infinite regress of self-scrutiny has begun to take over, that Markheim to his horror hears a step on the stairs and sees the handle of the door turning. The Devil has arrived, stepping into the room and blandly telling of the foreknown consequences of his deed. Markheim remains 'free', of course, to carry on and invest the money on the Stock Exchange, but he will lose it, and so on. Markheim (who, we learn, not to our surprise, has been a 'revivalist') is told what he will do to save his life, when the maid arrives in a few minutes. At this point, he reveals his real guilt, and decides to frustrate the course of events by giving himself up. And, instantly, the countenance of his visitor begins to undergo a 'wonderful and lovely change'. He turns out to have been the angel of Providence, disguised by Markheim's suppressed guilt as the Devil. By impersonating the Devil he tempts Markheim to reject him, and the story ends with Markheim giving himself up to the maid who duly arrives on time. This is precisely the structure, incidentally, of Maturin's *Melmoth the Wanderer*. But how do we read it? Again, from an anti-puritan Christian point of view, it is an impeccable piece of theology, and no doubt it was received as a didactic story, revealing that murder will out. God's Providence works by negatives, and Markheim's final speech to the 'Devil' shows this, quite clearly:

> 'Though I be, as you say truly, at the beck of every small

temptation, I can yet, by one decisive gesture, place myself beyond the reach of all. My love of good is damned to barrenness; it may, and let it be! But I have still my hatred of evil; and from that, to your galling disappointment, you shall see that I can draw both energy and courage.'[53]

But the impeccable theology is a mental labyrinth, which ends in 'free' suicide. Durkheim found in his classic study of suicide that in mid-nineteenth-century Germany, the rate was significantly higher amongst Protestants and this story of Stevenson's doubtless rehearses the logic by which some of them died. Technically, since Markheim will be judged by society, that is, his suicide is indirect; but the story cannot be read simply on that level because its details are set up in such a way that they demand to be translated back into psychopathology. It is about consciousness *masquerading* as action: the projections of the self are spread out into causation, on a thin social backdrop, but the landscape is still finally mental. As such, it is written out of a stock of mental manoeuvres which cluster round the social transmission of Protestant Christianity, but so rich is Stevenson's grasp that he reveals the implied contradictions.

Dickens's understanding of self-fragmentation and his accompanying analysis of guilt has been frequently commented on. It is highly complex, and I can do no more here than sketch out one or two points. It is clear that he is fascinated by the labyrinth and that he sees many of its implications early on in his career. Jonas Chuzzlewit's state of mind, for example, after the murder of Chuffy, corresponds perfectly to the model of a repressed conscience which we have been looking at already; and Dickens shows how, once the mechanism of conscience, ineradicable of course, has been displaced, it does its work on the self. Chuzzlewit is obsessed by getting back to his room in an attempt to convince himself that he hasn't performed the murder for which he is explicitly *not* remorseful. The transition is brilliantly described: the room to which he is inexorably drawn is also hateful to him:

Dread and fear were upon him, to an extent he had never counted on, and could not manage in the least degree. He was so horribly afraid of that infernal room at home. This made him, in a gloomy, murderous, mad way, not only fearful *for* himself, but *of* himself; for being as it were, a part of the room: a something supposed to be there, yet missing from it: he invested himself with its mysterious terrors; and when he pictured in his mind the ugly chamber, false and quiet, false and quiet, through the dark hours of two nights; and the tumbled bed, and he not in it, though believed to be; he became in a manner his own ghost and phantom, and was at once the haunting spirit and the haunted man.[54]

The third-person narrative makes sure that the reflexive logic of this doesn't spill over into the formal dimension; were Jonas at this point confessing, a third observer, even in his mode of address, would spring into being, or would have to be artfully concealed by an unresonant 'I'. Nevertheless the passage clearly uses the logic of the internalised conscience to initiate the split; like Browning's Johannes, Jonas's plate-glass feelings are dialectically reversible. He is outside looking in, and inside looking out at the same time, or in such rapid switches that his 'position' appears to be the same. Primitive Christianity, before Cartesianism, is responsible for the image of the mind as a room; one can see it quite plainly for example in Augustine's *Confessions*, in his discussion of the insoluble paradox, with which he batters himself into submission, of how something can be 'in' his memory and yet not 'in' it (that is, not remembered) at the same time.

Dickens pushes his analysis further and further into the prevalence of social conditioning; and in doing so moves away from strictly 'Gothic' effects; it is the comedy of repressed guilt which begins to obsess him, not the terror. And that comedy, in moment after moment, is the perfect demonstration of Marcuse's 'double morality'. When Harold Skimpole, in *Bleak House*, is arrested for debt, he appeals explicitly to the separation of the office and the person. His elaborate rhetorical flourish is so much double-Dutch to poor Coavinses, the bailiff who is the very image of debt, but to the reader it is the *exact* equivalent of Luther's argument to the Christian slaves – it behoves you not to take the condition of your body too personally. Skimpole, though apparently harmless, finds it quite easy to think of himself in two quite distinct ways. And Esther Summerson comments that he often seems to be referring to himself in the third person.

But the apotheosis of this is the famous confrontation in *Great Expectations* between Jaggers and Wemmick, both of whom are the perfect examples of the 'separation of office and person'. Wemmick is the more obvious, with his Aged P. and Walworth sentiments, his drawbridge and cannon, versus his 'office' persona; but it is Jaggers, the very scales of justice, who is the more severely repressed, as the form of his 'confession' to Pip clearly shows:

> Mr Jaggers nodded his head retrospectively two or three times, and actually drew a sigh. 'Pip', said he, 'we won't talk about "poor dreams"; you know more about such things than I, having much fresher experience of that kind. But now, about this other matter. I'll put a case to you. Mind! I must admit nothing.'
> He waited for me to declare that I quite understood that he expressly said that admitted nothing.
> 'Now, Pip', said Mr Jaggers, 'put this case. Put the case that a woman under such circumstances as you have mentioned, held her child concealed, and was obliged to communicate the fact to her legal adviser . . .'[55]

Finally, he makes his appearance in his own story in the third person. The theatre of alienation, finally a mental theatre and a mental court of judgement, is peopled by judge, advocate and criminal alike. Dickens is exposing the way in which social roles provide ways in which people can transform their self-scrutiny into action without destroying themselves; but at a price so severe that it makes human behaviour a mass of absurdity.

But at the end of his life, Dickens renewed his interest in the Gothic expression of this structure. In Jasper, the organist of Cloisterham, Dickens follows the logic of the repressed conscience through to its conclusion. Or at least, he would have done. The famous plan for the end of the book which he communicated to John Forster shows that he was going to have Jasper 'confess' in his prison cell in the person of another. This is how Kate Perugini wrote about the final scene in the *Pall Mall Gazette*:

> If those who are interested in the subject will carefully read what I have quoted, they will not be able to detect any word or hint from my father that it was upon the Mystery alone that he relied for the interest and originality of his idea. The originality was to be shown, as he tells us, in what we may call the psychological description the murderer gives us of his temptations, temperament, and character, as if told by another.[56]

Jasper feels that his life is 'lined and dotted out for him like a surveyor's plan'; Dickens's joke is that he has 'found his niche' and strait-jacketed himself into a social occupation. As he says, he must 'subdue himself to his vocation', and, in his description of it, that 'vocation' comes to have a familiar literalness:

> 'I hate it. The cramped monotony of my existence grinds me away by the grain. How does our service sound to you?'
> 'Beautiful! Quite celestial!'
> 'It often sounds to me quite devilish. I am so weary of it. The echoes of my own voice among the arches seem to mock me with my daily drudging round. No wretched monk who droned his life away in that gloomy place before me can have been more tired of it than I am. He would take for relief (and did take) to carving demons out of the stalls and seats and desks. What shall I do? Must I take to carving them out of my heart?'[57]

The setting, of course, is Anglican not Puritan; and Dickens's joke about the monk satirises the established, socialised product of the Reformation. But the isolation of the consciousness (the world of echoes) and the interiorised self-hatred of the final image belong to a different kind of religious tradition. Dickens has left us in this novel with one scene of extraordinary eroticism and power, which seems to me amongst the finest things he has written. Jasper, as is hinted by the image of carving demons out of the heart, is a masochist. He identifies his repression as 'social' only, so that he thinks of his inner self as entirely 'free'. So free that it is like a vacuum, a state of existential boredom that yearns to be punctured and violated and destroyed. The other side of the dialectic is the total egotism which will kill in order to obtain that kind of erotic satisfaction. This is the side of him which gives Rosa plate-glass feelings of an unmistakably erotic nature:

> 'What is this imagined threatening, pretty one? What is threatened?'
> 'I don't know.' I have never even dared to think or wonder what it is.'
> 'And was this all, tonight?'
> 'This was all; except that tonight when he watched my lips so closely as I was singing, besides feeling terrified I felt ashamed and passionately hurt. It was as if he kissed me, and I couldn't bear it, but cried. . . .'[58]

The hypnosis or 'animal magnetism' is merely a vehicle for the eroticism here, and even the celebrated opium serves as an artificial release of the 'other' self, which, like Hyde, is a bolus of repressed energy. The climax of the fragment of the book which we have is the chapter called 'Shadow on the Sundial', where the two confront each other in the centre of the garden at the Nun's House. Here, surrounded by windows, Jasper confesses his love for her, while pretending to make polite conversation. The windows all round them are insistent; they ensure that Jasper's public self will remain totally calm and unruffled, and it is this conscious repression that causes the growing excitement of the scene, as Jasper artificially arranges their positions according to an imagined idea of plausibility: and Rosa against her will adopts the theatrical posture of a casual listener in response: he then pours out his masochism.

> His preservation of his easy attitude rendering his working features and his convulsive hands absolutely diabolical, he returns, with a fierce extreme of admiration:
> 'How beautiful you are! You are more beautiful in anger than repose. I don't ask you for your love; give me yourself and your hatred; give me yourself and that pretty rage; give me yourself and that enchanting scorn; it will be enough for me.'
> Impatient tears rise to the eyes of the trembling little beauty, and her face flames; but as she again rises to leave him in indignation, and seek protection within the house, he stretches out his hand towards the porch, as though he invited her to enter it.[59]

This last sentence is a stroke of genius; it reveals how all their behaviour is constructed for the benefit of an unseen observer, who watches for the slightest sign of impropriety. Jasper's impromptu theatre of alienation, the logic of his fantasy, seems like (objective) magic here; it surrounds all their behaviour with 'doubleness':

> Again Rosa quails before his threatening face, though innocent of its meaning, and she remains. Her panting breathing comes and goes as if it would choke her; but with a repressive hand upon her bosom, she remains.
> 'I have made my confession that my love is mad. It is so mad that, had the ties between me and my dear lost boy been one

silken thread less strong, I might have swept even him from your side when you favoured him.'

A film comes over the eyes she raises for an instant, as though he had turned her faint.[60]

He is telling her that he *has* killed for her, without acknowledging it, and the thought begins to excite her, as one might say, 'despite herself'. What is the meaning of the 'repressive hand' here? It too is surely at some level for the benefit of an observer. But Dickens is only beginning to turn the screw. The scene mounts to a frenzy of sexual excitement as they act out the gestures of statuesque decorum, while Jasper pours out his masochistic ravings:

'Reckon up nothing at this moment, angel, but the sacrifices that I lay at those dear feet, which I could fall down among the vilest ashes and kiss, and put upon my head as a poor savage might. There is my fidelity to my dear boy after death. Tread up on it!' with an action of his hands, as though he cast down something precious.

'There is the inexpiable offence against my adoration of you. Spurn it!' with a similar action.

'There are my labours in the cause of a just vengeance for six toiling months. Crush them!' With another repetition of the action.

'There is my past and my present wasted life. There is the desolation of my heart and my soul. There is my peace; there is my despair. Stamp them into the dust, so that you take me, were it even mortally hating me!'

The frightful vehemence of the man, now reaching its full height, so additionally terrifies her as to break the spell that has held her to the spot. She swiftly moves towards the porch; but in an instant he is at her side, and speaking in her ear.

'Rosa, I am self-repressed again. I am walking calmly beside you to the house. I shall wait for some encouragement and hope. I shall not strike too soon. Give me a sign that you attend to me.'

She slightly and constrainedly moves her hand.[61]

It is hard to imagine anyone watching this who would not see what was going on; but then, no one *is* watching. This projection of unacknowledged guilt is powerful and grotesque; it creates a kind of mental theatre of alienation in which this erotic melodrama can be

acted out in all its contradictions. And there are plenty of those. The
language has moved into theology again. Jasper casts her as the
angel, and he quite clearly steps into the role of the Devil speaking in
her ear. But Dickens makes it quite clear that what is devilish about
him is his self-repression, not his eroticism. His confession is
'framed', but nevertheless it exhibits the same logical structure as
many of the other confessions examined in this chapter – that is, the
statement 'I am self-repressed' is an impossible one; it instantly
spawns another 'self' to monitor the struggle of the other two.
Dickens, with great brilliance, now mounts the erotic climax of the
scene; at the very moment of 'self-repression':

> She moves her hand once more.
> 'I love you, love you, love you! If you were to cast me off now –
> but you will not – you would never be rid of me. No one should
> come between us. I would pursue you to the death.'
> The handmaid coming out to open the gate for him, he quietly
> pulls off his hat as a parting salute, and goes away with no greater
> show of agitation than is visible in the effigy of Mr Sapsea's father
> opposite. Rosa faints in going upstairs, and is carefully carried to
> her room and laid on her bed. A thunderstorm is coming on the
> maids say, and the hot and stifling air has overset the pretty dear:
> no wonder; they have felt their own knees all of a tremble all day
> long.[62]

Claustrophobia and orgasm are inseparable here; the tone of the
maids is coy, and of the narrator, knowing. Together they diffuse
the eroticism into the environment; and in doing so save it up no
doubt for a further occasion. The 'comic' comparison of Jasper to the
statue of Sapsea's father only serves to conclude the symbolism of
niche and effigy. The writing is a rhetorical *tour de force*, reminiscent
of the structure of the central scenes from *Measure for Measure*, in
which Angelo and Isabella the two puritans (technically they are
Catholics, but the satire of that play is also directed towards puritan
Protestantism) goad each other, through the very rhetorical energy
of their holiness, into a lust that finally has to be acknowledged.

Now that Deirdre Bair's biography has emerged, after his notorious
reticence, we can see something of the relation between Samuel

Beckett's life and his work. Beckett is an Irish Huguenot, who displays the true gloom of Calvinism. Solitary, austere, puritan by his own admission, Beckett, after hundreds of sessions of analysis in the 1930s, appears to have taken self-loathing to the extreme. His first hero Belacqua was a 'low down low church Protestant Highbrow' and his work is full of all manner of theological ideas. Beckett is a lover of Augustine's Latin, to which he has assimilated his English style, and of Thomas à Kempis's *Imitatio Christi*. He has made the logic of self-scrutiny the territory of his major trilogy of novels, *Molloy*, *Malone Dies* and *The Unnamable*.

Beckett writes about the horrors, necessities and impossibilities of self-contemplation as well as its uproarious, hallucinatory absurdity. His novel *Molloy* is a 'double' story, in which one character turns into another, and the final picture of the dissolution of the precise pious Catholic Jacques Moran into the shambling toothless (Protestant?) Molloy is very close to some of the motifs I have been discussing. Compare, for example, this passage from *Molloy* in which Beckett takes the complexity but also the rigour of the internalised conscience to new heights, questioning even the language in which it is expressed. The process of writing itself has now become the subject; but the logical structure, the jokes about talking about yourself in the third person, and so on, are all familiar:

> And every time I say, I said this, or, I said that, or speak of a voice saying far away inside me, Molloy, and then a fine phrase more or less clear and simple, or find myself compelled to attribute to others intelligible words, or hear my own voice uttering to others more or less articulate sounds, I am merely complying with the convention that demands you either lie or hold your peace. . . . And then sometimes there arose within me, confusedly, a kind of consciousness, which I express by saying, I said etc., or Don't do it Molloy, or, Is that your Mother's name? said the sergeant, I quote from memory. Or which I express without sinking to the level of oratio recta, but by means of other figures quite as deceitful.[63]

The idea of lies and deceit here have a moral 'yield' as well as a philosophical one – they give rise to the association between guilt and consciousness itself. The rigour with which this process of self-examination is exploited by a writer is quite unparalleled; but the paradoxes themselves, of self-monitoring producing self-fragmentation, are really all part of what Marcuse describes as the negative concept of liberty in the Protestant internalisation of the conscience, the *a priori* freedom which the truly Christian mind cannot ever catch up with and take hold of. Here is how Moran, the bourgeois Catholic, talks of Molloy:

> I knew then about Molloy, without however knowing much about him. I shall say briefly what little I did know about him. I shall also draw attention, in my knowledge of Molloy to the most striking lacunae.
>
> He had very little room. His time too was limited. He hastened incessantly on, as if in despair, towards extremely close objectives. Now, a prisoner, he hurled himself at I know not what narrow confines, and now, hunted, he sought refuge near the centre.
>
> He panted. He had only to rise up within me for me to be filled with panting.[64]

It is not surprising that Moran wishes to teach his son double-entry bookkeeping. The passage above records a change into his 'other' for the unpleasantly self-satisfied Catholic, obsessed with neatness and ritual, whose house and garden are his whole world, who is seized by fits of unaccountable rage, and who treats his son with hideous cruelty. Moran is ordered to go on a 'journey' to seek Molloy by a Kafka-like organisation headed by one Youdi (Yahweh) which is almost certainly internal. On the journey, he hears himself 'hailed by a voice' and a man emerges out of the darkness. In the dialogue which follows we can feel Moran getting increasingly irritated with this 'pest' who keeps asking him questions:

> What is your business here? he said. Are you on night patrol? I said. He thrust his hand at me. I have an idea I told him again to get out of my way. I can still see the hand coming towards me, pallid, opening and closing. As if self-propelled. I do not know what happened then. But a little later, perhaps a long time later, I found him stretched on the ground, his head in a pulp. I am sorry I cannot indicate more clearly how this result was obtained, it would have been something worth reading. But it is not at this late stage of my relation that I intend to give way to literature. I myself was unscathed, except for a few scratches I did not discover till the following day. I bent over him. As I did so I realised my leg was bending normally. He no longer resembled me.[65]

The lack of description is even more effectively horrible than a blow by blow account; and the repressed politeness of Moran in talking of 'this result' as if it were an algebraic equation is also pathological. Moran's dreadful final joke here – *all* humans resemble each other, by definition – throws us right back to Hogg and the nineteenth-century obsession with the relation between 'the criminal mind' and the moral law. Moran's independence is undermined by the suggestion that he is looking in a mirror. This is another mythic version of Cain and Abel.

His final return to his dark house is pure Gothic. There is, of course, the usual double-take about giving way to literature:

But I shall not dwell upon this journey home, its furies and treacheries. And I shall pass over in silence the fiends in human shape and the phantoms of the dead that tried to prevent me from getting home, in obedience to Youdi's command. But one or two words nevertheless, for my own edification and to prepare my soul to make an end. To begin with my rare thoughts.

Certain questions of a theological nature preoccupied me strangely. As for example.

1. What value is to be attached to the theory that Eve sprang, not from Adam's rib, but from a tumour in the fat of his leg (arse?)

2. Did the serpent crawl, or, as Comestor affirms, walk upright?

3. Did Mary conceive through the ear, as Augustine and Adobard assert?

4. How much longer are we to hang about waiting for the antechrist (sic)?[66]

Beckett has a unique way of modulating horror into hysterical laughter; but here, if we take this passage schematically, we see the last gasp of the Catholic Moran, his goodbye, as it were, to the concept of external rule, before he takes the inward plunge for ever.

The house is decaying, and the passage which describes his return at the end of the novel is packed with motifs from the tradition I have been discussing:

I skirted the graveyard. It was night. Midnight perhaps. The lane is steep, I laboured. A little wind was chasing the clouds over the faint sky. It is a great thing to own a plot in perpetuity, a very great thing indeed. If only that were the only perpetuity. I came to the wicket. It was locked. Very properly. But I could not open it. The key went into the hole, but would not turn. Long disuse? A new lock?[67]

He finds his creatures dead, this God returning to his universe: he is, like Hyde, a stranger in his own house:

My bees, my hens, I had deserted them. I went towards the house. It was in darkness. The door was locked. I burst it open. Perhaps I could have opened it, with one of my keys. I turned the switch. No light. I went to the kitchen, to Martha's room. No one. There is nothing more to tell. The house was empty. The company had cut off the light. They have offered to let me have it back. But I told them they could keep it. That is the kind of man I have become. I went back to the garden. The next day I looked at my handful of bees. A little dust of annulets and wings. I found some letters, at the foot of the stairs, in the box. A letter from Savory. My son was well. He would be. Let us hear no more about him. He has come back. He is sleeping. A letter from Youdi, in the third person, asking for a report. . . .[68]

The 'report' *is* the narrative we are reading, its famous 'post-modernist' end returns to its beginning. One can regard the circularity as an illusionist trick, an existential paradox, and so on, but if we think of the way, for example, Poe throws us back to the beginning of 'William Wilson', the circularity can also be seen as part of the infinitely regressive mechanism of self-awareness.

Sylvia Plath's poetry, when it appeared in the 1960s, was labelled 'confessional'. The imagery of her more familiar, later poems is explicitly 'Gothic' (for her, this word means 'Prussian', which in its turn, means 'father') although it has taken some time for this to be taken into account by critics. What concerns me here is the connection between imagery and point of view which forms a subterranean network whose formal characteristics owe a great deal to the workings of the internalised conscience.

Sylvia Plath's mother was an immigrant German Roman Catholic. After the death of Otto Plath (a presumably atheistic German entomologist), Aurelia Plath was converted to evangelical Protestantism, and joined the Unitarian Fellowship, of which she was a devoted member. The Plath household was pious; and, according to at least one eye-witness, it was 'a real Calvinist

family'.[69] At Wellesley, Sylvia Plath wrote a dissertation on the
Double in Dostoievsky's fiction; she was well-versed in the tradition
of Christian self-scrutiny, and she understood very well, and,
indeed evolved a distinctive technique for the poetic evocation of
what Laing refers to as the installation, in the recesses of the inner
self, of 'a persecuting observer'. At what was to be the end of her
life, in its most fruitful poetic period, she lived below the graveyard
in an English village. The symbolism and the atmosphere of these
powerful poems is part of a ready made Gothic tradition.

> And the wall of old corpses
> I love them.
> I love them like history.[70]

At Court Green Sylvia Plath became highly preoccupied with
theology. She was married to a descendant of Nicholas Ferrar. She
carried on a long and involved correspondence with a Jesuit group
in Cambridge. She attended Protestant Evensong at the church next
door, and was generally excited by the tradition and ritual of a
twelfth-century parish church. But her opposition to the ex-colonial
Rector's High Church theology, and in particular to the doctrine of
the Trinity, betrays perhaps the survival of the non-conformism of
her Unitarian childhood. The Rector becomes a character in these
poems, one of the sinister shapes who populate this endlessly
metamorphosing world. On this level, her theological struggles
smack of a classic conflict between Anglicanism or Anglo-
Catholicism and Puritanism; between ritual and a dynamic, even
demonic, energy of self-awareness. This makes the use of 'I' in the
poems recessive, contradictory, metamorphic; in a way which is
more familiarly describable in the terms of existentialist psychology.
As Laing puts it, 'the I-sense is disembodied, and body becomes the
centre of a false self-system'. Consider, for example, the way in
which imagery and the point of view relate to one another in
'Tulips':

> I am nobody; I have nothing to do with explosions.
> I have given my name and my dayclothes up to the nurses
> And my history to the anaesthetist and my body to surgeons.
>
> . . .
>
> I am a nun now, I have never been so pure.

> I didn't want any flowers, I only wanted
> To lie with my hands turned up and be utterly empty.
> How free it is, you have no idea how free –
> The peacefulness is so big it dazes you,
> And it asks nothing, a name tag, a few trinkets.
> It is what the dead close on, finally; I imagine them
> Shutting their mouths on it, like a Communion tablet.[71]

The 'I' here is dramatising (that is, confessing) the *failure* of self-renunciation, while the images convey its effectiveness. The two are linked, but opposed. The fantasy of 'purity', of being able to slough off the organic process, mediated by some final ritual, is intimately related to a final act of self-scrutiny; yet that self-scrutiny creates the familiar audience of another self looking on:

> Nobody watched me before, now I am watched.
> The tulips turn to me, and the window behind me
> Where once a day the light slowly widens and slowly thins,
> And I see myself, flat, ridiculous, a cut-paper shadow
> Between the eye of the sun and the eyes of the tulips,
> I have no face, I have wanted to efface myself.[72]

'Eye', as in the Christian tradition of confessional autobiography, tends to be a sound pun (cf. the most famous example, 'Ariel' itself).

The poetry, rather reminiscent of Dylan Thomas in its mode of address, mimes a kind of Orphic explosion in which the body is viewed from afar by the 'I' as an institution, a landscape, anything imaginable. Take 'Medusa', for example. Here again one can see the connection between the dissociation of address and the fear of suffocation in the Catholic body:

>   I could draw no breath,
> Dead and moneyless,
>
> Overexposed, like an X-ray.
> Who do you think you are?
> A Communion wafer. Blubbery Mary?
> I shall take no bite of your body,
> Bottle in which I live,
>
> Ghastly Vatican.[73]

Sylvia Plath is an expert at plate-glass feelings, as this passage suggests; and how strange the 'I' becomes in the phrase 'bottle in which I live'; it shows, I think, how one 'I' will spawn another until the imaginative process itself is a form of inertia. The ingestion of the body and blood of Christ is linked with vampirism here, as it is more obviously perhaps in 'Nick and the Candlestick', where the 'I' mines its way down the body:

> Old cave of calcium
> Icicles, old echoer,
> Even the newts are white,
>
> Those holy Joes.
> And the fish, the fish –
> Christ! they are panes of ice,
>
> A vice of knives,
> A piranha
> Religion, drinking
>
> Its first communion out of my live toes.[74]

The white of the final bloodless wafer of a body is dialectically opposed in the structure of the imagery to the red of the 'impure' living blood-pump. 'Getting There' is a complex version of this structure of association:

> I am a letter in this slot –
> I fly to a name, two eyes . . .
> It is a trainstop, the nurses
> Undergoing the faucet water, its veils, veils in a nunnery,
> Touching their wounded,
> The men the blood still pumps forward. . . .[75]

What looks like memory, or rather fantasy-memory, is also self-description. The picture of the central European holocaust is stylised; the veils are part of a series of false selves, the blood is the blood of Jewish victims and her own blood (the imaginative pedigree of her present role, plus the thump of her heart). The poem inverts the logic of a conversion narrative, as it moves towards the present, or rather in Laingian terms from 'there' to 'here' on a pilgrimage through her genes, through various resurrections of the self:

> How far is it?
> There is mud on my feet,
> Thick, red and slipping. It is Adam's side,
> This earth I rise from, and I in agony.
> I cannot undo myself, and the train is steaming. . . .[76]

The veils are often what prevent the 'Eye/I' from getting through. They are false versions of the self ('old whore petticoats') which obscure and suffocate the 'pure' I. Compare the images in 'Totem' for example:

> There is no terminus, only suitcases
>
> Out of which the same self unfolds like a suit,
> Bald and shiny, with pockets of wishes,
>
> Notions and tickets, short circuits and folding mirrors.[77]

The alienated 'I' lives in a series of mirrors; but the agony of these poems lives in the simultaneous acceptance and rejection of the notion of self-integrity. The 'clear cellophane/I cannot crack' defines and confines simultaneously. Thus imaginative activity takes place in a kind of mental theatre, a sort of cabaret act watched by 'the peanut-munching crowd'. Being trapped in the body is inseparable from looking on at herself being trapped, as the terrible lines about the woman she saw totally encased in plaster show: 'I shall never get out of this; there are two of me now'.

The imagery of mirrors is common, but it is often attached to an almost impossible perspective, as in the little poem called 'Contusion':

> Colour floods to the spot, dull purple.
> The rest of the body is all washed out,
> The colour of pearl.
>
> In a pit of rock
> The sea sucks obsessively,
> One hollow the whole sea's pivot.

> The size of a fly,
> The doom mark
> Crawls down the wall.

> The heart shuts,
> The sea slides back,
> The mirrors are sheeted.[78]

This is an inversion of the idea of a life-force. The white and red are opposed again; but here the return of the life-blood is a form of death as 'the mirrors are sheeted' suggests; they are *un*sheeting, as the self glimpses its own extinction in a moment of unbodied 'oceanic' intimation. But the paradox in the presence of the mirror at such a moment, the paradox of self-scrutiny, is evident behind the logic of this witty inversion of life and death; and it is a paradox that is built into certain uses of the confessional form. The opening of *Fever 103°*, for example, is a deliberate pastiche of Puritan self-examination:

> Pure? What does it mean?
> The tongues of hell
> Are dull, dull as the triple

> Tongues of dull, fat Cerberus
> Who wheezes at the gate. Incapable
> Of licking clean

> The aguey tendon, the sin, the sin . . . .[79]

The fantasy of this poem is that, given this degree of self-loathing, sickness becomes a form of purity. The higher the temperature, the more the self is levitating out of the body:

> I think I am going up,
> I think I may rise –
> The beads of hot metal fly, and I, love, I

> Am a pure acetylene
> Virgin
> Attended by roses,

> By kisses, by cherubim,
> By whatever these pink things mean.
> Not you, nor him
>
> Not him, nor him
> (My selves dissolving, old whore petticoats) –
> To Paradise.[80]

The Magdelenian self, is finally naked; pure, spiritual body ascending, shedding as she goes the selves given to her by fathers and husbands and sons, the men in her life. This 'Apotheosis of Magdalen' is lit by a hideous acetylene glare; and it is the very violence of this conceit which reveals the paradox lying beneath the the poem's apparently conclusive rhetoric; turning the welding torch upon yourself, and *being the torch* are not the same thing, though the poem seeks to make them so.

'A Birthday Present' on the other hand seeks not so much to suppress the split self or obliterate it in a blaze of glory as to get it out, as it were, into the open; monologue modulates almost instantly into dialogue:

> What is this, behind this veil, is it ugly, is it beautiful?
> It is shimmering, has it breasts, has it edges?
>
> I am sure it is unique, I am sure it is just what I want,
> When I am quiet at my cooking I feel it looking, I feel it
>   thinking
>
> Is this the one I am to appear for,
> Is this the elect one, the one with black eye-pits and a scar?
>
> Measuring the flour, cutting off the surplus,
> Adhering to rules, to rules, to rules.
>
> Is this the one for the annunciation?
> My God, what a laugh![81]

If ever one wanted proof of the connection between horror and domesticity, this is it. In fact, there was a windowless inner room at Court Green, and the biographers report how Sylvia Plath was always afraid of it. She felt there was *another* room behind it, waiting for her. But the shape of this alienated meditation is governed by a set of theological jokes; the nun-self on the other side of the 'veil' is watching the monitoring self adhere to the rules. The 'obsession with the quotidian' here is purely symbolic. The central conceit of the poem is the opening of a parcel which contains this 'it', this new, non-bodied self. The final fantasy again is of death as a kind of virgin birth. Sylvia Plath's 'I' dreams of confronting itself, outside time. It is the final look in the mirror:

> Only let down the veil, the veil, the veil.
> If it were death
>
> I would admire the deep gravity of it, its timeless eyes.
> I would know you were serious.
>
> There would be a nobility then, there would be a birthday.
> And the knife not carve, but enter
>
> Pure and clean as the cry of a baby,
> And the universe slide from my side.[82]

She becomes the new Eve here, taken from her old tainted Adamite self by Caesarian section. The parcel of the body is violently opened, and the poem's address is rhetorically split between 'pure' present and monitoring receiver. 'You' is almost always (as in Dylan Thomas's rhetoric) reducible to 'I', for the pronouns enter and metamorphose into each other.

This process of inertial metamorphosis, of ultimate self-address, is the rhetorical symptom of a resistance to history. The poems assign fake provenance to their subjects and materials; in fact what they are doing is substituting a version of Providential irony, unearthing the tell-tale traces of final causation, for historical process. They purport to be tracing a line from origins, geographical, racial, to the present moment, but the present, usually that of an imagined death, is in fact casting its shadow backwards, converting history into myth, and myth into psychodrama. This is the pattern, for example, of the most famous of her poems, 'Daddy', and her most obvious piece of 'Gothic'. She casts the patriarchal presences in her biography, father and husband, as Nazi stormtroopers and herself as Jewish victim. The geographical and historical search through Europe for 'origins' implied in the rhetoric of the poem ends at its remotest point, a myth of Eastern European culture, which yet is suddenly the present:

> If I've killed one man, I've killed two –
> The vampire who said he was you
> And drank my blood for a year,
> Seven years, if you want to know.
> Daddy, you can lie back now.
>
> There's a stake in your fat black heart
> And the villagers never liked you.
> They are dancing and stamping on you.
> They always *knew* it was you.
> Daddy, daddy, you bastard, I'm through.[83]

The final effect of this is to seal the past in the present. Like 'Getting There', the retrospective movement of the poem is not structurally distinct from the exemplary pattern of Christian confessional autobiography, though, of course, it pastiches the mode for quite different purposes.

David Storey's biography has not yet emerged, but his novel *Radcliffe* is an explicit analysis of the existential aspects of puritan self-awareness. The Radcliffe family has both puritan and Catholic elements in it; and the story of the relationship between Leonard Radcliffe and Tolson, which culminates in violent murder is the story of a search for an impossible unity between two men. Leonard's theological argument with the Anglican Provost half-way through the book is crucial to its structure. Leonard Radcliffe, whose consciousness is totally alienated, seeks to confront the fact that he is trapped within his body. His interpretation of the incarnation is an extension, a sort of allegory, of his perception of his own alienation:

> 'What a contemptible and putrid thing the body is,' he said in a reflective tone. 'It does nothing but destroy us, hanging on us like a sickness, devouring us until we're assimilated by it, and die with it. . . . And Christ was separate. He destroyed His body, showed His contempt for it, hung it up like a bit of canvas. He cast it in the face of men who have to live *within* their bodies, taunting them with salvation, His spiritual grace.'[84]

Christ for Leonard is a kind of demon, who explains his own passionate vision of a prior unity of self that must include the body. The orthodox Pauline position is for him a mockery:

'What a trivial thing you've made of Christ. You've cut His body away from His soul, and condemned *us* to live with the body and to be ever wanting for the soul. You've condemned us to be separate things when our only salvation lies in wholeness and completeness. When the body and the soul are *one thing*.'

'God is our vision of everything that transcends our own physical lives,' the Provost said quietly, no longer interested in the theoretical interpretation of his own beliefs but in trying to control Leonard's outburst by his own calmness and manner. 'Our physical nature is an impediment to that state of Grace, to the spiritual world which, in one form or another, we all long for. To separate the Body from the Soul was Our Lord's gift to man. He *freed* the soul from the human body and gave us the true gift of immortality.'

'His gift! It was his *damnation!*'[85]

Leonard's search for an authentic form of action that welds knowing and being together leads to his relationship with his 'other half' Tolson and to a violent and horrific act of murder. It is, in a sense, Blakeley, the self-styled Catholic, who sews the idea of overcoming the dissociated self through violent action in Leonard's mind. Blakeley's speech is a monumental expression of the effect of installing a persecuting observer in the head:

'. . . But what I'm trying to say is that, however depressed or upset I get, there's a part of me that remains separate. A part that just watches me being depressed. It's as if I don't really *take part in* my depression. As though, because I can watch my feelings, that somehow, they're valueless . . . synthetic . . . put on. Though I know they're not. . . . It's hellish. . . . Hellish . . . watching your own suffering to such an extent that you begin to suspect that it's not really suffering at all . . .[86]

and he concludes with the kind of questions which Sylvia Plath was perpetually toying with:

'I mean, could this separate thing watch itself being destroyed, do you think? Suppose I'd turned the knife on myself, would that part of me which watches *still* go on watching or would something unusual, something *unique* happen? Would that part of me actually step in and *do* something? Commit itself?'

His eyes followed every stress and movement of Leonard's face, and greedily, with a voracious intentness. 'Is it that part of you that's called the soul? And when you die, or when you're dead, is it still separate, and can even leave you? Or leave its *body*. Do you think that's what Christ meant by the spirit, by his ascension?'[87]

But unlike the poetry of Plath, Storey's novel is obsessed by the nature of action. The almost Sartrian sense of commitment is grafted into the Christian paradox. The result is predictable, but no less horrific. Leonard destroys Tolson with his hammer; and Blakeley stabs his family to death, and then proceeds to the final look in the mirror:

> Blakeley himself, it was assumed, had spent some time after this writing his confession, one which was terminated by a simple but extremely articulate appeal for the strengthening and preservation of the monarchy, and for greater support for the unification of churches. He had then made several attempts to kill himself with the knife and, having failed, had seemingly walked aimlessly about the rest of the house for the rest of the night. Bloodied footmarks led repetitively through every room and up and down the stairs. He had finally succeeded in killing himself, it appeared, as the police knocked on the front door, and had done so by facing a mirror and cutting his throat. The mirror, for some absurd reason, was displayed in court, its surface almost completely concealed beneath a dark tracery of stains.[88]

This novel never enacts the confessional mode, and therefore the issues tend to be presented more abstractly, through a third person. The language here is a pastiche, not of Christian self-description, but of something between a local newspaper and a police report. This may be why its author has repudiated it as 'intellectualising'. But the structure of self-perception is very strongly related to the tradition I have been discussing. Again, the history of the Radcliffe family is converted into psychodrama; yet the class and sexual affiliations which separate, say, Richardson's heroines and heroes are at the centre of the book.

But despite Storey's determination to avoid the dialectics of 'I–he' in the style of the book, he still succeeds in making us *inhabit* the paradox of what Sylvia Plath calls 'the awful god-bit in him / Dying to fly and be done with it'. The summing-up of the prosecuting counsel at Leonard's trial is a brilliant inclusion by Storey because it forces us to apprehend the gap between Leonard's inarticulate, heroic struggles and the 'rational' explanation for his actions. What Leonard does not hear, so dissociated is his consciousness, is what the reader feels to be correct, but bland and schematic:

> As he listened to the closing speeches of the trial he appeared calm and reflective, only turning his head slightly at certain phrases as though he caught some fragment of their implication. '. . . A guilt so monstrous that, like all the other emotions his puritanical mind finds intolerable, it is manufactured into some heartless theory about the destiny of men in general. . . . He has asked us to look at his crime as if it were the simple illustration of an elaborate theory which he is holding up for our *approval*. . . . Asking us to approve of *his* sensations: sensations he has twisted into a logic that would not only explain with indifference the death of seven people, but seventy, seven thousand, seven million. Every action that this man has ever committed has been a blind attempt to deny his own intolerable conscience.'[89]

But we are made to understand what Leonard means when he shakes his fists at the court and shouts: 'I wanted something huge and *absolute*. . . . I wanted an order for things!' He has tried to catch up with the tantalising *'a priori* freedom' that Luther opposed to the moral law. Both he and Blakeley, from their different sides of the Anglo-Catholic and puritan fissure, have tried to mount their own individual revolution and counter-revolution. Like Sylvia Plath's 'I', Blakeley yearns to undo the world by dying, to kill off his historically unauthentic legacy of the internalised conscience. Leonard, on the other hand, seeks to transcend the moral law and, acting strictly in accordance with his conscience, perform 'justified' homicide. Ironically, the verdict of a Protestant Monarchy is 'diminished responsibility'.

It is a commonplace that the hero of Gothic fiction is the villain; for the Victorian, but still for us today even though police talk has demoted it to lower case, the Villain was the Criminal. Satan, however, did not cease to be a Christian when sin, in Milton's allegory, sprang from his head; on the contrary, the character who puts *aside* the internalised conscience, who attempts to perceive himself and his relation to the moral law without the benefit of this traditional apparatus, provides the novelist or poet, through his testimony, with the imaginative conditions in which to examine that apparatus or, at the very least, describe its consequences and its hidden logic. In this sense, the Criminal, whether suicide or murderer, *is* the perfect Christian; but with the graph of the Protestant psyche projected to its theological vanishing point.

4
Commodious Labyrinths: Testimony and Fictional Credibility

The narrative technique of the horror novel is usually clumsy and labyrinthine. The hallmark of the form appears to be narrative redundancy. It tends to be presented as an apparently inconsequential bundle of 'found' papers – documents, records, diaries, letters, manuscripts found in drawers or old chests, and so on. Jane Austen's satirical contrast between Catherine's romantic expectations and the bathos of real laundry bills in *Northanger Abbey* is not really apposite, because it is too close: Gothic novelists are actually more reliant on laundry bills than romantic expectations. Such expectations, in the reader at least, tend to be justified, especially in the realm of horror, by the provision of records, the more trivial the better. Before it could begin, every episode of the TV space romance of the 1960s, 'Startrek', was solemnly prefaced by the phrase: 'Captain's Log: Star Date . . .'. It is too easy, I think, to see this feature as a commercial excuse to produce more 'episodes'; or 'anthropologically', as a ritual; or, aesthetically, as a form of self-referential 'nesting'. None of these approaches quite satisfied, because the habit of fragmentation in this kind of fiction goes very deep, even in the popular context. The explosion of popular 'Gothic' in the magazines at the end of the eighteenth century, for example, tends to take the form of 'fragments':

> Most of the fragments are quite brief, and they often pretend to be shreds of ancient manuscripts, affording mere glimpses into the life of a darker and more barbarous age. It is only because of this that they were widely indulged in their use of the marvellous. The practical and didactic prejudices of readers and editors alike could tolerate 'superstition', only in diminutive doses and in the authorized manner.[1]

It is true, as the author points out elsewhere, that the non-existence of copyright laws at the time allows the Magazine, or Miscellany, to consist of plagiarised chunks of already-existent novels. But the originals, the novels themselves, tend also to be presented in the 'authorized manner' – even where they are 'spoken' accounts, or formed into something approaching narrative; tend to be set, one within the other, in recessive layers, so that reading them becomes like stripping the skin off a metaphysical onion; or, to change the metaphor, entering a maze, whose connecting links are not fully evident at any one time. Narrators tend to step back from the ironies and the intimacies of social tone into an 'editorial' role; they are truth-seekers, investigators, detectives or, crucially, witnesses, one perhaps among several who possess only certain fragments of evidence.

This 'authorizing' process, in other words, is characteristically 'legalistic'. As such, it tends to introduce a complicated, even paradoxical set of roles for the reader: the writing obviously works towards, and perhaps finally demands, some form of imaginative assent, but at the same time, its very form appears to stimulate an essentially *judgemental* response, which depends upon, and may even finish by maintaining, a degree of scepticism in the reader's mind.

These two roles need not be paradoxically opposed to one another, if one broadens the context of a hypothetical reader's experience of 'doubt' or 'belief'. The question of 'superstition' for a seventeenth- or eighteenth-century reader is not merely a legal one, but a theological one too. The form of 'evidence-giving' invited an introspective vigilance, which is the characteristic ground of the rational individual's belief. Of course, 'vigilance' and scepticism, as we shall see, are not the same thing; but if we prise open the concept of 'rationality', as a part of the reader's expectations, we shall immediately find its unity a kind of shadowplay from several different contexts. In theology, for example, the standard 'democratic' argument for the validity of internal (that is, *a priori*) evidence for the truth of revealed religion, instituted by Locke, was that, since God could not have dealt less fairly with any one section of the human race (that is, the Jews) than any other, such evidence was therefore always as strong as the individual's unassisted reason, at any moment in time, could make it.[2] Thus the strong demand in Protestant theology for the individual measure of faith is not at all incompatible with an individual measure of scepticism.

Rather, it is founded upon it. Indeed, after the attacks of the Deists, the orthodox position is marked by an extreme degree of scepticism. 'Speculative difficulties,' as Butler has it in the *Analogy*, 'are probationary in the same sense as external temptations.' And, as Sir Leslie Stephen observes, in thinking this 'he comes near to converting the deficiency of proof into a positive ground of belief'.[3] Butler here expresses a response to an increasing difficulty for orthodox theologians after Locke – how to leave room, not for doubt, but *assent*. Throughout the eighteenth century, what modern readers might think of as a psychologically 'alienated' position becomes, increasingly, the 'rational' one for orthodox apologists; the final argument against scepticism appears to be to assimilate it into faith. In the words of Tindall; 'the very attempt to destroy reason by reason is a demonstration that men have nothing but reason to trust to'.[4] Rational belief shares its process even with atheistical argument.

Now there is, I think, an interesting parallel in aesthetic debate about 'superstition'. The penultimate section in Bishop Hurd's *Letters on Chivalry and Romance* (1762) argues in defence of 'Gothic' romance against classical prejudice, by appealing, in a fashion that might appear perverse if not self-destructive, to the incredulity of the rational reader:

> But here, to prevent mistakes, an explanation will be necessary. We must distinguish between the *popular belief*, and *that of the Reader*. The fictions of poetry do, in some degree at least, require the *first*; (They would, otherwise, deservedly pass for *dreams* indeed). But when the poet has this advantage on his side, and his fancies have, or may be supposed to have, a countenance from the current superstitions of the age, in which he writes, he dispenses with the *last*, and gives his Reader leave to be as sceptical and incredulous as he pleases.[5]

Of course, by 'Gothic' Hurd means something else here than Jane Austen would later. But there is an important sense in which Ariosto, Tasso and Spenser raise similar, *general* problems for the concept of Probability, as the later prose romances do. Johnson's famous 1750 *Rambler* paper illustrates this, I think; there, he wheels in the qualitative, essentially Aristotelian, notion of Probability against the writers of romances (ancient and modern), making the identical point that Jane Austen does in *Northanger Abbey*: that an exposure to 'incredibilities' in the formative years of a reader corrupts the sense of probability which is one of the primary guarantees of rational civilisation.[6] But elsewhere, in other contexts (in the contemporary debates about miracles, for example), the arguments about where the lines of demarcation in what constitutes an 'incredibility' are to be drawn, are fully in flux.[7] Hurd, who, as a bishop (despite Leslie Stephen's slanderous account of his character), had a vested interest in the major debates of the eighteenth-century theologians, supports his notion of romance form by appealing to the idea that the text leaves room (that is, *makes* room) for the judgement of the individual reader. This notion is perfectly compatible in theory with Hurd's theology; I am even inclined to think that it is a latent expression of some of the theological arguments of the period. Here Johnson, the more profound thinker, is the inconsistent one because his classical prejudices do not 'sit' at all easily with that same sense of the individual measure of truth which, in a theological context, he accepted with such gloomy alacrity.

Whatever may be the case, one of Hurd's other, more familiar, arguments for the strength of 'Gothic' design in art is based on its 'irregularity', its labyrinthine or maze-like structure:

> This Gothic method of design in poetry may be, in some sort, illustrated by what is called the Gothic method of design in Gardening. A wood or grove cut out into many separate avenues or glades was amongst the most famous of the works of art, which our fathers attempted in this species of cultivation. These walks were distinct from each other, had, each, their several destination, and terminated on their own proper objects. Yet the whole was brought together and considered under one view by the relation which these various openings had not to each other, but to their common and concurrent centre.[8]

Despite the idea of a common or concurrent centre, this structure is presented as the opposite of classical unity: the particular, local aspects of the work of art, the way in which from moment to moment the reader experiences it, are like the features of a maze or labyrinth: essentially fragmented blocks of texture – corners, angles, prospects, open out on to whatever is common to them, from their own points of view.

It seems to me, that there is a connection here between the inevitable fragmentation of the process of giving evidence, that is to say, the invocation, in narrative form, of a corroborative principle; and the aesthetic fragmentation of 'Gothic' style. Hurd may well be thinking of the influence of Spenser on eighteenth-century formal gardening, in his use of such an analogy; but his insight into the principles of organisation of this kind of art, is, even so, part of a theological tradition.

I suppose the standard way of thinking about this is to make the 'legalistic' presentation of horror fiction a part of the special case of the development of the novel form as a whole, including the realistic novel. Ian Watt, for example, identifies formal realism in the novel from Defoe onwards by analogy with the law, when he describes its particularising rhetorical habits as 'an authentic report of human experience', based on 'a circumstantial view of life', whose 'mode of imitating reality . . . may be . . . summarized in terms of the procedures of another group of specialists in epistemology, the jury in a court of law'.[9] But this account is not what I mean by a 'legalistic' presentation, because his analogy assumes the real convergence of text and reader's expectations, not the conflict, or the mere coincidence between them. The legal format, as it were, works only one way – to identify reader and text. It is assumed that 'circumstantial evidence' really does generate authority and 'probability', in an almost Aristotelian, moral and aesthetic rather than legal or technical sense. And it is also assumed that this kind of particularising presentation is a narrative technique.

More recently, Professor Hillis Miller, again thinking about realism, has commented, with an odd kind of nostalgia for purity, on the way the novel has always been parasitic upon other forms of expression. He draws our attention to

the curious tradition, present in the modern middle-class novel from its sixteenth-century beginnings on, whereby a work of fiction is conventionally presented not as a work of fiction but as some other form of language. This is almost always some 'representational' form rooted in history and the direct report of 'real' human experience. It seems as if works of fiction are ashamed to present themselves as what they are but must always present themselves as what they are not, as some non-fictional form of language. A novel must pretend to be some kind of language validated by its one to one correspondence to psychological or historical reality.[10]

The obvious problem with this account is that so-called direct reports of human experience are themselve *parasitic*; they are the results of a consensus about representation, which is essentially cultural. Historically, the criteria for a 'representational form' are in a process of slow but perceptible change, as the needs and pressures of the social context change; and the assumption that these forms are (organically) 'rooted in history' is more difficult to make, especially if we take a limit case like that of horror fiction, where it is perhaps easier to see that human testimony is just as much a cultural epiphenomenon as the aesthetic form which is supposed to be based on it. Professor Kermode has issued a timely warning on this subject:

> We should never underestimate our predisposition to believe whatever is presented under the guise of an authoritative report and is also consistent with the mythological structure of a society from which we derive comfort, and which it may be uncomfortable to dispute. This desire for comfort, this willingness to believe what bears the ordinary signs of the credible, explains the rhetorical success of such works as Defoe's 'Apparition of Mrs Veal'. There is an agreed way of registering reality; and it has authority over us. There is also authority in the person making the report or maintaining its veracity; part, but not all, of this, is the mere authority of the printed word.[11]

Defoe's pamphlet is a notorious borderline case. Modern readers will think of it as a 'ghost story', perhaps; and it does indeed anticipate the 'legalistic' features of the genre as it has survived to the present day. But it is a profoundly ambiguous text, as the history of responses to it will show.

'Mrs Veal' was written in the context of a movement in late seventeenth-century thought against the increasing pressure of dogma – of dogmatic atheism, coming through from Hobbes. In all sorts of ways, this movement consciously adopted new methods of presenting material evidence, generally associated with the 'empiricism' and 'scepticism' of the Royal Society, in order to present, by analogy, evidence for spiritual experience. Signs of an 'overlap' of this kind had, indeed, appeared earlier. Where, for example are the boundaries between Science and Religion in the following scheme of the Mass Observation of providential occurrences:

> Towards the end of the Cromwellian Protectorate an even more elaborate 'design for registring of Illustrious Providences' was initiated by the Presbyterian Minister, Matthew Poole, in collaboration with other divines at home and in New England. The idea was that a complete list of fully documented providences should be compiled as a co-operative venture which would cross denominational barriers. Every county should have a secretary who would gather together the material sent in to him and forward it on to Syon College, to be analysed by Poole. The close parallel with the methods used by the scentists of the Royal Society for collecting and classifying natural phenomena is obvious enough, and it is worth recalling that Francis Bacon had himself urged the desirability of compiling a definitive history of the workings of providence.[12]

With such an overlap of contexts, testimony tends to assimilate itself to 'fact' and 'evidence'. This assimilation, especially in the realm of theological debate, is a general tendency throughout the eighteenth century, and one may be tempted to regard it as the workings of 'authority' on the responses of individuals. But even this argument needs another step because in the eyes of many orthodox, as well as dissenting, Protestants, 'testimony' was also a guarantee of the Christian faith which *opposed* itself to 'authority', the latter having 'superstitious' connotations. Thus the Anglican divine Leslie, for example, laid down with enormous confidence a series of four cardinal points, by which the rational man could receive the truth of the miracles on which the Scriptures were founded, one of which alone makes the point:

> 'I receive the Scriptures upon the testimony, not authority, of the Church; and I examine that testimony as I do other facts, till I have satisfied my private judgement there is no other way.'[13]

Given that such strenuously anti-authoritarian associations were embedded in the concept of testimony, it is not surprising that Defoe's pamphlet was read as fact by generations of the pious. Soon after its original printing, it became readily available as an anonymous 'factual' appendix to Charles Drelincourt's *Christian*

Man's Defence against the Fears of Death, a seventeenth-century work
of popular theology which went on being reprinted in huge
numbers until well into the nineteenth century. Such works as
Drelincourt, and the *Sadducismus Triumphatus* of Glanvill, himself a
member of the Royal Society, marry intellectual and popular
traditions of 'scepticism'; Glanvill, for example, divides his work
into a learned essay on the subject of belief, and a compendium of
popular testimonies, the 'authentication' of which involved him in
much correspondence. And, through assiduous reprinting, these
two texts were available as source material for such more obviously
'Gothic' writers as M. G. Lewis, Poe and R. L. Stevenson.[14] Johnson
had almost certainly read 'Mrs Veal' in Drelincourt, if not in Defoe;
but he had, apparently, also independently heard of the 'case',
which made quite a stir in Oxford when he was there in 1705; he
regarded it as fact. Though twenty years later, when questioned
about it by Boswell, he regarded it as discredited fact, as testimony
retracted by Mrs Bargrave on her death-bed.[15]

Edgar Allan Poe, on the other hand, was in no doubt that 'Mrs
Veal' was a hoax, claiming that Defoe had let his mask slip, and that,
at a certain point in his rhetoric towards the end, one could detect
signs of 'banter'. It is clearly a precedent for the rhetorical method of
one of his own hoaxes, as his letters show.[16] Interestingly, the
modern essays which succeed in throwing some further light on the
piece by Defoe themselves invoke the corroborative principle,
bringing further testimony in the manner of Johnson, to confirm or
deny the truth of Defoe's account; but as soon as one begins to bring
testimony in this manner (and independent accounts have been
found), one implicitly treats the material as 'fact', in order to attempt
to show its fictional outlines; once this road has been embarked
upon, it is extremely difficult to avoid the consequences of having
responded to the legalistic challenge.

This concentration on the direct provision of testimony, written or
spoken, is a demonstrable link between many horror texts. It is not
merely a literary convention; it is also a cultural pressure on any
writing which deals with either the marvellous, or the miraculous
(not the same thing, as we shall see), whether fictional or not. For all
writers, of whatever shade, testimony is a human necessity. It is also
a supremely ambiguous cultural form, because it generates a web
of opposing, but perhaps overlapping, expectations at the same
time. It reaches inwards, as we have seen in earlier chapters,
towards that interiorised act of witnessing, which has the strongest

possible connections with the theology and political history of the Protestant tradition. Sincerity, as Defoe tells us in the famous remark in the *Serious Reflections*, is ultimately in the mind of the reader, not the words of the writer: 'he that reads this essay without honesty, will never understand it right'. But also, increasingly from the late seventeenth century onwards, the cultural form of testimony projects outwards towards law; and, beyond that, but acting as a pressure upon it, science. It arouses increasingly active expectations of 'objectivity' and rational 'proof'.

To illustrate the flux of expectation around the concept of testimony, one has only to consider the impact of Hume's 'Essay of Miracles'. I will not rehearse this well-known set of arguments, except to quote the devastating conclusion:

> Upon the whole, then, it appears, that no testimony for any kind of miracle has ever amounted to a probability, much less to a proof; and that, even supposing it amounted to a proof, it would be opposed by another proof; derived from the very nature of the fact, which it would endeavour to establish. It is experience only, which gives authority to human testimony; and it is the same experience, which assures us of the laws of nature. When, therefore, these two kinds of experience are contrary, we have nothing to do but subtract the one from the other, and embrace an opinion, either on one side or the other, with that assurance which arises from the remainder. But according to the principle here explained, this subtraction, with regard to all popular religions, amounts to an entire annihilation; and therefore we may establish it as a maxim, that no human testimony can have such force as to prove a miracle, and make it a just foundation for any such system of religion.[17]

Hume also uses an analogy with the law; but what he succeeds in doing here is to threaten to the point of extinction the *a priori* connection, which was, as I have implied, a *theological* relationship between testimony and whatever it may assert. How dogmatic he can seem, when compared with the 'sceptical' rhetoric of belief:

> The death of man, and the fact that he is subsequently alive, are both matters which may be fairly established by evidence. The assertion that this or another such cases are 'contrary to the course of nature', means merely that they are contrary to the inferences

which we have drawn from observation. When men talk of the course of nature, they really talk of their own prejudices and imaginations, and in assuming that things cannot be otherwise than we have known them to be, we outrun the information of our senses, and the conclusion stands on prejudice, not on reason. When we consider how ignorant we are of the nature and causes of the simplest vital phenomena, we must see our incapacity for pronouncing the absolute possibility or impossibility of a resurrection.[18]

The Anglican Thomas Sherlock's position here is a good example of the manner in which orthodox apologists tended to 'exchange foils' with their sceptical opponents. The analogy with the law in the thinking process is, however, not at all the same as Hume's. The appeal to individual judgement here is infinitesimally close to an expression of humility. Testimony, for Sherlock, forms an endlessly escalating ladder of checks and balances, leading from rational incapacity to the *a priori* truth of revealed religion. The paradox, philosophically latent, in this process of thought is pushed to its limits by Sherlock's ingenious pamphlet 'The Tryal of the Witnesses' (1729), in which an English judge puts the Apostles on trial for bearing false witness, and, after hearing counsel for and against, proceeds duly to acquit them. That pamphlet is a marvellous example of the uses of legalism in matters of faith, because it calls upon, tautologically, all of the political assumptions of rational judgement and objectivity, endorsed in the law and the constitution since 1688, in order to justify the faith of the individual. Its parade of scepticism amounts to nothing more than a defence of adversary law, underwritten by a constitution which, in its turn, is an expression of a Protestant settlement.

But to return to Hume for a moment. There is, nevertheless, an ambiguity in his argument, which arises in part from the tricky semantics of terms like 'proof' and 'evidence'. And it is this: that 'evidence', especially in a legal context, tends to refer both to inert facts, as it were, or what came later to be called 'real' evidence, *and* to human testimony. This is true of 'fact' too, which refers to the *recounting* of fact, where it refers to testimony. This is how Richard Wollheim, Hume's modern editor, phrases the difficulty:

Hume's argument has often been criticised, and often unfairly or ignorantly. It seems, however, that its claim to definitiveness is not substantiated. For Hume in trying to show that a miracle must always be less credible than the corresponding natural law contrasts the testimony in support of a miracle with the observed regularities in which the law consists. But of course what Hume should have done is contrast the testimony in support of the miracle with the testimony or other evidence that can be adduced in support of the observed regularity.[19]

This is a pragmatic, rather than a logical point, perhaps; but it does tend to introduce another step into the argument. 'Observed regularities' are, at least in part, the result of a prior process of testimony.

Thus for orthodox apologists like Campbell or Beattie (whose 'Essay on Truth', as her Oxford editor tells us, Mrs Radcliffe was very fond of reading) testimony makes its reappearance, after Hume's attempt to banish it, as the founding shape of human experience, even experience of the laws of nature. And witnessing, in this no-man's-land of analogy between theology and law, carries a 'charge' of integrity. It amounts, in the orthodox position, to a selection from the full complexities of legal procedure, which acts as the most powerful metaphor possible for spiritual experience. Since there is no independent check from experience, testimony can only either be corroborated, or confuted by the discrediting of the witness, or the bringing of other testimony of a stronger nature against it. Bishop Sherlock's lawyer, arguing in defence of the Apostles, quite overtly distinguishes the legal from the 'scientific' point:

'Tis very true, that Men do not so easily believe upon Testimony of others, things which seem improbable or impossible; but the Reason is not, because the Thing itself admits no Evidence, but because the Hearer's preconceived Opinion outweighs the Credit of the Reporter, and makes his Veracity to be called in question. For instance: 'Tis natural for a stone to roll down Hill; 'Tis unnatural for it to roll up Hill; and all Men in their Senses are as capable of seeing and judging, and reporting the Fact in One Case, as in the Other. Shou'd a Man then tell you, that he saw a Stone go up Hill of its own accord, you might question his Veracity, but you cou'd not say the thing admitted no Evidence, because it was contrary to the Law and usual Course of Nature: For the Law of Nature formed to yourself from your own

Experiences and Reasoning, is quite independent of the Matter of Fact which the Man testifies.[20]

It is as if one kind of specificity ('Matter of Fact', as the legal phrase has it) can be brought against another ('experience and reasoning'); and even that the latter can be made to seem less specific by comparison. 'Fact' is clearly ambiguous here; but the problem is not simply resolvable by reference to semantic confusion. It is a question of a difference of context that lies behind the language used: the circumstantial particularity, which one associates with 'probability', in its most familiar literary sense, is transferable, in the orthodox argument, into testimony which may *oppose* itself to the probable.

In its eighteenth-century form, the Gothic novel exposes Romish superstition. This at least is a recurrent part of its overt, propagandist tactic. It plays upon the unease in its audience at the continued existence in Southern Europe of the Inquisition; an audience whose national identity is underpinned by the traditional freedom given to the individual citizen by the Common Law. There is an interesting passage in Blackstone's *Commentaries*, for example, where this notion of an indigenous legal system is portrayed by analogy with restored 'Gothic' architecture:

And since the new expedients have been refined by the practice of more than a century, and are sufficiently known and understood, they in general answer the purpose of doing speedy and substantial justice, much better than could now be effected by any great fundamental alterations. The only difficulty that attends them arises from their fictions and circuities: but, when once we have discovered the proper clue, that labyrinth is easily pervaded. Our system of remedial law resembles an old Gothic castle, erected in the days of chivalry, but fitted up for a modern inhabitant. The moated ramparts, the embattled towers, and the trophied halls, are magnificent and venerable, but useless. The inferior apartments, now accommodated to daily use, are cheerful and commodious, though their approaches may be winding and difficult.[21]

The prospects which open on to this 'Gothic' castle are culturally

1. Melrose Abbey: engraving (1809) by F. C. Lewis of a painting by William Wilson.

2. The Octagon, Fonthill Abbey: engraving from J. Britton, *Illustrations Literary and Graphic of Fonthill* (1823).

3. H. A. Bowler, 'The Doubt: Can These Dry Bones Live?' (1854).

4. *Nosferatu* (1922; Director: F. W. Murnau).

"My eyes insist on gazing down upon a coffin . . .
my coffin . . . while I await my second death. . . ."

5. Illustration by Stephen Lawrence for a story by Claude Farrière, 'The House of the Secret' in *Famous Fantastic Mysteries* (February 1946).

6. *Psycho* (1960; Director: Alfred Hitchcock).

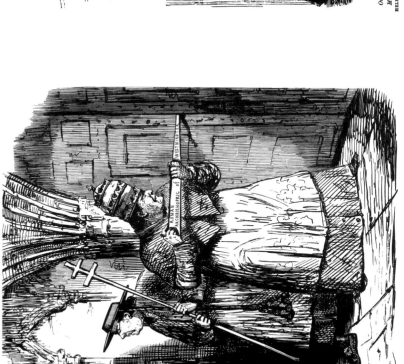

7. 'The Thin End of the Wedge' (*Punch* cartoon, 1850).

Oratorian. "Is your Mistress within, my dear!"
Maid-of-All-Work. "Oh, help! help! here's a Boogie, Missus!
help! help!"

8. 'The Oratorian as Bogey Man' (*Punch*
cartoon, 1850).

THE KIDNAPPER.—A CASE FOR THE POLICE

Kidnapper. "THERE 's A BEAUTIFUL VEIL !!! GIVE ME YOUR PARCEL, MY DEAR, WHILE YOU PUT IT ON."

9. 'The Kidnapper: a Case for the Police' (*Punch* cartoon, 1850).

10. 'Little Red Riding Hood' (*Punch* cartoon, 1850).

11. 'The First Time of Torture', illustration from Fox's *Book of Martyrs, 1865–7*.

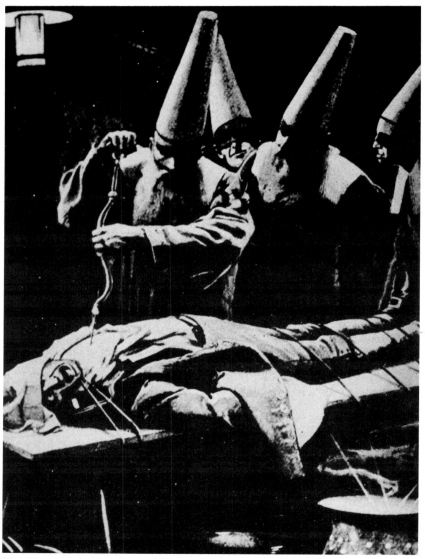

12. 'He uttered a low moan, which became a resounding shriek, as he felt the shining steel cut his flesh': an illustration by Piffard for Max Pemberton's 'Signors of the Night' in *Pearsons Magazine* (October 1898).

13. 'The Tortures of the Rack': illustration from Fox's *Book of Martyrs, 1908*.

14. 'Delirium': a painting from 'The Man of Genius' (1891) by Count Lombroso.

numerous; they depend to some extent on where one stands. Here again we have the irregularity of aesthetic form used as an analogy for something else; not for art this time, but law. Blackstone actually defends the labyrinthine structure of legal fictions and technical rules, which in the nineteenth century is to become the object of much agitation for legal reform, by reference to 'feodal' tradition. Whig aesthetics had since 1688 associated 'Gothic' architecture with the democratic tradition of the Germanic or 'Gothic' tribes. The notion of this passage, that the slow growth and adaptation of the English Common Law to contemporary life, irrational and cumbersome as it may appear, is preferable to any sweeping reform, is another basis for Henry Tilney's outburst in *Northanger Abbey*. The Abbey itself is a somewhat similar structure, whose menace has been outdated and whose alien-ness absorbed into the fabric of social life. The ruins of this 'Gothic' castle, into which modern equity judges have inserted the commodious, Strawberry Hill-like improvements of legal fictions, are not threatening or superstitious here – quite the reverse, in fact. They are the symbolic guarantee of a rational 'democratic' heritage.

The most important analogy, however, lying scarcely visible amongst the foundations of Blackstone's Gothic castle, has great relevance to the question of the cultural significance of testimony. This is the comparison, frequently found in the tradition of Germanic historiography, between the original throwing-off of Rome's yoke by the ancient, healthy, freedom-loving tribes from whom we trace our descent, and the later rejection of Rome by Luther. Our island heritage of law, which mirrors our political structure, is based on this double rejection of imperial rule from Rome, so runs the argument. This is the germanic myth of the so-called *translatio imperii*:

> The *translatio* suggested forcefully an anology between the break-up of the Roman Empire by the Goths, and the demands of the humanist reformers of Northern Europe for religious freedom, interpreted as liberation from Roman priestcraft. In other words, the *translatio* crystallized the idea that humanity was twice ransomed from Roman tyranny and depravity – in antiquity by the Goths, in modern times by their descendants the German reformers.[22]

To a large extent, it depends on which historiographical tradition one takes – that is, the Italian Renaissance or the Germanic Nationalist – which cluster of associations will be uppermost in the term 'Gothic' – barbarous and superstitious, on the one hand, or primitive and democratic, on the other. The English whig tradition, as scholars have shown, has a strong interest in the latter.

Now, the important part of this concerns the connection between testimony and the theological demand for private judgement, and its external image – a legal system whose decentralised nature mirrors the freedom of the individual, in a larger political sense. There is a saying, 'where conscience begins, law ends'; but for the eighteenth-century, orthodox Protestant, such a boundary did not exist. The primitive act of witnessing plays an important part in the historical development of a constitutional jury system, which has evolved its own rules, quite different in several important respects from those of continental systems, for the handling of testimony.

Here is part of the historical picture, sketched in a modern legal handbook. The political terminology is worthy of note:

> After about 1300 Roman and canon law ceased almost entirely to influence the development of the Common Law, but in their day they helped to make it a system not wholly unsuited to the needs of the English state, and thus it came about that when in the fifteenth and sixteenth centuries many continental states abandoned their own medieval law in favour of a wholesale reception of the law of Rome, in England, the medieval common law supplemented by equity and reformed by statute has survived into modern times to share the legal empire of the world with systems derived directly from the Roman jurisprudence.[23]

What distinctions are there between these two systems? The basic distinction between the inquisitorial and accusatory systems is sketched by the distinguished French legal historian, Esmein, in a manner which makes clear some of its ramifications for the psychology of the individual:

> In the accusatory procedure, the detection and the prosecution of offenses [sic] are left wholly to the initiative of private individuals – an initiative which may slumber through their inertia, fear, or corruption. The chances of impunity flowing from this system are still further enhanced both by the publicity which exists in all phases of the procedure, and by the necessity which compels the

judge to limit his investigation entirely to the evidence furnished him by the accuser. But, on the other hand, the inquisitorial procedure has very serious defects: under it, the prosecution and the detection of offenses are intrusted exclusively to the agents of the State; there is the atmosphere of secrecy and consequently of suspicion, in the midst of which the trial proceeds; and, finally, there is the absence of any real confrontation between prosecution and defense.[24]

Thus one can see how the code of Rome, and later of Continental Europe in general, comes to have associations of a sweeping, arbitrary, impersonal system, quite antipathetic to the open, contractual sense of English law as presented by Blackstone and others.

The Spanish Inquisition survived until the early nineteenth century, but it was not simply viewed even by the mid-century in England as an isolated ('Gothic') relic of a medieval past. The issue of 'inquisition' was a live one even in the later nineteenth century because of its legal implications. The wholesale acceptance of the legal system of the Roman Empire (not the Republic) was the acceptance of an inquisitorial system whose logic demanded torture, secrecy and a hampered defence of the individual. Torture is a popular theme for propaganda, and its visual representation has a striking continuity throughout the latter half of the century. Compare Plates 11 and 13 with Plate 12, for example. One could be forgiven for mistaking the horrific iconography of the *prima quaestio* in an edition of Foxe of 1865 for an illustration from an earlier Gothic novel by Mrs Radcliffe, or Maturin, or Monk Lewis. Similarly with the 'Tortures of the Rack' from the Working Man's Edition of 1908. On the other hand, the 1898 illustration for a horror story from *Pearson's Magazine* (Plate 12) draws upon exactly the same propagandist point, with illegality rather than heresy perhaps uppermost: the 'fictional' and 'factual' representations of horror are virtually indistinguishable: the stereotyped image of hooded, robed figures wielding instruments of torture is an immediate outrage – and therefore a source of potential titillation – to a complex mixture of theological and legal expectations in the audience, each it seems to some extent parasitic upon the other.

Let us take a literary example of the rhetorical use of these expectations. Lewis in *The Monk*, for all the *jeu d'esprit*, the affront to bourgeois sexual morality which – with the help of a lot of pastiche of *Measure for Measure* and *Faustus* – he manages to achieve in the early stages of the book, changes hats without effort in the latter part and turns himself from the narrator into a lecturer on the deficiencies of legal procedure in the Spanish Inquisition. Witness the change of tone in the following two paragraphs from 'narrative' to a kind of outraged information-giving:

At length a small door, opposite to that by which he (i.e. Ambrosio) had entered the hall, grated heavily upon its hinges. An officer appeared, and was immediately followed by the beautiful Matilda. Her hair hung about her face wildly; her cheeks were pale, and her eyes sunk and hollow. She threw a melancholy look upon Ambrosio: he replied by one of aversion and reproach. She was placed opposite to him. A bell then sounded thrice. It was the signal for opening the court, and the inquisitors entered upon their office.

In these trials, neither the accusation is mentioned, nor the name of the accuser. The prisoners are only asked, whether they will confess. If they reply that, having no crime, they can make no confession, they are put to the torture without delay. This is repeated at intervals, either till the suspected avow themselves culpable, or the perseverance of the examinants is worn out and exhausted; but without a direct knowledge of their guilt, the inquisition never pronounces the final doom of its prisoners. In general, much time is suffered to elapse without their being questioned; but Ambrosio's trial had been hastened on account of a solemn *auto da fé* which would take place in a few days, and in which the inquisitors meant this distinguished culprit to perform a part, and give a striking testimony of their vigilance.[25]

The present tense converts what looks like narrative into *example*. Lewis's cynicism – one can hardly call it irony – assumes a simple connection between the existent rules of the English adversary, or accusatory, system and the general idea of 'rationality': that the accused should be confronted with his accuser and that the burden of proof rests with the accusing individual. If we are a knowing audience, he is directly playing off expectations derived from the nexus of beliefs I have been describing above, touching a raw nerve which he knows is already there; if we are ignorant, he is supplying those beliefs, and we can take his tone to be earnest. Likewise, the superstition of Ambrosio's accusers, demonstrated both by the charge of sorcery itself and by their inability to further anything other than a ritual form of 'proof' is held up to ridicule:

> The abbot was not merely accused of rape and murder; the crime of sorcery was laid to his charge, as well as to Matilda's: she had been seized as an accomplice in Antonia's assassination. On searching her cell, various suspicious books and instruments were found, which justified the accusation brought against her. To criminate the monk, the constellated mirror was produced, which Matilda had accidentally left in his chamber. The strange figures engraved upon it caught the attention of Don Ramirez, while searching the abbot's cell; in consequence, he carried it away with him. It was shown to the Grand Inquisitor, who, having considered it for some time, took off a small golden cross which hung at his girdle, and laid it upon the mirror: instantly a loud noise was heard, resembling a clap of thunder, and the steel shivered into a thousand pieces. This circumstance confirmed the suspicion of the monk's having dealt in magic. It was even supposed that his former influence over the minds of the people was entirely to be ascribed to witchcraft.[26]

The Witchcraft statute, instituted in 1604 by James I, lapsed in 1736; after that date, witchcraft trials in England were trials for fraud or murder. According to Keith Thomas, the tendency to regard witchcraft and sorcery as heretical – as a theological state, rather than an antisocial action – was an infection from the continent, which received its sanction from a mixture of Catholic theology and Roman Law. What is interesting in the above passage is the way in which Lewis feels entirely free to shift the whole basis of his satire. The 'mirror' which is part of the 'evidence' has been used, earlier in the novel, to titillate sexually his hero, and his readers, by providing 'soft-porn' images to their voyeuristic gaze. But here Lewis establishes quite a different relationship with his audience; the word 'circumstance', for example, is chosen for its quasi-'legal' resonance: it implies the shallowness of a system which can erect judgements on such a basis: and it requires us to think that, whatever Ambrosio is charged with, this is no way to effect a proof. The appeal in this would go to almost any section of the audience, even to the Godwinians; on this point, even Coleridge, who objected to the sexual titillation in the book and initiated the charge of blasphemy against it, would have had no difficulty in feeling the required outrage.

The process of torture is presented, similarly, in such a way that it cannot affect the resolve of the monk; but it is not merely for heroic, 'Faustian' reasons. It is more like a *reductio ad absurdum* of the blind machine of the system:

> Determined to make him confess not only the crimes which he had committed, but those also of which he was innocent, the inquisitors began their examination. Though dreading the tortures, as he yet more dreaded death, which would consign him to eternal torments, the abbot asserted his purity in a voice bold and resolute. Matilda followed his example, but spoke with fear and trembling. Having in vain exhorted him to confess, the inquisitors ordered the monk to be put to the question. The decree was immediately executed. Ambrosio suffered the most excruciating pangs that ever were invented by human cruelty. Yet so dreadful is death, when guilt accompanies it, that he had sufficient fortitude to persist in his disavowal. His agonies were redoubled in consequence; nor was he released till, fainting from excess of pain, insensibility rescued him from the hands of his tormentors.[27]

From a Protestant point of view, there is something absurdly tautological about this process; the passage is not so much about the heroic fortitude of Ambrosio in the face of such horrifying treatment as about the irrationality of torture when employed in support of a system of justice which purports to be based on conscience. If, as is implied, Ambrosio is possessed of an interiorised account book whose credits and deficits only he and God can know, then, unless the law which judges him matches or acknowledges this fact, justice has no foundation: it is merely a piece of secular manipulation.

The assumption on which this rhetoric is founded may not have been consciously available to all of Lewis's audience: but it is clearly visible in certain aspects of the history of English legal procedure, aspects which have direct relevance to the question of authority and guarantees in relation to the production and reception of testimony in a court of law. Confession, for example, is the most powerful area of testimony, and therefore its role in English law is a sensitive one, precisely because of the situation played upon by Lewis. Almost all of Lewis's readers would have had a just horror of extorted confession; many of them would have a belief in its irrationality on religious grounds. Indeed, these religious grounds actually enter into the formation of the law of evidence, not only in the obvious case of the oath itself, but also in the rules which govern the admissibility of confession as a form of testimony. Sir James Stephen, the framer of the Indian Evidence Act, gives in his *Digest of the Law of Evidence* (1874) a nice example of the distinction between voluntary and involuntary confession, and the religious assumptions which governed that distinction in the early nineteenth century:

(a)   The question is, whether A murdered B.
A handbill issued by the Secretary of State, promising a reward and pardon to any accomplice who would confess, is brought to the knowledge of A, who, under the influence of the hope of pardon, makes a confession. This confession is not voluntary.
(b)   A being charged with the murder of B, the chaplain of the gaol reads the Commination Service to A, and exhorts him upon religious grounds to confess his sins. A, in consequence, makes a confession. This confession is voluntary.[28]

This latter illustration is based on *R. v. Gilham* (1828). With the growth of a police force, the worry about 'inducements' obviously increased. To be admissible as evidence, a confession had to be 'voluntary'. Sir James Stephen adds a footnote:

In this case the exhortation was that the accused man should confess 'to God', but it seems from parts of the case that he was urged also to confess to man 'to repair any injury done to the laws of his country.' According to the practice of the time, no reasons are given for the judgement. The principle seems to be that a man is not likely to tell a falsehood in such cases, from religious motives. The case is sometimes cited as an authority for the proposition that a clergyman may be compelled to reveal confessions made to him professionally. It has nothing to do with the subject.[29]

The last observation is made with a great deal of confidence; yet the whole example shows how complex the relations between religion and law might be in practice. What might seem at a distance to be a benign, conspiratorial embrace turns out, when one gets closer, to be a wrestling match. At any rate, it makes a nonsense of the traditional worries of Protestants (in contemporary pamphlets, for example) about the porousness of the Catholic confessional.[30]

As legal historians have shown, the law of evidence has evolved in intimate connection with the jury system and, in particular, with the historical emergence of the jury from its original role as part of the company of witnesses in a trial. This branch of the law, which Bentham called adjective, as opposed to substantive, law (because it was 'adjacent' to the content of the law), is really a system of rules administered by judges, which govern and control the admission of testimony to a court of law. These rules began to be written down in the early eighteenth century, though they are undoubtedly older. Perhaps the most complex and, in some ways irrational, of all is the hearsay rule. This rule develops in direct relation to the adversary system of English law. Where evidence is not direct and where testimony, for example, cannot be cross-examined and the usual securities of the English legal system applied to it, it becomes hearsay and is excluded from the court's attention, no matter how vital it may appear to be. The conditions for applying this rule are still in operation today,[31] and they have grown exceedingly complex; because, as the rule developed so a number of exceptions to it developed too, so that, under certain circumstances and conditions, evidence which was technically hearsay might be admitted. Some of these exceptions again are directly based on the assumption of an internalised conscience in the individual, tied to a belief in the Christian afterlife, as a modern writer on the law makes hilariously clear:

> In other cases, such as dying declarations, the exception is based on the supposition that a person who expects to die (having a 'settled hopeless expectation of death' as the legal phrase has it) will not wish to go to his Maker with a lie on his lips; 'a situation so solemn and so awful, is considered by the law as creating an obligation equal to that which is imposed by a positive oath administered in a Court of Justice'. The exception has been held not to apply in the case of the natives of Papua-New Guinea where the next life is believed to be spent on a neighbouring island.[32]

No wonder Bentham wanted to sweep away the exclusionary rules on the grounds of their irrationality. The second *verbatim* quotation here is from Chief Baron Eyre, in *R*. v. *Woodcock* (1789); and though no doubt the rule had been applied many times before merely on the grounds of expediency, we can see the 'guarantee' of individual conscience being made explicit, and translated as an 'authority', into the fabric of legal procedure, just seven years before the publication of those passages in *The Monk* which I have been discussing.

Much can hang on this. Perhaps the most spectacular example of the operation of the hearsay rule is *R*. v. *Bedingfield* (1879), where the victim had her throat cut from ear to ear at the time at which she implicated the accused. The court held that her statement was not admissable as a dying declaration because there was no evidence that she was aware that she was dying and she had no time for reflection. Another rather touching example, is *R*. v. *Jenkins* (1869) in which a magistrate's clerk took down a statement by a dying woman preceding a charge of murder. He wrote that she made the statement 'with no hope of my recovery', and read it over to her. But she asked for the words 'at present' to be inserted after 'hope', and this was done before she signed the statement. The Court for Crown Cases Reserved regarded this insertion as showing that she was not without hope of recovery, and held that the declaration was inadmissible.[33]

The point which seems to me to arise sharply out of these examples is that the bundle of things popularly assumed as 'rational' at the end of the eighteenth century, which acts in many ways as the traditional foundation of much nineteenth-century popular belief, is actually a composite, shaped by the gaps, or the edges, or the overlaps, between different social institutions. The process is in reality a form of mutual borrowing. Orthodox theology is borrowing its characteristic legalism from the legal process, especially with regard to the nature of testimony; and the legal process obtains its 'guarantees' in matters of the reception and treatment of testimony from Protestant theology. This is what I mean when I speak of cultural projection; that the invocation of one context, not just in writing but in social institutions, will draw along, perhaps unnoticed, part of another as a supporting factor in its train. The 'ordinary signs of credibility' for a reader of fiction whose subject matter is the marvellous, the incredible or the superstitious, are not just an unchanging set of expectations; objectively speaking they are the shapes of other factors, meshing out beyond themselves.

Both Lewis, for example, and, later, Maturin in *Melmoth the Wanderer* use the recessive structure I spoke of at the beginning of this chapter; and both include long passages of pseudo-narrative, in reality a kind of pamphleteering, in which the searchlight of Protestant rationality is turned on Romish superstition. Both concern themselves, in particular, with fraudulent claims to the miraculous. As we have seen, this was a vital subject for any eighteenth-century Christian to think about because, between them, Hume and the Deists had made enormous inroads into the internal evidence for revealed religion. In the novelists, the method itself of finding the story in a manuscript or enclosing it as part of a compendium of tales within tales, at times has the effect of a fake investigation, pushing us, as readers, through an apparently remote time-scale, but really turning our eyes towards the threat of current superstition. Lewis, for example, makes us examine the testimony for a miracle ourselves; despite his name, Lorenzo, the character in the following episode from *The Monk*, possesses a sense for the necessity of 'proof' for a miracle, which is 'scientific', 'legal' or merely Protestant, dependent on how we place the stress. He refuses to accept the testimony of the nuns that the statue which groans is a miracle – but it *does* groan:

> The nuns clasped their hands together, and sank on their kness. Lorenzo looked round him eagerly, and was on the point of yielding to the fears which had already possessed the women. Universal silence prevailed. He examined the vault, but nothing was to be seen. He now prepared to address the nuns, and ridicule their childish apprehensions, when his attention was arrested by a deep and long-drawn groan.
>
> 'What was that?' he cried, and started.
>
> 'There, Segnor!' said Helena; 'now you must be convinced. You have heard the noise yourself; now judge whether our terrors are imaginery.'[34]

The reader may object that this sort of thing is just a standard joke; but what is interesting about it is the invitation which is offered to us. We know that such terrors are imaginary, but what *is* the explanation? The nature of *fact* itself, and the relation between fact and human testimony, is brought into the foreground by the simple technique of restricting the narrative possibilities to the timing, as it were, of *investigation only*. We know that there is, as we say, 'some explanation'; but we have to look over the shoulder of the hearty, but uneasy, empiricist, Lorenzo. We, too, have to have proof of what we already regard as superstitious. Cases of witchcraft in the eighteenth century tended to become, as I have pointed out, cases of fraud. The expectation here is precisely that – yet testimony appears to support the case. This calls for an investigation:

> Not being convinced that this destruction would be so certain as Helena seemed to think it, Lorenzo persisted in his resolution. The nuns besought him to desist, in piteous terms, and even pointed out the robber's hand, which was in effect still visible on the arm of the statue. This proof, as they imagined, must convince him. It was very far from doing so; and they were greatly scandalised, when he declared his suspicion that the dried and shrivelled fingers had been placed there by order of the prioress. In spite of their prayers and threats, he approached the statue. He sprang over the iron rails which defended it, and the saint underwent a thorough examination.[35]

The tone is identical to Rider Haggard or the brisk, intrepid heroes of later Empire adventure stories; but it is interesting to ask oneself what 'proof' actually means here – is it, predominantly, 'scientific' or legal? In fact, it seems designed to provoke a misty bout of confidence in the reader, by the suggestion that it isn't clearly either so is probably both. 'Examination' is a medical joke about the anatomy of the statue; but the term also plays on a vague sense of a connection between empiricism and first-hand witnessing:

> The image at first appeared to be of stone, but proved on further inspection to be formed of no more solid materials than coloured wood. He shook it, and attempted to move it; but it appeared to be of a piece with the base which it stood upon. He examined it over and over; still no clue guided him to the solution of this mystery, for which the nuns were become equally solicitous, when they saw that he touched the statue with impunity. He paused, and listened: the groans were repeated at intervals, and he was convinced of being in the spot nearest to them. He mused upon this singular event, and ran over the statue with inquiring eyes. Suddenly they rested upon the shrivelled hand. It struck him, that so particular an injunction was not given without cause, not to touch the arm of the image. He again ascended the pedestal; he

examined the object of his attention, and discovered a small knob of iron concealed between the saint's shoulder and what was supposed to have been the hand of the robber. This observation delighted him . . .[36]

The touch about the nuns is charming here: how soon do the chains of superstition, even from the childish, idolatrous minds of Southern Europeans, begin to fall when one adopts a bold, no-nonsense approach to these matters. But for us, they have fallen already, because we all along placed our faith in causes and effects, in 'examination' and 'observation'. The elision is a cynical one, in the case of Lewis, but it is still an elision between different but mutually dependent areas of experience – physical vigour, intellectual problem-solving, and religious iconoclasm.

A more complex and interesting example of the way in which an eighteenth-century text uses this notion of testimony, and the ambiguous assumptions that lie embedded in it, is Mrs Radcliffe's *The Italian*. This novel begins from the premise that its hero, Schedoni (its real hero, that is) is a stereotypical villain. But the latter half of the novel, in which the effeminate young Vivaldi (the nominal hero) finds himself incarcerated in the bowels of the Roman Inquisition, is a remarkable deployment of this 'legalistic' technique and appears to depart from the stereotype altogether. Although the narrative is, technically, a third-person account, and not an explicitly fragmented sheaf of individual testimonies, Mrs Radcliffe, a lover of all kind of veils, is quite willing to lie by omission in order to confine her readers to the process of individual judgement. As we have seen, the image of Roman law involves the exclusion, and therefore the denial, of the English presumption that the accused be confronted in person by his accuser. The Roman Inquisition, like hell itself, is full of veiled accusers; and yet the conclusions of the narrative are radically ambiguous and quite unexpected, if we were expecting merely a stereotypical expression of anti-Catholicism.

Locked in his cell, Vivaldi receives a visitation from a mysterious, cowled figure, who urges him to make accusations against the villain of the novel, Schedoni. Although the reader, after what has happened in the rest of the novel, is cheering Vivaldi on at this point, he explains that his private judgement will not allow him to proceed in such a fashion:

'How can I do all this, and upon the instigation of a stranger!

Neither conscience nor prudence will suffer me to assert what I cannot prove. It is true that I have reason to believe that Schedoni is my bitter enemy, but I will not be unjust even to him. I have no proof that he is the Count di Bruno, nor that he is the perpetrator of the crimes you allude to, whatever those may be; and I will not be made an instrument to summon any man before a tribunal, where innocence is no protection from ignominy, and where suspicion alone may inflict death.'

'You doubt, then, the truth of what I assert?' said the Monk, in a haughty tone.

'Can I believe that of which I have no proof?' replied Vivaldi.[37]

So far so good. Vivaldi reacts as a good rational sceptic, or a good Protestant, should when faced with an irrational, potentially superstitious situation. We feel the strength of the British constitution gathering round him. But it is not as simple as this: the mysterious visit has strong overtones of the miraculous biblical visitation to Peter by the Angel. It is not only the 'legal' part of our and Vivaldi's assessment of testimony which is on trial, it is also the meaning of 'witnessing' itself:

'Yes, there are cases which do not admit of proof; under your peculiar circumstances, this is one of them; you can act only upon assertion. I attest,' continued the monk, raising his hollow voice to a tone of singular solemnity, 'I attest the powers which are beyond this earth, to witness the truth of what I have just delivered.'

As the stranger uttered this adjuration, Vivaldi observed, with emotion, the extraordinary expression of his eyes; Vivaldi's presence of mind, however, did not forsake him, and, in the next moment, he said, 'But who is he that thus attests? It is upon the assertion of a stranger that I am to rely, in defect of proof! It is a stranger who calls upon me to bring solemn charges against a man, of whose guilt I know nothing!'[38]

After he has left, it is discovered that the mysterious stranger has not been seen by the guards. We have here all the conditions of a miraculous visitation; plus all the apparatus of scepticism which brings a legalistic scrutiny to bear upon those conditions. In a cumbersome but interesting fashion, Mrs Radcliffe puts her readers in the position of her character. How to exercise judgement, while

responding to the 'fact' of testimony, even though you know that
the testimony is unsupported. The test is simultaneously one of
'faith' and 'reason', of emotional generosity and its opposite,
prudence.

This incident is to prove the foundation of a further scene in the
hearing which follows on the next day. This involves some reversals
of stereotype:

> As the monk had predicted, Vivaldi was asked what he knew of
> Father Schedoni, and, when he replied, as he had formerly done
> to his mysterious visitor, he told that he knew more than he
> acknowledged.
>
> 'I *know* no more,' replied Vivaldi.
>
> 'You equivocate,' said the inquisitor. 'Declare what you have
> heard, and remember that you formerly took an oath to that
> purpose.'[39]

We are amongst the Dominicans, but equivocation, for an English
audience, is the traditional sign of Jesuitism. Vivaldi's situation is
interestingly reversed here, because I think we are meant to feel
that, if he does not answer truly, then he *is* only playing with words.
In order to get him into this cleft stick, Mrs Radcliffe had to have her
inquisitor ask him to declare what he has heard. We expect to hear a
kind of ghostly defence counsel get to his feet at this point and
object that this is hearsay only. But poor Vivaldi, having repeated
the allegations made to him by the mysterious stranger, is steered
inexorably by his author towards what is, for a rational man of his
calibre, the moment of maximum humiliation:

> Vivaldi concluded with again declaring, that he had not sufficient
> authority to justify a belief in those reports.
>
> 'On what authority do you repeat them?' said the vicar-general.
>
> Vivaldi was silent.
>
> 'On what authority?' inquired the inquisitor, sternly.
>
> Vivaldi, after a momentary hesitation, said 'What I am about to
> declare, holy fathers, is so extraordinary –'
>
> 'Tremble!' said a voice close to his ear, which he instantly knew
> to be the monk's, and the suddenness of which electrified him. He
> was unable to conclude the sentence.
>
> 'What is your authority for the reports?' demanded the
> inquisitor.

'It is unknown, even to myself!' answered Vivaldi.[40]

Humiliation indeed, from one angle. But the pressure of interior witnessing, itself a form of guarantee to a judge of any perception, is also present. Ranged against this testimony of Vivaldi, whom we know to be of the most integrity, is the startling improbability of the incident, which we ourselves (the author, indeed, showing a fine disregard for *our* sense of probability, too) have been forced to witness. The judges, however, are themselves split over their interpretation; and again Mrs Radcliffe breaks the crude stereotype by making one judge, the inquisitor, a harsh legalist; and one, his superior, the vicar-general, a figure who displays a startling, almost an English, degree of humanity. More evidence is brought forward to damn the villain Schedoni, but on the grounds of prejudice only. In an extraordinary moment, as the vicar-general continues to insist that such evidence cannot constitute a proof, Vivaldi suddenly 'recognises' his judge:

> 'Here is no proof', said the vicar-general, 'other friars of that order might confess at the same hour, in the same church.'
> 'But there is strong presumption for proof,' observed the inquisitor. 'Holy father, we must judge from probabilities, as well as from proof.'
> 'But probabilities themselves,' replied the vicar-general, 'are strongly against the evidence of a man, who would betray another by means of words dropped in the unguarded moments of powerful emotion.'
> 'Are these the sentiments of an inquisitor!' said Vivaldi to himself, 'can such glorious candour appear amidst the tribunal of an Inquisition!' Tears fell fast on Vivaldi's cheek while he gazed upon the just judge, whose candour, had it been exerted in his cause, could not have excited more powerful sensations of esteem and admiration. 'An inquisitor!' he repeated to himself, 'an inquisitor!'[41]

A *real* inquisitor. The distinction between the approaches of the two men is between legal proof, that maze of technicalities which accompanies the inquisitorial system, and which Voltaire mocked so brilliantly,[42] and moral certainty, the judgement at a particular time of the whole man, according to common reason, which is the boast of the English judicial system. At the word 'presumption' above, carefully chosen by Mrs Radcliffe, the English reader's empiricist hackles rise, for, although presumptions exist in English law, they do not play the same role in the adversarial system. It is the pre-determined character of the machine which Mrs Radcliffe is hinting at here. This is how Esmein describes the role of the judge in the theory of legal proofs:

> This theory is the system known in the history of law as that of legal proofs. Its chief essential is that, before the judge can condemn, he must bring together certain pre-determined proofs; but, on the other hand, confronted with these proofs, he must, of necessity condemn; in either case, his personal opinion goes for nothing. The leading maxim of the ancient law in this respect is that judgement must be rendered 'secundum allegata et probata.' The judge may be likened to a harpsichord, responsive according to the particular keys which are struck.[43]

To an English mind, the harpsichord-judge is a nightmare. Vivaldi's moment of relief at the 'candour' of the vicar-general suggests that, for a brief period of time, we have been translated from the Roman Inquisition to a place where more equitable standards of human probability obtain – a Surrey Assize Court, perhaps.

The debate about these legal systems was a fierce contemporary issue, which affects, in all sorts of powerful but intangible ways, the concept of Probability. In revolutionary France, for example, the Cahiers of 1789 demanded trial by jurors in criminal matters, and they recommended a study of the English system. The arguments in the Assembly of 1791 are fascinating, for what they reveal instantly about the 'logic' of the systems. Here is the corresponding French nightmare, from the mouth of a magistrate:

> 'If legal proofs are no longer necessary to establish the guilt of an accused, everything must become conjectural, and the life and honour of the citizens are brought before a court of conjectures . . . the proof will lie in the individual perception of each juror.'[44]

The witnessing is *merely* interior. There is clearly a different sense of Probability at work altogether here, deriving from a different sense of authority and guarantee.

At the end of *The Italian* the truth prevails. But there is another shift of context. Remarkably, it is the Villain, Schedoni, who warns our hero, Vivaldi, of his 'prevailing weakness'. The moral prejudice which we would expect to operate against this cloaked, cowled Villain (putting aside, for the moment, the familiar question of his 'sublimity') falls away, in favour of a technical point of much greater importance:

> 'And what do you term my prevailing weakness,' said Vivaldi blushing.
> 'A susceptibility which renders you especially liable to superstition,' replied Schedoni.
> 'What! does a monk call superstition a weakness!' rejoined Vivaldi.
> 'But grant he does, on what occasion have I betrayed such weakness?'
> 'Have you forgotten a conversation which I once held with you on invisible spirits?' said Schedoni.[45]

There are other aspects of rational theology to be considered beside the threat of Roman 'authority'. Schedoni has, in a sense, doffed his cowl here, as he points out Vivaldi's dangerous tendency to irrational 'enthusiasm'. This could be an Anglican reproof:

> 'The opinions you avowed were rational,' said Schedoni, 'but the ardour of your imagination was apparent, and what ardent imagination ever was contented to trust to plain reasoning, or to the evidence of the senses? It may not willingly confine itself to the dull truths of this earth but, eager to expand its faculties, to fill its capacity, and to experience its own peculiar delights, soars after new wonders into a world of its own!'
> Vivaldi blushed at this reproof, now conscious of its justness; and was surprised that Schedoni should so well have understood the nature of his mind, while he himself, with whom conjecture had never assumed the stability of opinion, on the subject to which the Confessor alluded, had been ignorant even of its propensities.[46]

Vivaldi stands reproved; but the situation is a delicate one, because sheer dogmatic empiricism, though 'just', is not finally adequate either, Mrs Radcliffe hints. The long search for the 'facts' is over; but it has been, after all, Vivaldi's capacity to accept testimony *against* experience which has given his otherwise utterly unstable position providential support through this maze of legalism; ironically, it is is his own 'candour' which has been instrumental in defeating Schedoni; and it is the very 'susceptibility' which risks being manipulated, which also gives a 'leaven', as it were, to short-sighted dogma. 'Conjecture', in this novel, is the saving grace of 'opinion'.

These novelists convert narrative form to testimony, which is a form of presentation that taps deep-seated assumptions in the audience. In the case of Lewis, the process is part of a tactic to gain rhetorical acceptance. But Mrs Radcliffe is more interesting because she dramatises the contradictions and the profound unease, which are present in the cultural tradition which cultivates private judgements and direct testimony as the touchstones of rational belief. Neither writer is particularly self-conscious in the literary sense; nor, on the other, does either of them merely 'reflect' the culture in which their novels are produced. Their success, in dramatising the question of 'superstition' for the reader, whether they end up by confirming prejudice or confirming unease, depends upon their rhetorical manipulation of a set of expectations about what guaranteed the rational. And those expectations exist as a set of transactions between the contexts of theology and law.

In the course of his discussion of the question of why Bentham wrote his great treatise on the law in French, Elie Halévy in *The Growth of Philosophic Radicalism* gives one a panoramic insight into the atmosphere of late eighteenth-century Europe, which has some relevance to this notion of cultural 'guarantees':

> Now it happened that at this time there was no demand in England, for the supply of a systematised and codified law. In one of his manuscripts Bentham enumerates the rewards which had been offered, over the greater part of Europe, to encourage the reform of criminal law. In 1764 a medal worth twenty ducats was promised by the *Société Economique* of Berne to the anonymous author of *Dei delitti 'e della pene*, if he would disclose his identity. In 1777, a prize of fifty gold louis was offered by the same society for the best plan for a whole penal code: Voltaire and the Englishman Thomas Hollis added fifty louis for *accessits*, and Bentham considered competing. In 1773, a medal was offered by the Academy of Mantua for the solution of a problem relative to

the principles of penal law. Frederick II gave Prussia a code; the King of Sweden announced his intention of lightening and correcting the criminal laws; the Grand Duke of Tuscany simplified the procedure in his states; even in Spain and Poland we find codes in project. As a contemporary observed some years later, there was a general fermentation abroad: 'everything seemed to be pointing to an approaching revolution in the legislation of the whole of Europe; the philosophers were pointing out its abuses; the princes seemed to be seeking the means of doing away with them.' But it was the judicial institutions of England which were continually being cited by the reformers of Europe as a model to be imitated.[47]

Such reforms, and in particular the idea of a code being drawn up by a single individual, would be totally unacceptable to the sense of deep organic ties represented by Blackstone's Gothic Castle, the friendly, historic labyrinth rendered comfortable by equity judges. Essential to this view of legal history, is the sense of the slow, perceptible evolution of the common law, independent of necessities imposed on it from above or outside. To some Englishmen who looked outward to the Continent of Europe in the early nineteenth century, the spectacle of these sweeping reforms of the penal system, even of legal procedure itself, which spring, mushroom-like, overnight from the soil of an individual brain, appeared analogous to the hooded, cowled 'authority' of the Spanish Inquisition itself. Halévy also notes elsewhere that what to the disciples of Montesquieu was a guarantee of freedom, that is, a system which ties the individual response of the judge to a set of pre-determined rules, is to Bentham (profoundly English in this particular sense of his complete commitment to the virtues of an adversary system) a damaging technical redundancy, which will ultimately hamper his freedom to produce a just decision. And Bentham was in the van of reform.

In lesser spirits, who articulate popular prejudice, one sees the cultural projection in a clearer form. Take the example of the following anonymous writer in *The New Monthly Magazine*, Henry Colburn's miscellany which showed a great interest in Mrs Radcliffe, publishing her account of her European tour. This article, written in 1823, takes the form of a review of Abbé Calmet's treatise on Vampires and Apparitions, a work which, the author claims, virtually annihilated the Brighton season by its popularity. The author quotes with relish the details of one of Calmet's cases of vampires in Hungary in 1727, and finishes by describing with jocular contempt the legal procedures with which the case was 'authenticated':

> Among forty corpses, seventeen were found with all the indubitable characteristics of confirmed vampyres. The bodies were speedily decapitated, the hearts impaled, and the members burnt, and their ashes cast into the river Teisse. The Abbé Dom. Calmet enquired into these facts, and found them all judicially authenticated by local authorities, and attested by the officers of the Imperial garrisons, the surgeon-majors of the regiments, and the principal inhabitants of the district. The *procès verbal* of the whole proceedings was sent in January 1735 to the Imperial Council of War in Vienna, who had established a military commission to enquire into the facts. 'Procès verbaux' and 'juridical authentications' certainly are high-sounding things – but a sceptical critic has pretended, with a degree of malice prepense against the Vampyrarchy which we ourselves are far from applauding, that his Imperial Majesty's surgeons-major and counsellors of war might perchance be deceived in some respects; and admitting a great deal of what they attest to be true, that Vampyrism is not a necessary inference from it.[48]

This is as much a comment on the shortcomings of the continental system of law, as it is on the nature of the particular case of Vampyres; and the joke about the authorities, that they are the 'Vampyrarchy', is a witty condensation of a traditional riposte to the authority of Rome. Abbé Calmet is, as the writer points out later in the article, a Benedictine, with his own vested interest in finding vampires. But if we think, as many have, of the English treatment of suicides, the whole question of vampires seems to come much nearer home. According to Keith Thomas, a stake driven through the corpse's heart was the legally required method of burial for suicides until 1823.

This joke-anthropology encapsulates a complicated distrust of several features of European culture. One of these features is the difference in the role of documentation in the inquisitorial system. Our anonymous writer's jibe is against the 'procès verbal', and the lack of security, or openness to political manipulation, of a depositionary system. Perhaps a counter-example will throw the shape of this projection of anxiety into a greater relief. In 1808, after a test period of several years, the French provincial departments of justice, and in particular the Courts of Appeal for the departments, were asked to give their opinion on the jury system, for the purposes of deciding whether the Napoleonic Code would adopt it or not: 26 were against it; 26 were for it; and 23 merely presented remarks of detail without conclusion. In several of the submissions *against* the jury, we find an amusingly 'Gothic' caricature of English culture, which nevertheless has its relevance to the sense of guarantees. The French 'shape' derives from an immersion in documentation:

> 'The Englishman at the theatre only cares for apparitions, madmen, dreadful criminals, murders long drawn out; he runs to animal fights, and probably regrets [*sic*] those of the gladiators; who knows if he does not seek the functions of a juror for the sake of the pleasure of watching a criminal struggling with his conscience, with the death that awaits him? The Frenchman, on the contrary, is delicate in all his tastes; he eagerly flees from any sight which could disagreeably awaken his sensitiveness; could he have any pleasure in wielding the bleeding sword of justice?'[49]

This is just as absurd as Monk Lewis's version of superstition; but it reveals an alternative perspective. The system of oral proof is merely barbaric, and the Roman Empire is invoked as a forerunner of the typical English bloody farce. The truth seems to be, incidentally, that the Roman system changed from an essentially accusatory system in the Republic, which did not employ torture except in very special circumstances, to a system which, with the coming of the Empire, employed all the apparatus of contemporary European inquisitory.[50] Ironically, the occasion for worry is that the jury system was too *lenient* and that brigands were being acquitted in the French provinces by the local juries; but perhaps the Court of Appeal did see the sword of justice in a bloodier light. Whatever may be the case, we see that the French perspective clearly interprets the notion of 'proof' as 'test' only; a system which sacrifices justice to victory, rather than identifies it with truth, is only a piece of bad (melodramatic) theatre.

The French sense of 'private judgement' makes its appearance here (I was not supposing earlier that it did not exist), associated with the alternative to theatre and public spectacle: the private sifting of written depositions, whose admissibility is subject to very few conditions for exclusion, by a judge according to rules which have been provided for him: the half-proofs and the quarter-proofs which form the score for the harpsichord.

In an essentially depositionary system, the whole process of judgement is carried out with reference to documents. Some of the features of this process have survived today. Here, for example, is a description by a distinguished Australian lawyer of some of the obvious differences between the English and continental legal procedures, which gives one the clear sense of a completely different attitude towards documentation:

> Unlike the continental system of trials, based on the Civil Law, the English system is an adversary system, in which the contest is waged on a day in court. Under the Continental system, the witnesses are examined before the trial, and their evidence recorded and placed on the file. The documents which the parties wish to submit are also filed in advance, and their authenticity is taken for granted unless objection is taken beforehand. By contrast, unless a specific prior agreement is reached, every document (with very limited exceptions) that is to be used in an English trial has to be 'proved' by the testimony of some person who can vouch for its authenticity.[51]

Historically, the adversary system has come to imply a built-in suspicion of unauthenticated documents; but it was not always so. For example, this institutionalised suspicion did not exist in the Tudor period, when there existed a much greater sense in legal procedure (and this, I concede, might mean a much *lesser* sense in contexts outside the law) that, if a thing was written down, it had a greater authority than if it were merely delivered orally. No doubt this was convenient politically. Curiously, the deposition of Baines against Marlowe is given enormous authority in the average literary history. Of course, the authentication of a document is quite irrelevant, in one sense, to its truth or falsity; but it is because the historical development of legal procedure has *made* it irrelevant, that this point can come to be so much a part of the cultural sense of the guarantee. The sequences from the trial of Sir Walter Raleigh, for example, which were published in the first collection of State Trials in the early eighteenth century, make agonising reading for this very reason: for his life or death hangs, apparently, on the production by the prosecution of a piece of unauthenticated paper, deposing that he made treasonable remarks. In vain does Raleigh plead for the man to be brought to court to face him and be cross-examined on his evidence. In doing this, he is appealing to 'reason'; but it is a reason which did not, in the context in which he found himself, exist.[52]

The suspicion of documents began to be institutionalised in the eighteenth century, with the introduction of the so-called 'best evidence' rule, which specified that 'the best evidence should be given of which the case would admit'. This rather vague-sounding phrase begins to formalise the conditions on which documentary evidence shall be admissible in a court of law. Thayer in his *Preliminary Treatise on Evidence at the Common Law* (1898) concludes his discussion of this point by suggesting that the 'best evidence' rule develops out of the late medieval *praesumptio* of *profert*; and that in fact it was not one rule at all, but several. It is noteworthy that he too regards its modern form as a product of a cultural tradition. Baron Gilbert's attempt to synthesise what was, in Holt's time, merely a rough guide-line for judges is linked, in the eyes of Thayer, with the political philosophy of the Whig tradition:

> Upon the whole, then, it may be said that the Best Evidence rule was originally, in days when the law of evidence had not yet taken definite shape, a common and useful phrase in the mouths of judges who were expressing a general maxim of justice, without thinking of formulating an exact rule; and that Gilbert, in his premature, ambitious, and inadequate attempt to adjust to the philosophy of John Locke the rude beginnings and tentative, unconscious efforts of the courts, in the direction of a body of rules of evidence, hurt rather than helped matters. By holding up this vague principle as the 'first and most signal rule' of an excluding system, and imparting to our law at that period such systematized and far-looking aims in the region of evidence, he threw everything out of focus. A cheap varnish of philosophy took the place of an ordered statement of the facts.[53]

As the last, gruff remark indicates, Thayer's point of view is very much that of the practical lawyer not the philosopher of law. His late nineteenth-century evolutionary perspective is impatient of Benthamite 'intervention'; but even he, perhaps *a fortiori* he, sees this synthesis of rules as the result of particular cultural pressures.

The most comprehensive development of the eighteenth-century arguments about the relation of testimony to experience is Bentham's in *The Rationale of Judicial Evidence*; Bentham began writing this treatise remarkably early, the seeds of its argument having been sewn in his mind by his precocious but devastating attack on Blackstone's *Commentaries*. First written in French and circulated in the period of debate about the reform of the French penal code, the *Rationale* was not published in English until 1825 in a translation made by his French editor, M. Dumont. Bentham rejects the connection between law and constitutional guarantees from tradition. Instead, he tries to think the question through from first principles. From the outset, his stress is on the individual judging mind; as Halévy suggests, he translates older philosophical questions into the new psychology. And this approach makes his analysis uncannily relevant to the concept of expectation in the reading of fiction, because Bentham is, in effect, examining the question of belief with a startlingly fresh eye. He tends to push Hume's arguments about the testimonial support for miracles in a psychological direction, analysing just what is involved for the individual judgement in drawing the distinction between the improbable and the impossible.

The motives behind this are manifold. But one of his most important considerations is to cut a way for judicial process through the Gordian knot of debates about superstition. In childhood, he was grotesquely deceived by a servant into believing in a bogey-man called Palethorpe who lived in a dark cupboard below stairs. When he grew up, one of his primary aims was to lay out the rational foundations of knowledge, so that no false beliefs could again be admitted to hamper the course of individual or society.[54] But this ambition by no means turns Bentham into a crude Philistine, as the image of the father of utilitarianism might suggest. Throughout the seventeenth- and eighteenth-century furore about the role of testimony in human belief, the structure of arguments for miracles could be used to support testimony for other less salutary happenings. As Glanvill and More saw it, 'No Spirit, No God'. As Bentham himself is only too ready to recognise, when he suggests in the treatise that the writers of romances ought to be recognised as the benefactors, not the deceivers of mankind, there is a connection between these important debates and the question of the marvellous in literature. Bentham, of course, is anti-Christian; but he is not opposed to the notion of 'the marvellous': his sense of probability could not be more obviously anti-Aristotelian.

Bentham begins by outlining a further development of what I have been calling the 'alienated' position about testimony. Here, of course, he is not talking about law *by analogy*; but is attempting to lay ground rules for the judicial process. His main contention is that there is no absolute criterion for assuming the impossibility of any given fact. The will, he says, quoting Pascal with obvious relish, is the principal organ of belief. The impossible is only the highest degree of the improbable. And the improbable is really only the measure of our ignorance. Thus Bentham begins by sketching out an extreme form of cultural and individual relativity in matters of belief: that 'the credibility or incredibility of facts does not depend on their own nature, but on the disposition of our mind'. There is no universal scale that can be established of credibility:

> Every people has its own scale of credibility, graduated according to the state of its own knowledge. What do I say? This scale varies even in different parts of the same town. A story which would be readily believed in Wapping, merely on the faith of public report, would not be believed in St James' Square, even on the faith of direct testimony.[55]

So what of Hume's argument about the laws of nature? Bentham, to this extent like the Anglican divines before him, finds that the evidence in favour of Hume's argument is a presumed mass of testimony, which he terms the 'general counter-testimony', and which is only a species of 'circumstantial evidence'. He briefly inhabits the Humean position:

> But, it will be said, when a fact intrinsically impossible is in question, its impossibility is palpable; it is decided on, the very moment it is announced; there is no necessity for arranging other facts in opposition to it; we regret it without encumbering ourselves with evidence.[56]

But his use of this position is momentary and rhetorical: it exists only to parody its *popular* reception, as a form of prejudice. Here, the sudden flash of irony reveals how fresh are the witchcraft horrors in his mind, and how shallow he finds the 'orthodox' positions of both law and religion:

Take a case of witchcraft. It must be recollected, that, what, in our own days, is never spoken of seriously, was a source of terror to our forefathers. The alleged fact is, that an old woman travelled through the air on a broomstick. Do you believe it? No. Why? Because it is impossible. Impossible! how do you prove that? Where is the necessity for proof? To reason about such a thing is mere madness.

This is no doubt a most legitimate prejudice, and one which does honour to the knowledge of the age; but those whose opinions are founded only on this prejudice, would have condemned the very same witches, had they lived in the times when the prejudice was in favour of their existence.[57]

But even bringing Hume's philosophical arguments to bear upon the question, he is forced to admit that the so-called 'laws of nature' are founded on nothing more than circumstantial evidence:

But, when I refer to these laws of nature, and advance them as evidence, for the sake of shortening the discussion, have I done anything else than refer to an immense assemblage of facts which seem to me to be incompatible with the fact in question? All the bodies with which I am acquainted tend towards the centre of the earth. But how am I led to so general a conclusion? By my own personal experience, by the testimony of my fellow-men, by the testimony of learned persons who have made natural knowledge their particular study, and have written expressly on this subject. Were this regularly increasing mass of knowledge analysed, it would be resolved into so many distinct articles of evidence, perception, report, oral or written testimony etc. But to what does this all amount? There is not here any direct evidence against the supposed magical journey. What is it then? It is circumstantial evidence, and nothing else.[58]

What price here Ian Watt's 'circumstantial view of life' as an epistemological guarantee for aesthetic realism? Looked at from another point of view, 'circumstantial evidence' becomes the support for nothing more than prejudice, which, in its turn, can be overthrown by testimony to the marvellous.

This is the very difficulty in Hume's argument which the Anglican divines seized upon to justify their own beliefs in miracles. But Bentham uses it for a very different purpose. Here, it is thoroughly secularised. Indeed, it is the most radical, wholesale rejection of the 'orthodox' position, whether alienated or comfortable, which would establish guarantees for probability, by deriving them exclusively from tradition and social system. The foundations of Blackstone's position are rotten; and there is nothing which distinguishes his argument from precedent from that of witch-burners:

> If Blackstone partly refuses his belief (and it is only partly) to the sorcerers of modern times, it is merely because they are not stamped with the seal of a sufficiently remote antiquity. Had they borne on their heads a few additional centuries, his doubts would have been converted into certainty; and who knows but that in time, and in certain circumstances, the imagination of some successor of this celebrated lawyer may beget on the spectre of the witch of Endor, a new progeny of magicians and sorcerers, who will call up infernal spirits, and restore the reign of phantoms and terror?[59]

Bentham's concern is, as I have suggested, with the psychology of the individual mind in the act of judgement. He assumes the general model of an audience (whether it be made up of judges, whose task it is to attend to matters of law, or a jury, whose concern is with matters of fact) for testimony; and he assumes a graduated ability in that audience, according to education, intelligence, social grouping, cultural affinities, and so on, to receive with scepticism the 'general counter-testimony' or consensus about what constitutes the probable, which is a condition of any act of judgement. His treatise is thus a grammar of human expectation; and, as such, it is a blue-print for the rhetorical features of the romance genre in fiction. Take, for example, his maxim that 'distance diminishes incredibility'. One of the favourite argumentative examples from Locke onwards had been the Indian Prince who had scoffed at the Dutchman when he told him that in his country water formed itself, at a certain part of the year, into a white substance so solid that a man could walk on it. This example is used for different rhetorical purposes by almost everyone who quotes it; but Bentham's use is interesting because it supports his cultural relativism. He finds the Prince a perfectly reasonable figure, whose disbelief satirises those whose superior 'scepticism' would seek to make him into a comic butt. Bentham was obsessively interested in travellers' tales; and there is a sense in which his scepticism (his complicated awareness of the relations between imagination and fact) gives us an insight into the rhetorical function of 'distance'. The conflict between 'special testimony' and 'general counter-testimony', which for the reader of romance is revealed in its very form, has to be fought out anew in each individual case. Bentham's attitude is that there is no *given* place in the *gestalt* of expectation, where testimony inserts itself. His attitude towards the evidence of German Gothic manuscripts which tells of monsters is emblematic of his attitude towards all experience:

> I have before me a copy of the Chronicle of Nürnberg, which contains, in twelve folio plates, representations of twenty one species of men, or, in the usual mode of expression, twenty one monsters, taken from Pliny and other authors. Some of them appear to imply anatomical inconsistencies; others have really existed; some of the rest have existed in a certain degree; the eye of the Cyclops, for example; heads with horns, supernumerary arms and hands, and double bodies. Still, in these cases, the fact is an individual one and does not extend to the species. What is a species, however, but multiplied individuals?[60]

Later in the nineteenth century, Darwinism made it much more difficult to mount such a general argument; but the striking thing here is the readiness to dissolve the general, expected boundaries between fact and fiction on the basis of the individual *fact*. Bentham subjects experience to a relentless fragmentation; and the whole Aristotelian idea of a qualitative synthesis, which lies behind the social guarantees for Probability, is rejected by an attention to detail, which divides and subdivides experience into its component parts. Thus Bentham is positively fond of what M. Dumont calls *le fait déviatif*; and he quotes with obvious approval Bacon's famous desire to make an objective catalogue of monstrosities in nature, without the distractions of religious orthodoxy. The strange, for Bentham, is on a par with the everyday, the singular is on a scale with the ordinary. His accent is on seeing through the language and standards of judgement which we inherit or absorb from our immediate environment:

> The incredibility of any given fact diminishes as its distance increases; that is, we believe more readily what is related of a distant country. But why does distance diminish improbability?

Imagination has some share in it, but reason, too has her's. We know that what surrounds us is not to be the standard of our judgement concerning everything; singular facts, which at first surprised us, have turned out to be true, and this experience prevents us from deciding hastily on what we do not know.[61]

Viewed from this perspective, the rhetorical form of direct testimony undermines the reader's obvious securities, because the trial or case format tends to assume certain necessary symmetries between art and life. The distance, which decreases incredibility (Bentham gives the example of *Gulliver's Travels*), is based, partly, on an appeal to reason; thus the literary form becomes a kind of mock-argument. What is aesthetically a cumbersome labyrinth, a set of narrative redundancies, is also a test of the reader's judgement, which is disconcertingly *direct*.

Mary Shelley's *Frankenstein*, for example, employs the kind of structure I have been discussing; reading is a process of directly apprehending and judging testimony. The narrative is 'learnt' in the course of a series of apparently redundant records of journeys. In the beginning, we follow Captain Walton, as he first sets out from London on his search for the magnetic north, into the Arctic regions. This is the start of the labyrinth, for the reader, the first projection of 'distance', in the Benthamite sense, which bristles with the sense of a record set down:

Letter 1

To Mrs Saville, England

ST PETERSBURGH, Dec. 11th, 17—

You will rejoice to hear that no disaster has accompanied the commencement of an enterprise which you have regarded with such evil forebodings. I arrived here yesterday; and my first task is to assure my dear sister of my welfare and increasing confidence in the success of my undertaking.

I am already far north of London; and as I walk in the streets of Petersburgh, I feel a cold northern breeze play upon my cheeks, which braces my nerves, and fills me with delight. Do you understand this feeling? This breeze, which has travelled from the regions towards which I am advancing, gives me a foretaste of those icy climes.[62]

Here we have the beginning of indirection and, at the same time, the 'frame' of direct testimony. Walton, who in obvious ways is the forerunner of Victor Frankenstein, then meets the latter who tells him his story. But Walton, the imagery of whose letters introduces the reader to many of the major themes of the book, is only a witness to the testimony of another:

> He then told me that he would commence his narrative the next day when I should be at leisure. This promise drew from me the warmest thanks. I have resolved every night, when I am not imperatively occupied by my duties, to record, as nearly as possible in his own words, what he has related during the day. If I should be engaged, I will at least make notes. This manuscript will doubtless afford you the greatest pleasure; but to me, who know him, and who hear it from his own lips with what interest and sympathy shall I read it in some future day![63]

Pleasure may be the outcome for his sister (the 'you' referred to), but the reader of Captain Walton's 'record' is also setting out on a process of sifting, and comparing points of view, as we move on to the conveyor-belt of retrospection, in order to find out what the meaning of the 'present' of the recording process is. So we begin again at Chapter 1: 'I am by birth a Genevese.' This, however, is another layer of 'recording'. As such, it too is subject to the judgemental convention, which the context of testimony arouses. The famous 'Gothic' passages of his story are expressed in a language which reminds us of the debates about superstition and 'fact'. It is a double-take, for the theme of education, and the idea that 'horror' is socially caused, is also being used to tempt the reader's foreboding:

> In my education my father had taken the greatest precautions that my mind should be impressed with no supernatural horrors. I do not ever remember to have trembled at a tale of superstition, or to have feared the apparition of a spirit. Darkness had no effect upon my fancy; and a churchyard was to me merely the receptacle of bodies deprived of life, which, from being the seat of beauty and strength, had become food for the worm. Now I was led to examine the cause of the progress of this decay, and forced to spend days and nights in vaults and charnel houses.[64]

Into this darkness, which we, in our fallen state, leap to imagine, pours the light of truth; and, hard on the heels of a Shelleyan passage of great lyricism about light, comes the 'affidavit'; the distinction between the marvellous and the miraculous is self-consciously evoked in the testimony itself:

> Remember, I am not recording the vision of a madman. The sun does not more certainly shine in the heavens than that which I now affirm is true. Some miracle might have produced it, yet the stages of the discovery were distinct and probable. After days and nights of incredible labour and fatigue, I succeeded in discovering the cause of generation and life; nay, more, I became myself capable of bestowing animation upon lifeless matter.[65]

We realise that he, too, is an editor of the 'stages' which make this probable; but it remains 'probable', because we have his 'special counter-testimony' for it. This whole process of being made to pass from one witness to another, has the effect of forcing the reader into the position of reviewing the 'general counter-testimony' against what is being witnessed, which is supplied by our expectations of a familiar environment. Imaginatively, we travel away into a land distant from us in both time and space, yet due to the process of 'fading' from one testimony to another, we preserve the expectation of present judgement. The process is narratively redundant, but forensically direct; and this directness carries with it many of the expectations of judgement which take place in the courtroom.

Frankenstein himself then hands over the story to the 'daemon'; but not before the challenge to his own credibility has occurred. His testimony has become doubtful, because we begin to see through the apparatus of 'recording' to the speaker. But that, of course, is a response partly generated and aroused by the form of the testimony itself. The sequence of association in the following turns the reader into a juror:

> Unable to endure the aspect of the being I had created, I rushed out of the room, and continued a long time traversing my bedchamber, unable to compose my mind to sleep. At length lassitude succeeded to the tumult I had before endured, and I threw myself on the bed in my clothes, endeavouring to seek a few moments of forgetfulness. But it was in vain: I slept, indeed, but I was disturbed by the wildest dreams. I thought I saw Elizabeth in the bloom of health, walking in the streets of

Ingolstadt. Delighted and surprised, I embraced her, but as I imprinted the first kiss on her lips, they became livid with the hue of death; her features appeared to change, and I thought that I held the corpse of my dead mother in my arms; a shroud enveloped her form, and I saw the grave-worms crawling in the folds of the flannel. I started from my sleep with horror; a cold dew covered my forehead, my teeth chattered, and every limb became convulsed: when, by the dim and yellow light of the moon, as it forced its way through the window shutters, I beheld the wretch, the miserable *monster* whom I had created [author's italics].[66]

Here we become sensitised to the amount of projection which exists in Frankenstein's point of view; we look 'through' it, as it were. As critics have pointed out, to use the word 'monster' about the daemon is to fall into the very credibility trap which the novel sets for the reader. It is our disability, our disinclination to believe the word *monster* here (in metaphysical terms, our 'unfallen' response) which makes us want to invoke the corroborative principle and turn away from Frankenstein to another point of view: that of the daemon himself. For Frankenstein, retrospectively, appearance has become reality. The truths of vision which he has already articulated are no longer accessible to him at this point: what was a special testimony, has become stereotyped 'horror' (general counter-testimony) as we see the gap opening up between the events he recounts and the way he describes them.

But this general counter-testimony is met by further special testimony – that of the daemon himself; as Mary Shelley takes the trouble, or rather the opportunity, to give us his testimony direct. It is this directness of effect, still carrying us into the heart of the labyrinth, as it were, which results in the moral ambiguity that so characterises this novel. What appears redundant from a *narrative* point of view – because it, too could have been reported by Frankenstein, or, for that matter, Walton – is absolutely essential from a rhetorical point of view, because it is testimony which challenges the structure of authority set up in the previous testimony of the other narrators. This is the daemon's point of view, and our judgement, unless we are as corrupt in that judgement as Frankenstein himself, demands it. Notoriously, the beauty and the pathos, the dignity and the sensitivity of the testimony, combined with the *fact* of its appearance, forces a judgemental dilemma in the reader's mind and confirms the deep rift which has opened up in the structure of expectation. For the novel here has begun to raise the question of the singular life and the responsibilities of not only one human being towards another, but also, if he exists, of God towards humanity.

Frankenstein's own moral position is trite, and retrospective:

> Learn from me, if not by my precepts, at least by my example, how dangerous is the acquirement of knowledge and how much happier that man is who believes his native town to be the world, than he who aspires to become greater than his nature will allow.[67]

Here he is talking to Walton, and such a warning has some importance for him; but, for us, who read the record of this conversation, this whole piece of retrospective advice is contradicted by the rhetorical form in which we receive the following (brilliant and sad) *tour de force*:

> 'I am thy creature, and I will be even mild and docile to my natural lord and king, if thou wilt also perform thy part, the which thou owest me. Oh, Frankenstein, be not equitable to every other, and trample upon me alone, to whom thy justice, and even thy clemency and affection is most due. Remember that I am thy creature; I ought to be thy Adam, but I am rather the fallen angel, whom thou drivest from joy for no misdeed. Everywhere I see bliss, from which I alone am irrevocably excluded. I was benevolent and good; misery made me a friend. Make me happy, and I shall again be virtuous.'
>
> 'Begone! I will not hear you. There can be no community between you and me; we are enemies. Begone, or let us try our strength in a fight, in which one must fall.'[68]

We feel the gap here, almost instantly, between our responses and those of Frankenstein. Both of us have heard the same speech; and we are thrown back on our private judgement, and forced to weigh the expectation created by a familiar (Christian) moral scheme, and the evidence we are here confronted with. The testimony of the daemon is a crucial factor in this process, which cuts across the linear sense of narrative altogether. So, for example, the saddest and most complex moment of all, and yet the moment which most

obviously hands on the fall which Frankenstein himself has
undergone, involved only the daemon himself, looking for the first
time, in a pool of water:

> 'I had admired the perfect forms of my cottagers – their grace,
> beauty, and delicate complexions: but how was I terrified when I
> viewed myself in a transparent pool! At first I started back, unable
> to believe that it was indeed I who was reflected in the mirror; and
> when I became fully convinced that *I was in reality the monster that I
> am*, I was filled with the bitterest sensations of despondence and
> mortification.[69]

These are my italics; for the inversion of Narcissus becomes
immediately plain in that one simple phrase. The creature has now
begun to see himself as deformed, just as Frankenstein first saw
him. But we learn this from the testimony of the creature himself; a
gap opens up in the different perspectives contained in that single
phrase, because we see him differently. Far from restricting us to his
own view of himself, the directness of his testimony makes us see
beyond him; beyond the appearance, that is, which his fallen
perception, his acceptance of the general counter-testimony, has
imposed upon himself. His own socialised viewpoint is corrupt, a
failure of vision. The allusion in the passage is to Eve's first,
gloriously Narcissistic view of herself in *Paradise Lost*, Book IV; and
the intimate engineering of simultaneously internal and external
perspectives, which Milton seems so effortlessly to perform, is
harnessed by Mary Shelley to the device of direct testimony. The
technique of presenting evidence in both cases – Frankenstein and
the daemon – sets the dynamic apprehension of the reader against
the slack, conditioned retrospection of the speaker: 'But, reality was
only appearance!' we cry.

Few of the renditions of the novel on the screen have managed to
convey this conflict, partly because directors have been more
interested in playing on the simple paranoia of the situation, in
creating threat through visual disgust; but partly for formal reasons
too. The direct (verbal) testimony of the creature is either discredited
by a monstrous visual impression or suppressed altogether. When
this happens, the general counter-testimony has its way
unopposed. But the creature in the novel *is* his speech, and in the
ironic contrast between appearance and reality his direct testimony,
inelegant though the device of 'starting again' appears to be,

contradicts and relativises, turns inside out, the simple sub-Christian scheme which appears to be the shaping message of the book. The anxiety the novel raises, which is a fundamental part of its power, is precisely about the flimsiness of this 'general counter-testimony' by which we calculate the security of our place in the world. The radical attack on Christianity, which is at the centre of *Frankenstein*, is carried out by an invitation to the reader to respond judgementally to direct testimony. That invitation is essentially the same as the appeal to reason which Bentham describes in the legal context; and the ambiguity of this appeal (different readers respond, notoriously, in different ways to the novel's 'tragedy') stems partly from the ambiguous nature of testimony itself. The act of witnessing is not merely 'legal': it provides the model for individual judgement and carries a theological 'charge' in the arguments used throughout the eighteenth century to establish the existence of miracles.

Bentham himself recognises something of the complexity of this web of relationships which surround testimony, when he talks about the relation of fact to imagination:

If we go deeper into the human heart, we shall find in it a secret disposition to believe the marvellous, as if it extended our power, and gave us the command of supernatural means.

Besides, when these things of pure creation are the subject, reason is not sufficiently unbiassed to scrutinize the testimony. Fear comes in the way, doubt appears dangerous; we are afraid, lest we offend these invisible agents; there are numerous stories in the public mouth of the vengeance which they have taken on unbelievers.

These are the causes, which have established the belief in spectres, ghosts, possessed persons, devils, vampires, magicians, sorcerers – all those frightful beings, who have ceased to play a part in courts, but still appear in the cottage.

Among the extraordinary operations of the imagination, there is one directly the reverse of those of which we have been speaking. There we had facts which did not exist, attested as real facts, but here we have real facts produced by imagination; and which have no existence but through it. The history of medicine contains a multitude of examples of this kind, of diseases suspended or cured by the influence of mental belief – a simple, pure belief – without any foundation in the action of natural causes. *Fit medicina fides*. I need only to refer to animal magnetism.[70]

One gets a real sense here of the cultural limbo in which testimony, the frame of credibility itself, operates. While adopting the Humean position with regard to superstition, Bentham is fully alive to the consequences of part of Hume's argument, namely, that either a situation is miraculous, in which case for Hume it is impossible and the testimony for it is false, or it extends the laws of nature, and a new law has to be invoked to cover the case. But, he points out here, the relation between fact and imagination is not always the same; and he seemed to have no doubt (unlike many 'rationalists') in the existence of the power of 'mind over matter'.

Here it is worth pausing to note the semantic quagmire one enters, when charting the usage of some of these key terms. I have already referred to an ambiguity in the use of 'fact' and 'evidence', this latter, in its quasi-legal usage, being a name for the production of testimony. The same is true of 'proof' and the vexed term 'probability'. 'Proof', for example, meant in the old legal usage 'trial by arms': the modern sense of 'rationality' is only part of its meaning, and a part which, in legal contexts, only comes into its own in the later nineteenth century. The last actual case of the legal challenge being used by a defendant was as late as 1819. This shows how much the idea of legal 'reasoning' was associated with its adversary context. Again, unexpectedly at first, Bentham's moral antipathy to casuistry, and the merely technical standards of 'proving power' make his picture of the process of judgement an intimate, experiential, even an instinctual matter. It is not possible, he acknowledges, to form an objective scale on which the truth or falsity of evidence can be shown. Bentham's model for the law is ultimately a domestic tribunal – the judge is as a wise father examining his sons. This idea runs through his treatise, and forms the basis of his rejection of exclusionary rules. His version of 'proof' is not exactly the conventional enlightenment faculty of *le bon sens*; but of an instinct whose absence would involve us in a dizzying spectacle of solipsistic isolation:

> To say that one event is proof of another, is judgement founded on analogy, and the analogy itself rests on experience. It must be confessed, however, that this judgement must be considered as a sort of instinct, as well from the promptness of its operation, as

from the difficulty of explaining it, and the impossibility of finding rules to guide it. This instinct, so useful to men as a guide, would throw them into despair, if it were not nearly uniform in all; all that could be said on the connection between phenomena would be vain, if we did not set out from the supposition that two facts, which appear in the eyes of one person to be connected in a particular manner, will appear to be connected in the same way in the eyes of all others.[71]

Here there is no confusion at all, it seems, between the natural sciences (or even Bentham's own favourites, arithmetic and geometry) and legal reasoning; and it is precisely this kind of insight into the nature of proof in the law, which impels Bentham to attack the inhumanity, as well as the irrationality, of a purely technical system of exclusionary rules, based on a set of 'securities' which are theological in nature.

The same kind of broad point can be made about the concept of 'probability'. Bentham reduces the idea of probability to 'credibility', thus ridding it of a confusion between knowledge and belief at a single stroke. In this sense, he resembles Plato. Bentham's motive for this is to commit the *whole man* to a judgement at a single point in time. His counter to the eighteenth-century arguments about probability is typical. Price and others had used the standard analogy of the lottery, to describe the nature of probability as an enormous series of chances. It is almost incredible, they argued, that *this* ticket should have won: the chances against the return of a comet seem so vast that one feels the sense of wonderment swelling when it appears. Bentham's reply is typically pragmatic: that no analogy holds here, because one ticket *must* win. This makes the event an expected one, not something akin to a miracle. And if the lottery were increased to the size of millions, the same expectation would obtain, that a particular ticket would win. The Anglicans here are the ones who support the idea of the miraculous by the doctrine of chances. And this confusion between quite different senses of 'probability' seems to Bentham to have the most dangerous consequences:

This is not a mere metaphysical speculation; it is of great importance in judicial practice. If the mathematically improbable facts of Dr Price are confounded with facts physically impossible in the eyes of those who have some acquaintance with the

ordinary course of nature; if facts of the former, and facts of the
latter kind, are admitted on the same evidence, the reign of magic
and witchcraft is restored. Stakes may be raised and piles kindled,
for those into whom devils and demons have entered; the greater
the number of wizards that are burned, the more numerous will
be the reasons for continuing to burn them.[72]

What Bentham acknowledges here is the semantic ambiguity in the
use of a term which straddles different contexts; but more than this,
he is also pointing to a confusion of contexts.

But the most spectacular example of the relationship in the narrative
form of the horror novel between testimony and the corroborative
principle comes at the end of the nineteenth century in Bram
Stoker's *Dracula*. This novel takes the form of an enormous
international 'case', extended geographically throughout Europe,
whose labyrinthine ramifications reach politically across the
Atlantic to the Western Alliance. 'Distance decreases incredibility' is
demonstrably the law of its rhetorical procedure. The novel begins
in a fashion that seems leisurely, remote from its central concerns; it
creates 'distance' in cultural terms, while at the same time relying
heavily on the apparatus of testimony. The opening is lovingly
done:

JONATHAN HARKER'S JOURNAL – (kept in shorthand)

3 May.   Bistriz. – Left Munich at 8.35 p.m., on 1st May, arriving
at Vienna early next morning; should have arrived at 6.46 but train
was an hour late. Buda-Pesth seems a wonderful place, from the
glimpse which I got of it from the train and the little I could walk
through the streets. I feared to go very far from the station, as we
arrived late and would start as near the correct time as possible.
The impression I had was that we were leaving the West and
entering the East; the most western of splendid bridges over the
Danube, which is here of noble width and depth, took us among
the traditions of Turkish rule.[73]

The lawyer's clerk (Harker is a good allegorical name for a witness,
and Stoker may well have picked this up from Ambrose Bierce), who

records in shorthand, finicky, fearful and punctilious, yet determined to witness everything for the sake of his wife, is, ludicrously, the ambassador of Western Rationalism. He represents the 'liberal' belief in the progress of the human spirit away from backward looking, theologically dominated cultures – the kind of position celebrated in W. E. H. Lecky's *The Rise of Rationalism in Europe*, written at more or less the same time as this novel. The hints are there of technological progress: the shorthand feels 'modern'; and later, as the tissue of records thickens and different witnesses are brought into play, these materials are re-formed into a single 'case' on Dr Seward's phonograph machine. Mina, Harker's wife, is, among other handy things, a stenographer who can type up Seward's diary in emergencies. We are exposed, as readers, to letters, journals, telegrams, newspaper reports, naval log books and, within these forms, the oral testimony of individuals is also recorded. The effect is of a wanton scattering of forms: yet there is a thread of threat and irony: the very medium of the novel itself seems to betray a built-in frailty in the cultural guarantees that appear to support its method. The cultural thrill that Harker feels in his first diary entry, still familiar to us nowadays on trips across the border between East and West, accompanies the act of travelling away from a centre of security. In the *Rationale*, Bentham insisted on the asymmetry between geographical distance, the vehicle, as it were, of cultural relativism, and the journey in time from the present into the past, which for him, as a believer in the progress of reason, which had been only shakily achieved, was not to be subverted: witches were not burnt in England, and that meant a lot to him. The whole effect of Stoker's rhetoric in this novel is to create a symmetry between journeys in space and time, through the conduit of the isolated witnessing individual: he used the threat of an alien culture, still apparently in its darkest age, as a means of throwing into relief the decadence of 'scientific' attitudes in Western Europe. The point is made about half-way through the book by Van Helsing, when he is beginning to introduce, for the benefit of the purblind empiricist Dr Seward, a unified explanation of the scattered testimonies which we, as readers, have already long since begun to use corroboratively. The contrast is between the blind process of inductive reasoning, the Shibboleth of 'natural' explanation, and the nature of belief;

'Well, I shall tell you. My thesis is this: I want you to believe.'

'To believe what?'

'To believe in things that you cannot. Let me illustrate. I heard once of an American who so defined faith: "that faculty which enables us to believe things which we know to be untrue." For one, I follow that man. He meant that we shall have an open mind, and not let a little bit of truth check the rush of a big truth, like a small rock does a railway truck. We get the small truth first. Good! We keep him, and we value him; but all the same we must not let him think himself all the truth in the universe.'

'Then you want me not to let some previous conviction injure the receptivity of my mind with regard to some strange matter. Do I read your lesson aright?'[74]

I have abstracted part of this dialogue: in fact, it, too, is framed as part of his diary, and hence is a fragment of recessive testimony, a layer itself, rather than a directly perceived, dramatic encounter. The theme of their conversation is purely traditional, which the reader of this chapter will easily recognise by now: the intrusion of the railway may make the *vis a tergo* of the 'big truth' look modern; but the argument against the vanity of dogmatising empiricism takes us all the way back to the overlap between empirical method and spiritual testimony which Glanvill, More and Defoe were trying to exploit in the seventeenth century. The mere collection of evidence is a form of short-sightedness: it is the symptom of a decadent materialism in our culture. We must learn to draw other influences from 'evidence':

'You think then that those so small holes in the childrens' throats were made by the same that made the hole in Miss Lucy?'

'I suppose so.' He stood up and said solemnly:–

'Then you are wrong. Oh, would it were so! But alas! no. It is worse, far, far worse.'

'In God's name, Professor Van Helsing, what do you mean?' I cried.

He threw himself with a despairing gesture into a chair, and placed his elbows on the table, covering his face with his hands as he spoke:–

'They were made by Miss Lucy!'[75]

Seward plays Dr Watson to Van Helsing's Holmes here: such

Sancho Panza figures are the 'markers' for the residue of empiricist feelings in the reader, which are in the process of being evaded by the case format itself. Yes, this really *is* the explanation, the mythic one, and unless we are prepared to jump vigilantly ahead and infer the unknown from the known, we shall remain with only a series of fragments. Of course, by this time the reader already knows this because the narrative connections, hidden in their separate testimonies from each of the isolated characters, have become corroboratively evident: the reader has been forced already to draw the inference through recognising a series of potential convergences. Seward the empiricist, however, confined, mole-like, in the tunnel of experiment, lags woefully behind.

The book takes a qualitative leap at this point, as the scattered characters form themselves into a team and their individual testimonies are acknowledged to be part of a whole. In fact, as the book's rhetoric becomes more confident, we learn that it is 'empiricism' we are fighting against. Dracula is the ultimate empiricist, we learn, towards the end of the book:

> To begin, have you ever study the philosophy of crime? 'Yes' and 'No' – You, John, yes; for it is a study of insanity. You, no, Madame Mina; for crime touch you not – not but once. Still, your mind works true, and argues not *a particulare ad universale*. There is this peculiarity in criminals. It is so constant, in all countries and at all times, that even police, who know not much from philosophy, come to know it empirically, that *it is*. That is to be empiric. The criminal always work at one crime – that is the true criminal who seems predestinate to crime, and who will of none other. This criminal has not full man-brain. He is clever and cunning and resourceful; but he be of not man-nature as to brain. He be of child-brain in much. Now this criminal of ours is predestinate to crime also; he, too, have child-brain, and it is of the little child to do what he have done. The little bird, the little fish learn not by principle, but empirically; and when he learn to do, then there is to the ground to start to do more. *'Dos pon sto'*, said Archimedes, 'Give me a fulcrum, and I shall move the world!'[76]

The extraordinary jumble of scientific language and theological premise in which his theory of atavistic regression is couched lies directly behind some of the striking imagery in the book. It explains, for example, the strange touch of apparent tenderness which

Seward's relentless habit of observation intrudes into the following scene:

> His face was turned from us, but the instant we saw all recognised the Count – in every way, even to the scar on his forehead. With his left hand he held both Mrs Harker's hands, keeping them away with her arms at full tension; his right hand gripping her by the back of the neck, forcing her face down on his bosom. Her white nightdress was smeared with blood, and a thin stream trickled down the man's bare breast which was shown by his torn-open dress. The attitude of the two had a terrible resemblance to a child forcing a kitten's nose into a saucer of milk to compel it to drink.[77]

As a recent adaptation of this scene on television showed, it is certainly pornographic: it is a form of *fellatio*. It is also a moment of power, yet the child and the kitten are in danger of appealing to a kind of tenderness, or at least a 'cruel to be kind' feeling. Then why is this resemblance 'terrible'? The horror stems here from the moment of onto- and phylo-genetic regression: we have caught in the act (and, complicatedly, there is a distinct feeling of sexual thrill about it), that primitive, greedy, blind sucking which associates for Van Helsing with the blind mental habits of empiricism, the inverse of faith, principle and civilisation. It is not, in this sense, an observed event at all, but an *instance* of Van Helsing's speech above.

It is presented, however, as testimony, recorded at the time, a vivid detail caught in the process of observation, not explained, yet felt as threatening and 'terrible'. The explanation which I have just used is, in fact, inserted into the text long *after* the passage has struck us with all the force of sensitive 'observation'.

Stoker was a graduate in general science. He was very interested in 'new' scientific theory, and in the theories of the unconscious, which preceded Freud. The 'philosophy of crime', which Van Helsing refers to above, is a mixture of Nordau and Count Lombroso, in particular, backed by the theories of Charcot, who is mentioned several times in *Dracula*, and possibly B. A. Morel. One can see instantly, upon opening Count Lombroso's *Criminal Man*, that Stoker did not have to move very far into what was setting itself up in the 1890s as the foundation of the new science of 'criminal anthropology', in order to get most of the materials for the figure of Count Dracula. Lombroso and Nordau appeared to be extending the boundaries of positivism (Lombroso was the head of the 'New', the 'Modern', the 'Positive' school of the study of crime): whereas they were in fact extending the boundaries of Social Darwinism. The tendency of Lombrosianism is to erode the boundaries of crime, vice and insanity through the 'biological' study of the criminal and the insane. The idea was born that the criminal was a 'throwback', a 'ghost of the past' and 'the relic of a vanished race'. Here is the famous passage in which Lombroso, after studying the remains of a particularly vicious Neopolitan murderer, experiences a revelation, startlingly akin to that of St Paul or St Augustine, in which he sees before him the *true* nature of this figure of the criminal:

> At the sight of that skull, I seemed to see all of a sudden, lighted up as a vast plain under a flaming sky, the problem of the nature of the criminal – an atavistic being who reproduces in his person the ferocious instincts of primitive humanity and the inferior animals. Thus were explained anatomically the enormous jaws, high cheek-bones, prominent superciliary arches, solitary lines in the palms, extreme size of the orbits, handle-shaped or sessile ears found in criminals, savages, and apes, insensibility to pain, extremely acute sight, tattooing, excessive idleness, love of orgies, and the irresistible craving for evil for its own sake, the desire not only to extinguish life in the victim, but to mutilate the corpse, tear its flesh, and drink its blood.[78]

This inclines more towards Werewolf than Vampire, perhaps, but Lombroso was an expert in 'stigmata', and he made innumerable 'scientific' observations, whose data could provide the basis for a number of 'identikit' pictures of degeneracy. He reported, for example, that in four per cent of his sample (size not given), 'the canines are very strongly developed, long, sharp, and curving inwardly as in carnivores'. This sounds, again, werewolfian (see Plate 14). But later in his book he includes the vampire type:

> In criminals, especially if epileptics, the middle incisors of the upper jaw are sometimes missing and their absence is compensated by the excessive development of the lateral incisors.[79]

Invulnerability, apparently, is another characteristic of the 'criminal epileptic' or 'morally insane' individual, which has an obvious relevance to Dracula:

Invulnerability, another characteristic common to criminals, has been observed by Tonnini in epileptics, whose wounds and injuries heal with astonishing rapidity, and he is inclined to regard this peculiarity in the light of a reversion to a stage of evolution, at which animals like lizards and salamanders were able to replace severed joints by new growths. This invulnerability is shared by all degenerates: epileptics, imbeciles, and the morally insane.[80]

The degree of threat in this is potentially enormous, especially if, as in the case of the Vampire or Ghoul, it is projected to the point of violating taboo: the invulnerability to natural death.

Finally, perhaps, the other characteristic of degeneracy which Lombroso notes is of obvious, but puzzling, relevance to Stoker's novel:

The eyebrows are bushy and tend to meet across the nose. Sometimes they grow in a slanting direction and give the face a satyr-like expression.[81]

This is puzzling, at first, because Stoker makes a point of giving Van Helsing, the wise Magus from Eastern Europe, these symptoms of degeneracy. Can he be a parody of Dracula? But this puzzle is answered when one reads Lombroso's other book, *The Man of Genius* (1891), where Lombroso extends his unflinching search into the realms of truth from the subnormal into the supra-normal:

It is a sad mission to cut through and destroy with the scissors of analysis the delicate and iridescent veils with which our proud mediocrity clothes itself. Very terrible is the religion of truth. The physiologist is not afraid to reduce love to a play of stamens and pistils, and thought to a molecular movement. Even genius, the one human power before which we may bow the knee without shame, has been classed by not a few alienists as on the confines of criminality, one of the teratologic forms of the human mind, a variety of insanity.[82]

Here I think we do have a clue to the way in which testimony is used in this novel. Genius, according to theory, is a form of degeneracy; it, too, is a throwback. Van Helsing is thus a mirror-image of Dracula, a genius in this sense. They are the only people in the novel

who do not make records and keep diaries. They are *perceived*, but
not presented as directly perceiving agents to the reader. Instead,
the whole process of (mistaken, but significant) testimony is what
Lombroso calls 'one of the veils in which . . . mediocrity clothes
itself'.

Here again, for example, is a section from Dr Seward's diary, in
which his untutored observation is the medium through which we
observe events. He honestly records what appeared to him (the
psychiatrist) unconscious or instinctive behaviour on the part of Van
Helsing. We read it as a diary entry; and afterwards we are told that
Mrs Harker the protagonist typed it up from manuscript, so that it is
retrospectively converted into evidence:

> 'Now you shall speak, Tell us two dry men of science what you
> see with those so bright eyes.' He took her hand and held it while
> she spoke. His finger and thumb closed on her pulse, as I thought
> instinctively and unconsciously, as she spoke:–
>
> 'The Count is a criminal and of criminal type. Nordau and
> Lombroso would so classify him, and *qua* criminal he is of
> imperfectly formed mind. Thus, in a difficulty, he has to seek
> resource in habit. His past is a clue, and the one page of it that we
> know – and that from his own lips – tells that once before, when in
> what Mr Morris would call a "tight place", he went back to his
> own country from the land he had tried to invade, and thence,
> without losing purpose, prepared himself for a new effort . . .'
>
> 'Good, good! oh, you so clever lady!' said Van Helsing,
> enthusiastically, as he stooped and kissed her hand. A moment
> later he said to me, as calmly as though we had been having a sick
> room consultation:–
>
> 'Seventy two only; and in all this excitement. I have hope.'[83]

Van Helsing is the perfect combination of doctor and priest. Seward,
the witness, is an 'expert', whose responses are nevertheless wrong:
Van Helsing is a genius, prepared to deceive, even at the moment of
truth. Mina Harker's analysis of Dracula is elicited from her in order
to tempt her into excitement, so that he can measure her pulse: her
'message' is to us therefore thoroughly framed, even likely to go
unnoticed by a reader, in the patronising sick-bed drama which is
taking place. For *our* witness's (Seward's) eye is on Van Helsing, not
on her.

Mina is a reader of Nordau, and this is, no doubt, what helps to

save her from Dracula. Much of *Dracula* is obsessed with the notion
of 'consciousness' and what constitutes 'unconscious' behaviour.
As I have already suggested in Chapter 2 Stoker is contrasting two
women: the white and the red. The white woman is dangerous:
pallor denotes disease, cadaverousness, wantonness. The ability to
blush: health and shame. Nordau reveals in *Degeneration* (1895) a
physiological basis for the theory of degeneration, which reaches as
far as consciousness and conscious reasoning. The evidence comes
from the exposed part of the brain in trepanning and the
experiments of Mosso, which Nordau indicates as the source for his
remarks on this subject. Brain degeneration has to do with the will
which controls the blood-supply to the brain. Nordau regards
consciousness as a struggle for existence between 'representations',
that is, images or thought-processes, some of which are original and
clear, and others secondary or derived and murky:

> I myself conceive the interference of the will in this struggle for life
> amongst representations as giving motor impulses (even if
> unconsciously) to the muscles of the cerebral arteries. By this
> means the blood vessels are dilated or contracted as required, and
> the consequent supply of blood becomes more or less copious.
> The cells which receive no blood must suspend their action, those
> which receive a larger supply can, on the contrary, operate more
> powerfully.[84]

Nordau's theory of 'psychic health' is thus based on the conjunction
of will, physical vigour and reasoning. The consciousness is a
chamber, kept lit by willpower. One lapse, however, and the
shadows and superstition of degeneracy begin to invade:

> Culture and command over the powers of nature are solely the
> result of attention; all errors, all superstition, the consequence of
> defective attention. . . . Observation, which lies at the root of all
> progress, is thus the adaptation through attention of the sense-
> organs and their centres of perception to a presentation or group
> of presentations predominating in consciousness.
>   A state of attention allows no obscurity to persist in
> consciousness. For either the will strengthens every rising
> presentation to full clearness and distinctness, or, if it cannot do
> this, it extinguishes the idea completely. The consciousness of a
> healthy, strong-minded, and consequently attentive man,

resembles a room in the full light of day, in which the eye sees all objects distinctly, in which all outlines are sharp, and wherein no indefinite shadows are floating.[85]

The picture of a degenerate is therefore of a consciousness whose 'chamber' is beginning to grow dim, as the individual undergoes a kind of 'somatic sinking': the will refusing to do its job and carry the precious blood to the vessels of the brain. The external projection of this image of atavastic regression is, for Nordau, thoroughly 'Gothic':

> Like bats in old towers, they are niched in the proud monument of civilisation, which they have found ready-made, but they themselves can construct nothing more, nor prevent any deterioration. They live, like parasites, on labour which past generations have accumulated for them; and when the heritage is once consumed, they are condemned to die of hunger.[86]

What Stoker does in the novel is dramatise, from internal and external points of view, partly through the medium of testimony, the atavistic 'swoon'. Harker at the beginning of the novel, having entered the castle, describes his loss of vigilance as he sits writing his diary: and, as he does so, in his foolish, patronisingly 'romantic' tone, we begin to feel the shadows gathering in the dusty chamber:

> after trying a little to school my nerves, I found a soft quietude come over me. Here I am, sitting at a little oak table where in old times possibly some fair lady sat to pen, with much thought and many blushes, her ill-spelt love-letter, and writing in my diary in shorthand all that has happened since I closed it last. It is nineteenth century up-to-date with a vengeance. And yet, unless my senses deceive me, the old centuries had, and have, powers of their own which mere 'modernity' cannot kill.[87]

Harker is feeling something here; but it is an absurdly shallow version of what is to happen to him. The 'much thought and many blushes' is heavily ironic in the code of the novel, for he is to be faced with three of those ladies, who are bloodless and thirsty: the passage is a marvellous dramatisation of the atavistic swoon, as Harker prepares to monitor his own dissolution:

I was afraid to raise my eyelids, but looked out and saw perfectly under the lashes. The girl went on her knees and bent over me, simply gloating. There was a deliberate voluptuousness which was both thrilling and repulsive, and as she arched her neck she actually licked her lips like an animal, till I could see in the moonlight the moisture shining on the scarlet lips and on the red tongue as it lapped the white sharp teeth. Lower and lower went her head as the lips went below the range of my mouth and chin and seemed about to fasten on my throat. Then she paused, and I could hear the churning sound of her tongue as it licked her teeth and lips, and could feel the hot breath on my neck. Then the skin of my throat began to tingle as one's flesh does when the hand that is to tickle it approaches nearer – nearer. I could feel the soft, shivering touch of the lips on the supersensitive skin of my throat, and the hard dents of two sharp teeth, just touching and pausing there. I closed my eyes in a languorous ecstasy and waited – waited with a beating heart.[88]

The languor, the abnegation of the will, is counterpointed by his awareness of his beating heart – coursing the blood through his veins with excitement. Both blood and consciousness are on the point of being drained out of him; but for this moment, we get what for Stoker is the perfectly erotic state: impossible vigilance and impossible languor which blend in the equilibrium of sado-masochistic fantasy.

5

Strange Cases: Horror Fiction as Legal Process

The history of the law of evidence after Bentham is the history of a debate between his profoundly human advocacy of individual judgement and the ideal of a purely technical system based on the laws of logic and mathematics. Sir Richard Egglestone's recent book, *Evidence, Proof and Probability* (1978), for example, re-opens the notion, not unfamiliarly, of dispensing with the jury and applying Bayes's theorem to legal judgement. He argues that there is a strong tie between the mathematical idea of probability, of *prediction*, and the legal idea of proof. Again, the argument rests on the idea that 'proof' and 'fact' are not really what they are said to be. His account of these terms has some fascinating implications for the use of legal format as a fictional frame:

> the process of decision is closely analogous to that of prediction, but the words used to describe it imply a degree of certainty that is not at all essential. Thus we speak of 'finding the facts' as if they were there to be inspected, once their location had been ascertained, and we speak of 'the facts proved in evidence', 'proving the facts' and the like, as if when facts are sufficiently probable to be made the basis of a decision they have been 'proved' in the sense in which that term is used to describe the establishment of a fact to be proved in solving a problem in geometry.[1]

If one thinks of the format of a 'case' in fiction, this is an acute description of the strong set of expectations which are aroused by the use of that format. But such expectations derive from a context outside fiction. The author here is describing a set of popular assumptions about the nature of the process involved in judging human testimony in an actual legal situation.

The 'Strange Case' is one of the commonest conventional formats in which horror fiction is presented in the novels and, particularly,

187

the anthologised short stories of the nineteenth century. The ambiguity of the context of 'case' is acute; but, whatever the context, the form of presentation instantly calls up a strong and apparently unified set of expectations, of an 'objective' set of 'facts' which are there to be ascertained, regardless of whether the 'case' is a medical, a legal or a theological one. The strongest expectation of the rhetorical form of testimony is that there is something to be testified *to*: a 'case' persuades the reader that fiction conforms to a set of records, which appear to the reader in a particular relationship to a content, to what is recorded.

I have said 'theological' because there is an older sense of 'case' which runs parallel to the legal and medical developments of the term, forming the root from which the term 'casuistry' is derived – the *casus conscientiae*. In popular mythology, casuistry is the primary weapon of the evil, scheming Jesuit; and it is true that it does appear to originate in the niceties of the confessional in the medieval church. But the Reformation adapted it, as part of the psychology of interiorised witnessing, as Keith Thomas points out:

> Casuistry, that is the resolution of moral dilemmas by skilled theologians, had been a feature of medieval handbooks for confessors; and in the seventeenth century Protestant divines turned out many volumes of 'cases of conscience', in which the educated reader might find the resolution of some hypothetical problem close to his own.[2]

This is an interesting overlap with the idea of a 'strange case', because a 'casus' in this sense postulates that the dimensions of the moral life are known already; that the 'moral science' of the operating conscience can be known through patterns of hypothesis like the natural sciences, or according to rules, like the law.[3] Thomas goes on to link this Reformation adaptation of the confessional, which he seems to view as nostalgic, with the Puritan habit of diary-keeping. But, as we have seen above, the literary exploitation of such self-scrutiny, the obsession with the quotidian, is often associated not merely with 'release mechanisms' but also with extreme forms of psychopathology.

The clearest example of this interplay of contexts which I can find in horror fiction is Poe's famous story, 'The Facts in the Case of Monsieur Valdemar' (1845). The opening paragraph of this singularly unpleasant tale places it very firmly in the context of truth-bearing testimony:

> Of course I shall not pretend to consider it any matter for wonder, that the extraordinary case of M. Valdemar has excited discussion. It would have been a miracle had it not – especially under the circumstances. Through the desire of all parties concerned, to keep the affair from the public, at least for the present, or until we had further opportunities for investigation – through our endeavours to effect this – a garbled or exaggerated account made its way into society, and became the source of many unpleasant misrepresentations; and, very naturally, of a great deal of disbelief.
>
> It is now rendered necessary that I give the *facts* – as far as I comprehend them myself. They are, succinctly, these. . . .[4]

The rhetorical effect of this is strong and apparently clear: it turns on the familiar distinction between 'fact' (that is, the direct evidence of an eye-witness) and hearsay or non-swearable testimony. The narrator begins by presenting himself as a witness; and the idea of the 'extraordinary case' has strong legal implications. But as he goes on to tell us of his interest in Mesmerism, and of his curiosity to see what were the effects of mesmerising someone *in articulo mortis*, we begin to sense, perhaps, that 'case' here shades over into a more 'scientific' or 'medical' sense. The narrator is clearly not just a witness; he is also the initiator of an experiment. As such, he is also a man (though anonymous) who is clearing his name from possible or implied imputations of quackery, fraud or even possibly magic. In 1844 in the state of Massachusetts, for example, you could still be arrested for necromancy. The story was published in 1845; and at this point in time, mesmerism might have become legitimised as a form of anaesthetic. The medical profession in England was split over its authenticity, but certainly it was not merely a pseudo-science or quackery for many, as Bentham's remark quoted above might indicate. The issue, however, was resolved in the following year, as a recent writer shows:

> So far as orthodoxy was concerned, there was no need to pay any attention even to Carpenter's contention that surgery could be painlessly performed with the patient mesmerised. It came just

too late; in 1846, ether and laughing gas were coming into use as anaesthetics in the United States; and that winter, Robert Liston performed the first operation in Britain with ether. . . . Very soon, chloroform was in standard use, rendering it unnecessary for surgeons to contemplate hypnosis as an alternative.[5]

And hypnotism and 'electro-biology' afterwards, as Brian Inglis puts it, 'fell into a limbo'. Poe's story draws upon a historical moment in the fortunes of a phenomenon not fully recognised, but certainly open to belief. Whether his readers understood 'fact' and 'case' in a fully medical sense, presumably, varied from individual to individual.

At any rate, the reader is left in no doubt about the controlled conditions under which this experiment took place. Not only do we have a barrage of medical evidence, in suitably technical language, on the advanced state of decay of the 'patient's' lungs, we also have a record of his consent. Further precautions are elaborately provided, which contain all the apparatus of reassurance – an appeal, for example, to the now familiar snobbery of expertise, and an origin for the account which we are now reading – but which, oddly, raise the tempo of the narrative, and even serve perhaps to generate a flicker of suspicion in the reader's mind – after all, the medical men are *not* there:

> A male and female nurse were in attendance; but I did not feel myself altogether at liberty to engage in a task of this character with no more reliable witnesses than these people, in case of sudden accident, might prove. I therefore postponed operations until about eight the next night, when the arrival of a medical student, with whom I had some acquaintance (Mr Theodore L . . . l), relieved me from further embarrassment. It had been my design, originally, to wait for the physicians; but I was induced to proceed, first, by the urgent entreaties of M. Valdemar, and secondly, by my conviction that I had not a moment to lose, as he was evidently sinking fast.
>
> Mr L . . . l was so kind as to accede to my desire that he would take notes of all that occurred; and it is from his memoranda that what I now have to relate is, for the most part, either condensed, or copied *verbatim*.[6]

The reader is now, mentally, firmly seated amongst the jury; that is, intensely preoccupied with the question of credibility. For a moment here we hear the sound of the narrator justifying himself, which prompts the suggestion, in its turn, that we are perhaps going to learn of something about which he *needs* to justify his action.

The mesmeric passes are made, the physicians return, their curiosity 'greatly excited' about M. Valdemar's condition – deeply mesmerised and approaching the moment of dissolution. The description of his demise contains a sudden flash of grotesque vehemence, ending in complete hyperbole, which is far from either medical or legal registers:

> While I spoke, there came a marked change over the countenance of the sleep-walker. The eyes rolled themselves slowly open, the pupils disappearing upwardly; the skin generally assumed a cadaverous hue, resembling not so much parchment as white paper; and the circular hectic spots which, hitherto, had been strongly defined in the centre of each cheek, *went out* at once. I use this expression because the suddenness of their departure put me in mind of nothing so much as the extinguishment of a candle by a puff of the breath. The upper lip, at the same time, writhed itself away from the teeth, which it had previously covered completely; while the lower jaw fell with an audible jerk, leaving the mouth widely extended, and disclosing in full view the swollen and blackened tongue. I presume that no member of the party then present had been unaccustomed to death-bed horrors; but so hideous beyond conception was the appearance of M. Valdemar at this moment, that there was a general shrinking back from the region of the bed.
>
> I now feel that I have reached the point of this narrative at which every reader will be startled into positive disbelief. It is my business, however, simply to proceed.[7]

The vehemence, which expresses itself in the italics of '*went out*', occurs at the perfectly conventional point of death – the point, theologically, of 'consolation' – except that we know that M. Valdemar has been mesmerised. The 'death-bed horrors', even evoked in loving detail as they are, even 'hideous beyond conception', are characterised still as part of our belief, and the hyperbole, as soon as it is uttered, is brought back within the purview of our 'ordinary' responses – only to remain there, however, as a further stepping-stone in an increasing intensity of tone. Our disbelief is openly challenged, as the narrator, willing now to sacrifice his carefully nourished credibility for the sake of the *truth*, comes to the climax of his testimony. M. Valdemar *speaks* posthumously; and the narrator is at a loss to describe this. Still within the frame of evidence-giving, he searches for metaphors which will truthfully convey the 'sound' of his voice. Here the legalistic framework gives a detachment which, throughout a carefully-orchestrated struggle, fails to suppress a mounting excitement:

> There were two particulars, nevertheless, which I thought then, and still think, might fairly be stated as characteristic of the intonation – as well adapted to convey some idea of its unearthly peculiarity. In the first place, the voice seemed to reach our ears – at least mine – from a vast distance, or from some deep cavern within the earth. In the second place, it impressed me (I fear indeed, that it will be impossible to make myself comprehended) as gelatinous or glutinous matters impress the sense of touch.[8]

These metaphors, if read in a poetic fashion, anticipate the story's end in an obvious manner; but they fit perfectly into the frame of witnessing. Even the qualification he gives ('to reach our ears – at least mine') serves the purpose of enforcing the 'rational', until we regard it as a sign of his solipsism, an authorial joke. But the honesty, the modesty, of this narrator, in persevering with his testimony in spite of our disbelief and the sudden incapacity of all the witnesses, is relentlessly preserved:

> I have spoken both of 'sound' and of 'voice'. I mean to say that the sound was one of distinct – of even wonderfully, thrillingly distinct – syllabification. M. Valdemar *spoke* – obviously in reply to the question I had propounded to him a few minutes before. I had asked him, it will be remembered, if he still slept. He now said:
> 'Yes – no, – I *have been* sleeping – and now – now – I am *dead*.'
> No person present ever affected to deny, or attempted to repress, the unutterable shuddering horror which these few words, thus uttered, were so well calculated to convey. Mr L . . . l (the student) swooned. The nurses immediately left the chamber, and could not be induced to return. My own

impressions I would not pretend to render intelligible to the reader'.[9]

If we wish to treat this legalistically, a host of missing explanations for the behaviour of these people, which lie beyond the narrator's account, insert themselves into our minds. Students do swoon, nurses may well feel their job is over for the present. But the 'horror' is now, fairly openly, a theological business: the fear, against which the purely symbolic interpretation of St Paul provides a bulwark, of the soul's entrapment in a heap of decaying matter firmly enters the 'case'. But this still plays off against the idea of a scientific investigation in a spirit of 'objective' curiosity into the ways of matter. The synaesthaesia implied in the account of the 'voice' looks, from one point of view, terribly nineteenth-century and 'symbolist', but it is completely ambiguous in its effect. It represents the extension of sensory perception into matter itself, which was the contemporary view of animal magnetism, that it worked through laws as objective as those of Newton. It also satisfies the ancient criteria for direct evidence of *vidi et audivi*, that is, what the witness has seen and heard (for hearsay, of course, is quite a different matter). Our narrator is what used to be called an 'ear-witness'. And there is another frame of reference which swings silently into place too; it is the most traditional, ancient form of testimony to *spiritual* perception. Compare the following, fairly typical passage from Drelincourt's *Book of Christian Man's Consolations Against Death*:

> Is that man truly converted, who cannot witness with Isaiah, The Lord hath wakened my ear as the learned; and with the Psalmist, Mine *ears* hast thou opened. Had not the believers at Ephesus *heard* Christ, and been taught of him? When St Paul was caught up into the third heaven, did he not *hear* words unspeakable? And far from thinking spiritual hearing absurd, or impossible, did he not question whether he was not then out of the body?[10]

Horror, like the entry of the Godhead in Italian Renaissance painting, enters often through the *ear*. Compare, for example, the incidents given above from Lewis and Mrs Radcliffe. It gives one the terrifying sense that the straining of the sensory organs for the *external* perception is a kind of implosion. Compare the auditory stress in Stevenson's climax in *Jekyll and Hyde*:

He thought of Hyde, for all his energy of life, as of something not only hellish but inorganic. This was the shocking thing; that the slime of the pit seemed to utter cries and voices; that the amorphous dust gesticulated and sinned; that what was dead, and had no shape, should usurp the offices of life. And this again, that that insurgent horror was knit to him closer than a wife, closer than an eye; lay caged in his flesh, where he heard it mutter and felt it struggle to be born.[11]

This rhetoric is perfectly centred in the Pauline tradition of 'consolation'; the sense of its being, in some manner tilted, or askew, comes, I think, from the ambiguity of the frame of testimony.

The final paragraph of 'M. Valdemar' is a *tour de force*, which yet need not prise apart these overlapping contexts for its language. The truth-telling role of the narrator, though still providing impetus and rhetorical direction, certainly clashes on the surface with his immense excitement, his solipsistic insistence on the *absolute* unexpectedness of what he is testifying to. M. Valdemar has remained in this condition of living death for seven months. At last, for reasons not really given to us, but which no doubt have as much to do with our collective impatience as anything more 'probable', the narrator determines to awaken him:

In this attempt I soon saw that I should be successful – or at least I soon fancied that my success would be complete – and I am sure that all in the room were prepared to see the patient awaken.

For what really occurred, however, it is quite impossible that any human being could have been prepared.

As I rapidly made the mesmeric passes, amid ejaculations of 'dead! dead!' absolutely *bursting* from the tongue and not from the lips of the sufferer, his whole frame at once – within the space of a single minute, or less, shrunk – crumbled – absolutely *rotted* away beneath my hands. Upon the bed, before that whole company, there lay a nearly liquid mass of loathsome – of detestable putridity.[12]

If St Paul had been given to joking, this is the kind of thing we would expect from him. The image is indeed disgusting, but curiously relieving too; the relief stemming from the consoling sense, for many readers brought up on popular theology like Drelincourt, that the terrible, suffocating torment of the imprisoned soul is over. Many readers today laugh at our release from a threat to natural death. Historically, that relief was more precise, for natural death involved the Resurrection of the Spirit:

> The natural death is a separation of the soul from the body. . . . As soon as this angelical guest leaves its mansion, the body, it loses all its beauty, and falls of itself into a state of ruin; for this flesh that we are so careful of, and feed with all manner of dainties, then corrupts and rots. After that it hath been stretched awhile upon beds of gold, and richly attired in purple and scarlet, it is cast upon a bed of worms, and covered with the vilest insects of the earth. Notwithstanding all its former perfumes, it yields then a most horrid stink. Before, it ravished the eyes of the beholders with its admirable beauty; but now it becomes so odious and offensive, that the living care not to see it. [13]

Poe's narrator, then, is a 'witness', who offers 'testimony' in several different senses at once. He is close to the primitive testimony of the Christian tradition to the miraculous. He is also a 'legal' witness – even a 'defendant' in a 'case'. He is a mesmerist, a kind of medical expert, who, for some people, was a genuine scientist.

What, then, is M. Valdemar's 'case' a case 'of'? Put like this, if one takes into account the story's overlapping frames of reference, the question is scarcely answerable – the answer will hover, occupying the penumbrae between a number of different contexts, almost like a matrix, all of which act as pressure-points on the expectations of a reader. This makes the question seem inappropriate; yet the power of the story comes from the feeling in its whole shape and rhetorical direction that the question has been answered.

For some contemporary readers, however, both question and answer were simple: it was a case of mesmerism. The story was published as a factual article in the *Morning Post* and the *Popular Record of Modern Science*. It was then published separately as a pamphlet by a different set of editors. Two out of these three publications contained prefaces indicating that the editors thought the case to be true. Ten years later in France, the story was again published in several places as a factual piece:

> Edgar Poe est un partisan determiné du magnetisme; et si vous voulez savoir justqu'où va sur ce point la frénésie de sa credulité

. . . lisez tout entier le conte intitulé: la Verité sur le cas de M. Valdemar.[14]

So the *Journal des débats* assured its readers in 1856. But the 'frenetically credulous' Poe, as his letters show, was delighted. The 'Valdemar Case' was one of several stories deliberately intended as hoaxes in 'the plausible or verisimilar style'. In England, Elizabeth Barrett Browning was one of the people taken in. Poe's correspondence is very amusing on this point; but what is also interesting is his belief that he could expose the credulity of his readers to themselves, by exposing them to each other: I think that Poe really believed, for example, that he could stop the California gold rush by fictional means. At any rate, at the height of the controversy over animal magnetism, his story appears as fact, either as credited fact or, precisely as in the example of Dr Johnson and Mrs Veal, *dis*credited fact, which is still quite different from 'fiction'. As Léon Lemonnier observes, there is a more refined level of acceptance even than the *Journal des débats*:

> Il y a mieux encore. Ouvrez le 'Dictionnaire de Superstitions' edité en 1856, à l'article 'Magnétisme animal'. Vous y lirez en entier *La Verité sur ce qui s'est passé chez M. Valdemar*.[15]

The motives for producing a dictionary of superstitions are often themselves mixed; and, even if they are purely positivistic, they are liable to misinterpretation by an audience whose expectations are different. The retitling of Poe's piece here loses the reflexive exploitation of cultural ambiguity in the word 'case' and gets rid of the frame altogether: but if readers are reading about superstition with a mixture of scientific incredulity and theological dread in the first place, the removal of the frame 'case' exacerbates, rather than removes, the ambiguity of testimony because it makes it easier to believe: the frame 'case' simply gets absorbed into the frame 'Dictionary'.

What looks rhetorically 'weak' in all this has its own power. The audience for a written 'case' is, in some important respects, in a similar position to that of an audience in court. Sir Richard Egglestone comments on the nature of the investigative process in the courtroom, in a way which throws some light on its overall logic:

> The facts on which a legal decision must be based are usually past

and closed, and discoverable only by an examination of the recollection of untrained observers, often emotionally affected by the events they are being asked to describe.[16]

The logic of response to a written 'case' – with all the attendant ambiguities of the label – is similar in certain ways. We stand in an apparently retrospective relation to materials, contents, evidences, facts. This apparent relation is real, to the extent that it creates a powerful expectation, carried over from the legal context itself, of sifting and penetrating the materials of the case by rational judgement. It is too easy, I feel, to dissolve this expectation into mere rhetoric, by pointing to the fact that it is not fulfilled; this is not *really* what is going on, and that what we are *really* getting is a disguised form of narrative. Nor will it do, in this instance, to rely on the idea of narrative. W. B. Gallie, for example, in his influential *Philosophy and the Historical Understanding* claims that 'following a narrative' is a universal phenomenon, which ultimately makes history indistinguishable from fiction. But this argument will not quite apply in the instance of 'case' format; because the nature of the expectations mobilised by the format itself are not reducible to the idea of either passively or actively 'following a story'. The testimonies themselves are set within a prior framework, they have an often unspoken 'further point'. If following a narrative is, as Gallie's famous phrase has it, a 'teleologically guided form of attention', then sifting testimony is a different, or even a reverse teleology: for the reader opens a closed world of storytelling to prior or further processes of judgement.[17]

Poe's story is striking, because a lot of its ambiguity clusters around the reception, and the origin, of a single testimony. The formula of the 'case' format, however, can be more recessive, as another more simple, but extremely effective example will show. Ambrose Bierce's short story 'The Damned Thing' remains a favourite of the horror omnibuses of the twentieth century. This piece begins in a completely defamiliarising way, with a man reading a book:

By the light of a tallow candle which had been placed on one end of a rough table a man was reading something written in a book. It was an old account book, greatly worn; and the writing was not, apparently, very legible, for the man sometimes held the page, close to the flame of the candle to get a stronger light on it. The

shadow of the book would then throw into obscurity a half of the
room, darkening a number of faces and figures; for besides the
reader, eight other men were present. Seven of them sat against
the rough log walls, silent, motionless, and the room being small,
not very far from the table. By extending an arm anyone of them
could have touched the eighth man, who lay on the table, face
upward, partly covered by a sheet, his arms at his sides. He was
dead.[18]

We are at an inquest in the Californian outback; and the
defamiliarised opening reduces us to the barest bones of civilisation.
The 'account book' turns out to be the diary of the deceased man,
Hugh Morgan, and it is to be revealed as a crucial piece of evidence
in the 'case'. The journey from the metropolis to the provinces has,
as it were, already been made; but the itinerant coroner who reads,
though not merely a farmer or a woodsman like the jury, does not
simply represent the values of urban civilisation. The key witness,
Harker, who is a young newspaper man, to some extent does; and it
is his testimony we are all waiting for:

The young man smiled. 'I am sorry to have kept you,' he said. 'I
went away, not to evade your summons, but to post to my
newspaper an account of what I suppose I am called back to
relate.'
   The coroner smiled.
   'The account that you posted to your newspaper', he said,
'differs, probably, from that which you will give here under oath.'
   'That', replied the other, rather hotly and with a visible flush, 'is
as you please. I used manifold paper and have a copy of what I
sent. It was not written as news, for it is incredible, but as fiction.
It may go as part of my testimony under oath.'
   'But you say it is incredible.'
   'That is nothing to you, sir, if I also swear that it is true.'[19]

The joke is a complicated one; it rests, obviously, upon literary
tradition and the aesthetic sense of probability. But it also requires
an awareness, at some level, of Bentham's point about the relative
differences in the currency of fact and fiction in different parts of the
country: Wapping *vs* St James's Square. What can only be presented
as imaginative fantasy to the readers of San Francisco is true in the
backwoods. More than that, however, testimony has its own claim

on our attention, its own 'charge' of truth; and when matters which, in any other context, would be thought of as fictional are offered as sworn testimony, a new form of guarantee comes into play.

By this relatively simple beginning the reader is displaced, manoeuvred into an oblique position. Already, our responses are multiple; our disbelief is challenged, but, simultaneously, our judgement is invited. We are somewhere up in the public gallery perhaps, looking over the shoulders of the jury. Harker takes out his manuscript and reads to the court the account of Hugh Morgan's death. We encounter narrative evidence. He tells how the two of them, out hunting, hear a noise in some bushes. They have shotguns; the wrong guns for deer, thinks Harker; but the intensity of Morgan's expression seems to suggest that they have jumped a grizzly. But these 'natural' explanations cease all of a sudden:

' "What is it? What the devil is it?" I asked.
' "That Damned Thing!" he replied, without turning his head. His voice was husky and unnatural. He trembled visibly.

'I was about to speak further, when I observed the wild oats near the place of the disturbance moving in the most inexplicable way. I can hardly describe it. It seemed as if stirred by a streak of wind, which not only bent it, but pressed it down – crushed it so that it did not rise; and this movement was slowly prolonging itself directly toward us.'[20]

Natural explanation has acquired a theological element. As the rhetoric of the story intensifies, the sense of working our way through a labyrinth of partial explanation intrudes itself: this is one man's testimony, and therefore it is only a fragment of the whole case. We are confined, by the very form of the inquest, to *vidi et audivi*; but, beyond that, further testimony is to be brought, for, as the legal maxim has it, *unus testis, nullus testis*, 'one voice, no voice'.[21] This maxim is founded in the guarantees, not merely of judgement, but simultaneously of faith. As the evidence unfolds, the lyricism, and the threat, increases:

'Nothing that I had ever seen had affected me so strangely as this unfamiliar and unaccountable phenomenon, yet I am unable to recall any sense of fear. I remember – and tell it here because, singularly enough, I recollected it then – that once in looking carelessly out of an open window I momentarily mistook a small tree close at hand for one of a group of larger trees at a little distance away. It looked the same size as the others, but being more distinctly and sharply defined in mass and detail seemed out of harmony with them. It was a mere falsification of the law of aerial perspective, but it startled, almost terrified me. We so rely upon the orderly operation of familiar natural laws that any seeming suspension of them is noted as a menace to our safety, a warning of unthinkable calamity. So now the apparently causeless movement of the herbage and the slow, undeviating approaching of the line of disturbance were distinctly disquieting. My companion appeared actually frightened, and I could hardly credit my sense when I saw him throw his gun to his shoulder and fire both barrels at the agitated grain!'[22]

The theological idea is familiar; it is the notion that evil is not directly perceptible, but appears as a trace in the physical world. Many of M. R. James's stories, for example, were founded on the same premise. The illusion is created of an almost sensory perception of the spiritual world; done here, however, by an extension of natural law. The reader looks through the filtering lens of one man's testimony to the reactions of another. We are left, despite the fact of some 'soft heavy substance' being thrown against Harker, with only a handful of external signs. Morgan's actions are reported as a grotesque kind of shadow-play, as 'evidence', the negative shape, of the Thing's attack upon him. He, the victim, shows us that it is there:

Inexpressibly terrified, I struggled to my feet and looked in the direction of Morgan's retreat; and may Heaven in mercy spare me from another sight like that! At a distance of less than thirty yards was my friend, down on one knee, his head thrown back at a frightful angle, hatless, his long hair in disorder and his whole body in violent movement from side to side, backward and forward. His right arm was lifted and seemed to lack the hand – at least I could see none. The other arm was invisible. At times, as my memory now reports this extraordinary scene, I could discern but a part of his body; it was as if he had been partly blotted out – I cannot otherwise express it – then a shifting of position would bring it all into view again.[23]

Conventional exclamations in this testimony ('may Heaven in

mercy spare me') have become intensified, as the theological counterpoint increases. As its name suggests, the Thing is the ultimate *material* manifestation; but it is only indirectly perceivable. Testimony, however, is *direct*; it is a striking image, which has for its source the same beliefs which, in part, underwrite the value of individual testimony against general counter-testimony.

But we have only a fragment, and a fragment postulates two things: corroboration or denial. Now that Harker has come to the end of his testimony, we are given the jury's reaction:

> 'Gentlemen,' the coroner said, 'we have no more evidence, I think. Your duty has been already explained to you; if there is nothing you wish to ask you may go outside and consider your verdict.'
>
> The foreman rose – a tall, bearded man of sixty, coarsely clad. 'I should like to ask one question, Mr Coroner,' he said. 'What asylum did yer last witness escape from?'[24]

The self-conscious 'marker' for the reader's ('yer') scepticism and good sense appears on time here, just as it often does in the horror film, of which this story is the nineteenth-century counterpart; but, for the reader, the idea of disbelief is being raised from an angle which the testimony of Morgan has already implicitly challenged. The *boni homines* bring in their verdict – that 'the remains met their death at the hands of a mountain lion, but some of us thinks, all the same, they had fits'. The foreman's caricature-demotic signals two things here: that this verdict is perfectly probable from the point of view of an ignorant backwoodsman; and perfectly wrong.

The final section of the story, 'An Explanation From the Tomb', reveals the contents of the diary which the Coroner was reading as the story opened. Apparently, he has suppressed this evidence from the jurors (and, so far, the reader) possibly because 'he thought it not worth while to confuse the jury'. It is corroborative; it has 'scientific value'; it is also the heart of the story's journey to individual experience. Here is the evidence of interior witnessing (the account book I have analysed above) placed in the position, simultaneously, of *external* evidence. It is a kind of confession, the 'true fact', of Morgan's experience. And here Bierce, the son of Calvinist parents, places maximum rhetorical weight on the idea of evil, not only surviving, but also competing, in a world of progressive science:

'As with sounds, so with colours. At each end of the solar spectrum, the chemist can detect the presence of what is known as "actinic rays". They represent colour – integral colours in the composition of light – which we are unable to discern. The human eye is an imperfect instrument; its range is but a few octaves of the real "chromatic scale". I am not mad; here are colours that we cannot see.

'And, God help me! the Damned Thing is of such a colour!'[25]

The interior of the labyrinth, the appeal to one man's witnessing of his own experience, overlaps perfectly with the external corroboration, evidence in a legal sense, judged inadmissible by the coroner but given to the reader.

Here again there is some evidence that the story does not merely create the overlap between its major frames of reference. The tradition of popular science, for example, has a close relation to theology in the eighteenth century. The *Encyclopaedia Britannica*, for instance, was founded explicitly to combat the effects of the French encyclopaedists, as its dedication to George III makes perfectly clear:

The French Encyclopédie has been accused, and justly accused, of having disseminated far and wide the seeds of anarchy and atheism. If the Encyclopaedia Britannica shall in any degree counteract the tendency of that pestiferous work, even these two volumes will not be wholly unworthy of your Majesty's attention.[26]

So Dr Gleig, writing in 1801, in his capacity as editor of the two-volume supplement. There is a strong tradition of Scottish piety in the writers who contributed articles all through the nineteenth century too. Tytler, Gleig, Robison and the Hutchinsonian William Jones who has an interesting place in Church History:

He was of the High Church School, which formed the link between the non-jurors, and the later Oxford School. Here we trace a line northward of the Tweed, for the Scottish Episcopalians, particularly the more northerly were both non-jurors, and Hutchinsonian. As Jacobites they suffered under penal statutes which were removed in 1792, largely as a result of efforts by Horne, Jones and their friends.[27]

Many of the early articles contained the same kind of mish-mash of languages and contexts which Bierce's story depends on for its articulation of threat: the three-in-oneness, for example, of fire, light and air; or Robison's extraordinary article on 'Stones' which has a bizarre fusion of ideas, quite worthy of Glanvill. The line north of the Tweed referred to above has some relation to such 'Gothic' as Hogg's *Confessions of a Justified Sinner* and Stevenson's *Jekyll and Hyde*, as I have implied above. Leslie, who founded the study of radiant heat, incurred *odium theologicum* for some of his speculations; and, when he was appointed successor to Playfair, his inclination towards Hume was an objection against him.

Thus one can see that Ambrose Bierce, in revealing a theological content in Herschel's discovery of 'actinic' or ultra-violet rays, or rather in appealing to the recent scientific discovery as a kind of 'authority', is part of a tradition. Later, for example, Conan Doyle experimented with photography, whose images were produced, it was discovered almost contemporaneously with Bierce's story, by 'actinic' rays. Thus the technology for reproducing the image of the spiritual gives it a new literalness because image and original share the same physical process: photographs of ectoplasm, for example, are powerful; not because of an anthropological form of sympathetic magic (though that is what this is) but because they claim implicitly, by their very process, that the spiritual exists within the realm of natural law.

Another and slightly different example of the uses of case format is Sheridan Le Fanu's brilliant horror story, *Green Tea*. Here the displacement of the origins of the narrative is presented in an elaborate 'editorial' flourish at the opening by an anonymous doctor who has been prevented from practising his true profession by the amputation of two of his fingers. Instead, he has become a recorder, an editor and a literary, if not a legal, executor to the man he admired: wanderer, fellow-physician, and German genius, Dr Martin Hesselius, 'whose grasp of a case was an intuition'. The creation of a spectrum of responses in the following could be put down to mere literary fussing; or the slightly bored, leisurely air of the clubman, but its elaboration is not merely that:

For nearly twenty years I acted as his medical secretary. His immense collection of papers he has left in my care, to be arranged, indexed and bound. His treatment of some of these cases is curious. He writes in two distinct characters. He describes what he saw and heard as an intelligent layman might, and when in this style of narrative he had seen the patient either through his own hall-door, to the light of day, or through the gates of darkness to the caverns of the dead, he returns upon the narrative, and in the terms of his art, and with all the force and originality of genius, proceeds to the work of analysis, diagnosis and illustration.

Here and there a case strikes me of a kind to amuse or horrify a lay reader with an interest quite different from the peculiar one which it may possess for an expert. With slight modifications, chiefly of language, and of course a change of names, I copy the following. The narrator is Dr Martin Hesselius. I find it among the voluminous notes of cases which he made during a tour in England about sixty-four years ago.[28]

Some of this is like a clumsy-looking version of modern documentary introductions and disclaimers. But the rhetoric of 'through the gates of darkness to the caverns of the dead' and the avowed intention to 'amuse or horrify' (dependent on what kind of reader we regard ourselves) give the 'Gothic' undertone immediately. The term 'case', in all its attendant cultural ambiguity, is hammered home; and one can see the active spreading of contexts which it creates. The notion that papers must be *proffered*, fetishistically, to the reader has its origins in the 'best evidence' rule of the eighteenth century, developed by Baron Gilbert. Documents themselves, however, as I have implied above, have a suspiciously 'continental' association, especially when they are the records of a German. The back-dating also, which may look casual and evasive at first sight, is also important here because it recalls the apparently dead theological pressures of Swedenborgianism at the end of the eighteenth century, with which the story is to be concerned: I say *apparently*, because this is a common pattern of sleight-of-hand in Le Fanu – to reactivate a threat of a theological nature, as Dissent still was in the latter half of the nineteenth century, by back-reference.

This 'case' is another intersection. Throughout, the idea of 'explanation' is confused with 'narrative'; but, although we have the common sense version of it, for Hesselius reserves 'all that borders on the technical for a strictly scientific paper', it is no easier than with Poe to answer our common sense question: what is the case of the Reverend Jennings a case *of*? The clergyman hallucinates a monkey, which pursues him everywhere, causing him eventually to cut his throat. It seems clear that the story is a pre-Freudian allegory of unconscious guilt, and that Hesselius's explanations via his theory of 'metaphysical Medicine' are at least in part a form of psychoanalysis. This is one level of 'explanation'. But Hesselius is not called 'Martin' for nothing: even if only innocently named after the father of the Reformation (and Le Fanu is by no means an innocent author) he is still a representative of a certain theological tradition. The following, for example, purports to be a description of a new 'interface' between medicine and theology, but its theological meaning seems perfectly traditional:

> I may remark, that when I speak here of medical science, I do so, as I hope some day to see it more generally understood, in a much more comprehensive sense than its generally material treatment would warrant. I believe the entire natural world is but the ultimate expression of that spiritual world from which, and in which alone, it has its life. I believe that the essential man is a spirit, that the spirit is an organised substance, but as different in point of material from what we ordinarily understand by matter, as light or electricity is; that the material body is, in the most literal sense, a vesture, and death consequently no interruption of the living man's existence, but simply his extrication from the natural body – a process which commences at the moment of what we term death, and the completion of which, at furthest a few days later, is the resurrection 'in power'.
>
> The person who weighs the consequences of these positions will probably see their practical bearing upon medical science. This is, however, by no means the proper place for displaying the proofs and discussing the consequences of this too generally unrecognised state of facts.[29]

There is in fact nothing in this account which strays far from orthodox Pauline theology; yet, ironically, it is presented as a 'new' or a secret form of 'explanation', whose technical aspects would be too dull to give to the lay reader. The case format here depends on a deliberate acknowledgement of an overlap between contexts, which the reader must, at some level, grasp explicitly; but Le Fanu has it both ways very nicely, within this fiction of separating narrative from explanation, because this allows him to intertwine the two very closely, creating the aura of a seamless web between religion and objective science.

Hesselius is the forerunner of Van Helsing in *Dracula*; a white magician, a magus, posing as a higher form of scientist. The fascination, displayed in the very structure of the story, with turning inside out empirical methods of presenting fact, is similar; and so, also, is Hesselius's claim to have discovered that spirit is 'organised substance' – perhaps the one point in the above declaration where St Paul, had he been listening, would have baulked. The dream of a higher synthesis of matter and spirit leads, it seems, in each work, to an orthodox expression of the resurrection of the spirit.[30] The reservation, for example, expressed in the above passage, is a well-known theological compromise: thus, the most 'progressive' and 'modern' position turns out, after all, to 'vindicate' the most ancient and traditional.

> I went upstairs with him to the room – what I saw there I won't tell you. He had cut his throat with his razor. It was a frightful gash. The two men had laid him on the bed, and composed his limbs. It had happened, as the immense pool of blood on the floor declared, at some distance between the bed and the window. There was carpet round his bed, and a carpet under his dressing-table, but none on the rest of the floor, for the man said he did not like a carpet on his bedroom. In this sombre and now terrible room, one of the great elms that darkened the house was slowly moving the shadow of one of its great boughs upon this dreadful floor.[31]

Here the legal sense of 'case' swings into place, and the evidence which might have been simply medical and theological acquires a different dimension; but, interestingly, the 'inner' structure of testimony appears to have been censored. Le Fanu teases the reader all through this story with the fiction of censorship, so that we are, as it were, off-balance, looking all the time for something that isn't there. The above passage is not *really* censored at all – though 'what Hesselius saw' appears under the sign of a negative – because the rhetorical climax of the passage is precisely the suggestion, conveyed in the shadowy animation of the boughs on the floor, of an evil much greater than the mere 'horror' of the police-report details of a suicide. And this suggestion gains weight from the ambiguity of its status as testimony; so that, one is finally receiving a form of theological witnessing.

As I have suggested, this is the rhetorical climax of the story. But the analytic fiction of multiple explanation is pursued to the literal end. Again, the pretext of the story, 'green tea', which assumes the status of what Aristotle would have called the 'efficient cause' of depression, is introduced as part of a 'new' psychological theory, which appears anachronistically pre-Harveian, or Galenic even:

> You know my tract on 'The Cardinal Functions of the Brain'. I there, by the evidence of innumerable facts, prove, as I think, the high probability of a circulation arterial and venous in its mechanism, through the nerves. Of this system, thus considered, the brain is the heart. The fluid, which is propagated hence through one class of nerves, returns in an altered state through another, and the nature of that fluid is spiritual, though not immaterial, any more than, as I before remarked, light or electricity are so.[32]

This looks like nothing more than the 'animal spirits', which provided the sixteenth- and seventeenth-century theologians with the perfect account of the contact between spirit and body for the defence of their systems, here presented as a 'new' synthesis. But even this explanation is fragmented and compartmentalised, so that the 'case' of Jennings is, we learn finally, *two* cases: the suicide of Jennings is diagnosed by Hesselius as a much more conventional disorder ('hereditary suicidal mania'), which 'projected itself upon that disease which was established'. The terminology here ('projected') is anticipatory of Freud, though the diagnosis itself is conventional enough.

Finally, then, the frame of the 'case' is used in this story to preserve a fragmentation in the reader's responses. It is more elaborate, more playful than Bierce's piece, because it preserves the fiction of multiple explanation. Narrative is indistinguishable from a strongly aroused set of expectations of sifting, sorting, proving, explaining and witnessing.

A familiar yet also a subtle use of case format is *The Strange Case of Dr Jekyll and Mr Hyde*. Here again, we have the characteristic structure of testimony: the characters in the story are all, essentially, witnesses, each of whom has a partial or fragmentary sense of the true nature of the events they have witnessed. We begin in a remote, apparently contingent manner; and we carry on through a series of false trails of 'explanation'. The forward drive is not narrative *per se* but the urge, harnessed rhetorically by the evidential form, to recover the facts. Thus we are allowed to glimpse events through the testimony of the characters concerned, but *only* through them. The dramatic irony, beautifully handled by the author, occurs when we become aware at certain points that, though sincere, the testimony of the characters does not contain its own explanation; that what they see and hear has another dimension to it. Like M. Valdemar's, the 'case' is partly medical and scientific, partly legal and theological. For it is a *casus conscientiae*, whose theme of guilt and the contours of repression in the individual, internalised conscience, is also finally indistinguishable from its external manifestation in law. The interface between these two aspects is presented in the first paragraph, during the course of the apparently irrevelant description of Mr Utterson:

> He was austere with himself; drank gin when he was alone, to mortify a taste for vintages; and though he enjoyed the theatre had not crossed the doors of one for twenty years. But he had an approved tolerance for others; sometimes wondering, almost with envy, at the high pressure of spirits involved in their misdeeds; and in any extremity inclined to help rather than reprove. 'I incline to Cain's heresy', he used to say quaintly, 'I let my brother go to the devil in his own way.' In this character, it was frequently his fortune to be the last reputable acquaintance and the last good influence in the lives of down going men. And to such as these, so long as they came about his chambers, he never marked a shade of change in his demeanour.[33]

The counterpoint here is between the man's profession and his moral and psychological make-up: he is a lawyer, and he is masochistic, or at least guilty about his own hedonism; this is the internal registration of guilt in the conscience. But his remark about Cain (and by implication, Abel) is a theological jest, which situates itself at the point where conscience meets law – the 'primal elder's curse'. The figures of Cain and Abel are the originals of Jekyll and Hyde in the story; and Utterson's envy of the high spirits involved in his clients' misdeeds suggests that his detachment is won at a certain cost, which he is remotely aware of. In this way, he displays the pattern of Jekyll and Hyde in little.

Our first glimpse of Hyde is via the testimony of Utterson's friend, Enfield. It is a perfect example of the fragmentation of perspective which Stevenson achieves throughout the tale, and which, incidentally, makes such a vivid scene as the following difficult to render in visual terms; for, although the scene is strikingly visual, this quality is quite indistinguishable from the 'filter' of testimony:

> Well, sir, the two ran into one other naturally enough at the corner; and then came the horrible part of the thing; for the man trampled calmly over the child's body and left her screaming on the ground. It sounds nothing to hear, but it was hellish to see. It wasn't like a man; it was like some damned Juggernaut. I gave a view halloa, took to my heels, collared my gentleman, and brought him back to where there was already quite a group about the screaming child. He was perfectly cool and made no resistance, but gave me one look, so ugly that it brought the sweat out on me like running. The people who had turned out were the girl's family; and pretty soon, the doctor, for whom she had been sent, put in his appearance. Well the child was not much the worse, more frightened, according to the Sawbones; and there you might have supposed would be an end to it. But there was one curious circumstance. I had taken a loathing to my gentleman at first sight. So had the child's family, which was only natural. But the doctor's case was what struck me. He was the usual cut and dry apothecary, of no particular age and colour, with a strong Edinburgh accent, and about as emotional as a bagpipe. Well, sir, he was like the rest of us; every time he looked at my prisoner, I saw that Sawbones turn sick and white with the desire to kill him. I knew what was in his mind, just as he knew what was in mine; and killing being out of the question, we did the next best. We told the man we could and would make such a scandal out of this, as should make his name stink from one end of London to the other. If he had any friends or any credit, we undertook that he should lose them. And all the time, as we were pitching it in, red-hot, we were keeping the women off him as best we could, for they were as wild as harpies. I never saw a circle of such hateful faces; and there was the man in the middle, with a kind of black, sneering coolness – frightened, too, I could see that – but carrying it off, sir, really like Satan.[34]

The writing here is particularly good, because one is struck by the teller's honesty, and by his capacity for sensitive observation: we are tempted to look *through* it at the scene. The form of testimony carries the presumption that something is to be testified *to*; a presumption, which can only in part be attributed to the rhetorical or persuasive level of the writing. Yet what is being testified to is the existence of the Devil: the legalistic form supports a metaphysical theme. One can see the intersection between law and theology showing itself, momentarily, in the irony that not even a crime has been committed. But this simple support system between form and theme is undercut by other pressures on our response. Although Enfield is not a false witness, his testimony is not adequate either; the satire in the passage, characteristic of this piece as a whole, derives from our ability to *discount* 'horror' and the metaphysical language which he uses; for the 'good' in this story are the repressed and guilty, and the 'evil' are equivalent to the id of Freud. The passage reveals less than the speaker intends about the object of his automatic reaction, Hyde; and more about the conditioned responses of himself and the other people in the group. One can see this, for example, in the ambiguity of the phrase 'hateful faces', where one is not finally sure of its objective or subjective application: Enfield hates them and himself for hating Hyde. His own guilt feelings and sense of implication in a social guilt are hopelessly mixed up with his righteousness, his sense of virtue and public responsibility. Blackmail is the instant resort of the holy in this society; Enfield not only practises it himself with alacrity, but also leaps to it as the obvious ('rational') explanation of Hyde's relationship with Jekyll.

So we are drawn on, through a maze of partially discredited testimony, to the 'confession' of Jekyll which crowns and climaxes the 'case'. As with Bierce, 'Henry Jekyll's Full Statement of the Case' is both a confession, *and* a true explanation. It is therefore a vital piece of evidence. This sense is inseparable from the familiar literary feeling of rhetorical climax. The legal presupposition is that 'confession is the best evidence', in the sense of the strongest testimony that one can have. Thus the final section of the tale carries a greater 'weight' in one part of our expectations than the other sections of more indirect testimony.

This is a pull on our expectation that I think any reader will feel. In fact, however, it also raises the question of guarantees and securities in the oral system, which I spoke of before. Interestingly, Stevenson takes care, while leading us through the misapprehensions of other witnesses in the case, to reveal the inextricability of sin and crime in their minds. The internal and external are clearly linked, for example, in the following meditation of Utterson on the analogical relationship between law and its metaphysical guarantees:

'Poor Henry Jekyll,' he thought, 'my mind misgives me he is in deep waters! He was wild when he was young; a long while ago to be sure; but in the law of God, there is no statute of limitations. Ay, it must be that; the ghost of some old sin, the cancer of some concealed disgrace: punishment coming, *pede claudo*, years after memory has forgotten and self-love condoned the fault.' And the lawyer, scared by the thought, brooded awhile on his own past, groping in all the corners of memory, lest by chance some Jack-in-the-Box of an old iniquity should leap to light there.[35]

Much of the 'case' is actually presented as a third-person narrative, in fact, interspersed with bouts of documentation: letters, wills, and so on. Formally, it is looser than, say, Ambrose Bierce's piece: but the dimensions of satire and allegory make it a more complex affair altogether. Both stories however have the confessional climax in common. This is an externally projected piece of evidence, a deposition, in effect, which, in the oral system, is technically hearsay because non-swearable testimony. The law of evidence regards it as admissible as evidence in a court only after certain securities have been applied and certain conditions met. As I have suggested above, the belief that 'no man will go to his Maker with a lie on his lips' is one of those conditioning securities in the matter of admitting dying declarations. There are two overlapping frames of reference in the cultural context on which this piece of writing is parasitic: it is a statement of 'what is', so that we know that we are going to have our itch for 'explanation' satisfied by external 'fact'; and it is the echo of the day of judgement which guarantees that 'fact'. Thus, the most *internal* point, the revelation of the man's internalised conscience, his final act of self-witnessing in the purely religio-moral sense, forms part of the guarantee for external fact: the centre of the labyrinth is its circumference.

Historically, the pressures exerted by other contexts on the image of the law shift back and forth throughout the nineteenth century. Bentham had thrown down the gauntlet, in many ways, on the question of the law of Evidence. The nature and extent of his influence is a matter for legal historians; and opinion appears sharply divided.[36] One pattern, however, is clearly discernible; that there are certain points in the history of the law of evidence, when attempts were made to 'rationalise' the process of legal reasoning – that is to say, to bring it closer to a strict form of logic, to assimilate it to a calculus. Bentham did much to formulate clear-minded principles, it seems, on a wide variety of aspects of this subject; but the age of Bentham is often thought of as the mid- to latter half of the century, after some of these reforms had passed piecemeal into judicial practice, owing to the support of a younger generation of distinguished Benthamite sympathisers. The unexpected thing about Bentham's treatise is the *basis* of its attack on anomalies and irregularities and superstitions in the contemporary law of evidence; as Halévy points out, he does it from a broad sense of rationality, not a narrow technical base. Bentham almost convinced the French, single-handedly, to adopt the jury system, the 'palladium of civil liberty' as the French magistrates of the revolutionary period called it. His attacks on the inherited system of exclusionary rules in the English system are made as a staunch defender of the adversary system, even though he attacks the oath and the theological 'securities' on which the rules of admissibility are founded. In this respect, his whole cast of mind seems quite different, for example, from that of Austin, whose thinking on this matter appears more conventionally Christian.

Much of Bentham, literally, comes down through Mill. But Mill's influence on the law of evidence is, in some respects, very different. Sir James Stephen, for example, the framer of the Indian Evidence Act, made an attempt in his *Digest of the Law of Evidence* (1874) to draw legal and logical reasoning together, by resting on Mill's inductive logic. His version of the law of evidence assumes the doctrine of 'relevancy' as its fundamental defining characteristic:

> The expression 'hearsay is not evidence' seemed to assume by the light of nature what evidence was, but I perceived at last that that was just what I did not know. I found that I was in the position of a person who, having never seen a cat, is instructed about them in this fashion: 'Lions are not cats, nor are tigers, nor leopards, though you might be inclined to think they were.' Show me a cat to begin with, and I at once understand both what is meant by saying that a lion is not a cat, and why it is possible to call him one. Tell me what evidence is, and I shall be able to understand why you say that this and that class of facts are not evidence. The question, What is evidence? gradually disclosed the ambiguity of the word. To describe a matter of fact as 'evidence' in the sense of

testimony is obviously nonsense. No one wants to be told that
hearsay, whatever else it is, is not testimony. What, then, does
the phrase mean? The only possible answer is: It means that the
one fact either is or else is not considered by the person using the
expression to furnish a premiss or part of a premiss from which
the existence of the other is a necessary or probable inference – in
other words, that the one fact is or is not relevant to the other.
When the inquiry is pushed further, and the nature of relevancy
has to be considered in itself, and apart from legal rules about it,
we are led to inductive logic, which shows that the judicial
evidence is only one case of the general problem of science –
namely, inferring the unknown from the known.[37]

But one of the perennial problems here with the English legal
system is that 'relevance' cannot be considered 'apart from the legal
rules about it'; so that legal reasoning cannot simply be subsumed
under the general rubric of inductive logic, because the materials
given to the judging mind are pre-selected, pre-shaped, by the
nature of the accusatory system itself. Thayer, for example, in his
classic *Preliminary Treatise On Evidence at the Common Law* (1898), still
an important work in the study of this subject, attacks Stephen
fiercely on this very point: he maintains that legal and logical
reasoning processes are asymmetrical, at the point where the law of
evidence comes into play:

> In stating thus our two large, fundamental conceptions, we must
> not fall into the error of supposing that relevancy, logical
> connection, real or supposed, is the only test of admissibility; for
> so we should drop out of sight the chief part of the law of
> evidence. When we have said (1) that, without exception,
> nothing which is not, or is not supposed to be, logically relevant is
> admissible; and (2) that, subject to many exceptions and
> qualifications, whatever is logically relevant is admissible; it is
> obvious that, in reality, there are tests of admissibility other than
> logical relevancy. Some things are rejected as being of too slight a
> significance, or as having too conjectural and remote a
> connection; others, as being dangerous, in their effect on the jury,
> – and likely to be misused or overestimated by that body; others,
> as being impolitic, or unsafe on public grounds; others, on the
> bare ground of precedent. It is this sort of thing . . . – the rejection
> on one or another practical ground, of what is really probative –

which is the characteristic thing in the law of evidence; stamping it as the child of the jury system.[38]

Thayer's view of the history of the law of evidence is cautiously accepted by Sir Frederick Holdsworth in his *History of English Law*. His argument is largely concerned with the organic growth of the modern law of evidence from the changes which occurred in the system of witnessing in the common law in the later medieval period. He even denies Bentham's confident distinction between 'adjective' and 'substantive' law, which gives a separate status to the law of evidence as prior or apart from the substantive content of the law. Thayer's stress is on the practical necessities of such rules; he regards as fallacious such ambitious attempts to systematise the law of evidence in terms of more general contexts. Thayer's appeal is necessarily to the *boni homines*; and he goes on to make the point that legal reasoning is tied to a non-mathematical concept of probability:

This does not, like mathematical reasoning, have to do merely with ideal truth, with mere mental conceptions; it is not aiming at demonstration and ideally exact results; it deals with probabilities and not with certainties; it works in an atmosphere, and not in a vacuum; it has to allow for friction, for accident and mischance.[39]

This argument is an important one throughout the nineteenth century, when the pressure of natural science as a lens through which to view all institutions is growing. Stephen recanted his view in old age, but his modern editors, in a fascinating appendix to the *Digest*, put forward a considered defence of it. The see-saw goes on in the twentieth century, because the tie between legal proof and probability needs reasserting; as one can see, for example, from the arguments over the viability of the phrase 'beyond reasonable doubt'. Here is Lord Maugham, framer of the 1938 Evidence Act, for example:

The object of evidence in a Court of Law is plain. It is to discover the truth in relation to the issues of fact involved in the case which is being tried. But here we are met at the outset with an important consideration. Truth in an absolute sense can seldom or never be ascertained, and what is sought for, what indeed alone can be aimed at, is evidence of facts sufficient to satisfy the mind of the judge or the jury that a certain proposition of fact is true. If that is done the proposition is said to be proved. The law does not and cannot require mathematical certainty.[40]

As I have suggested, there are counter-pressures to this view in an age of computers. Sir Richard Egglestone in *Evidence, Proof and Probability* (1978) has voiced dissent; and there are some interesting examples given in Joseph Weizenbaum's recent *Computer Science and Human Reasoning* of how computers can be programmed to manipulate the rules of evidence in many different contexts. The notion that legal judgement can be reduced to a calculus is less likely to go away now than it was in the nineteenth century.

Here I must return, however briefly, to Poe: these arguments about whether legal reasoning is a separate activity, or whether it is a branch of logic have an obvious relation to an underlying idea of probability. The question of whether logic is too narrow, or too wide a category for describing the treatment of 'evidence' is a vexed one, not only in its own terms; but because it also has historical and 'political' entailments of a far-reaching nature. Poe's 'Dupin' stories are generally concerned with the nature of reasoning and evidence, and its relation to probability; more specifically, with this very question of fact and relevance. The most difficult of these is the notorious 'Mystery of Marie Roget'; in which he appears to take the unfinished real case of Mary Rogers, and attempts to solve it by fictional means. The story is the most legalistic, and the most difficult to read, of all this group of tales; partly because it specifically encounters, in a fashion that seems almost Benthamite, this issue of the exclusionary principles of the law of evidence:

> I would here observe that very much of what is rejected as evidence by a court, is the best of evidence to the intellect. For the court, guided itself by the general principles of evidence – the recognised and *booked* principles – is averse from swerving at particular instances. And this steadfast adherence to principle, with rigorous disregard of the conflicting exception, is a sure mode of attaining the maximum of attainable truth, in any long sequence of time. The practice, *in mass*, is therefore philosophical; but it is not the less certain that it engenders vast individual error.

Poe sites his 'narrative' in the centre of a debate about forensic procedure and evidence. He quotes Landor in a footnote:

Thus the jurisprudence of every nation will show that, when law becomes a science and a system, it ceases to be justice. The errors into which a blind devotion to *principles* of classification has led the common law, will be seen by observing how often the legislature has been obliged to come forward to restore the equity its scheme had lost.[41]

Poe's story rests on the notion of a parallel between two cases: the contemporary case of the murder of Mary Rogers in New York, and its fictional, 'historical' equivalent, the mystery of Marie Roget in Paris. The details from the present case are set back and transposed into the fiction of the French case. Poe boasted that he would use fictional means to solve a real case, publishing the story in serial form, while the real case was yet unsolved. The result is an intensely legalistic invitation to the reader to behave like a real jury in a trial. The narrator acts in the capacity of advocate, analysing chunks of real newspaper reports, quoted and sometimes parodied, which were published at the time the story was written. The structure of the story challenges the empirical idea of evidence-giving, by associating the parallel between the two cases with a technical or mathematical calculus of probability. The 'coincidence' between the two cases is claimed to be 'in' the evidence, that is, the testimony presented to the reader in the story.

French reviewers took Poe to have been a pupil of Laplace, whose treatise on probability theory had been published in 1820. In this treatise, Laplace discusses the possible relation between his mathematical theory of probability and legal testimony in the French inquisitory system. In 1846, delightedly, the *Revue des deux mondes* commented on Poe's story:

On voit qu'il a lu, dans l'Essai philosophique de Laplace, le chapitre consacré à la probabilité des jugements de tribuneaux.[42]

The French response to Poe's technique of documentation in his stories appears to have been enthusiastic. They believed it supported his 'fantastique' effects. And their response appears to have derived from a different set of expectations about the process of giving evidence. One can clearly discern the presence of the *procès verbal* for example, as an assumption, in the response of the following reviewer from the *Revue française* to Poe's 'Descent into the Maelstrom':

Il specifie si bien . . . qu'il paraît vraiment d'avoir vue; on dirait un juge d'instruction traçant le procès verbal de quelque drame étrange plutôt qu'un poète créat un fiction . . . .[43]

The device of documented testimony here can be seen (so dramatic, so obviously an adventure does it appear) without the slightest difficulty, as existing on an axis with the marvellous.

Recent American scholarship, however, shows a quite different reaction to 'The Mystery of Marie Roget'. John Walsh, for example, has researched the real case of Mary Rogers minutely, and comes to the conclusion that Poe fiddled his fictional books, as it were (introducing changes into the text at proof stage, delaying publication of the story because fresh evidence in the real case threatened to ruin the credibility of his fictional deductions), in order to engineer the coincidence between fiction and empirical fact. For him, the story is an elaborate cheat.[44]

These differences in response are partly determined by cultural expectations of what is involved in assessing 'evidence'. The curious effect of Poe's story lies in the delicate, teasing way it encourages and also depends upon the gaps in the contexts from which such expectations are derived. The two kinds of response are to quite different aspects of the story's central conceit. In the story, Poe playfully acts out exactly what Bentham feared happening in the English legal context: he deliberately assimilates quite different senses of 'probability' together – aesthetic, moral and mathematical.

He erects Laplace's fourth principle of mathematical probability into a parallel; this parallel is no more or less than a miracle, a glimpse into the other world, which reveals the same structure of relationships between testimony and its relation to probability as those of the eighteenth-century English theologians. His epigraph from Novalis gives away the curious transcendent overtone to all this concern with 'probability', 'fact' and 'evidence':

There are ideal series of events which run parallel with real ones. They rarely coincide. Man and circumstances generally modify the ideal train of events, so that it seems imperfect, and its consequences are equally imperfect. Thus with the Reformation; instead of Protestantism came Lutheranism.[45]

This may be only an illustration of the relation between the ideal and material; but the connection between Luther and *Materialismus* is more than a merely witty or fortuitous one. It is clear, from other parts of *Moralische Ansichten*, that Novalis is simultaneously rejecting Jesuits *and* French Protestants as equally worldly and corrupt: and his objection is a 'theological' one, as much as it is an assertion of German nationalism. In Poe's text, the connection between this epigraph and Laplace is inspired: behind the shadowy realm of particular events, Poe suggests, stands the shining platonic form of ideal reality, Laplacian in its mathematical cleanliness, betrayed by history into imperfection. The conceit is double-edged: it tempts yet mocks the empirical expectations of the reader who sees the search for particular facts as the way to truth – half of the testimony in the story follows contemporary forensic medicine very closely indeed, and half of it is mumbo-jumbo. But, on the other hand, it also mocks the relationship between faith and common sense, which tends to reduce our concept of 'possibility' to a mere projection of ourselves:

> It will be understood that I speak of coincidences *and no more*. What I have said on this topic must suffice. In my own heart there dwells no faith in praeter-nature. That Nature and its God are two, no man who thinks, will deny. That the latter, creating the former, can, at will, control or modify it, is also unquestionable. I say 'at will'; for the question is of will, and not, as the insanity of logic has assumed, of power. It is not that the Deity *cannot* modify his laws, but that we insult him in imagining a possible necessity for modification. In their origin these laws were fashioned to embrace *all* contingencies which *could* lie in the Future. With God all is *Now*.[46]

It seems a marvellous irony, not an indictment of the author, that Poe should have inserted this passage after the galleys had been set up: all *is* now indeed. Walsh discovered by historical research that Poe's story 'deduces' a naval officer in the real case of Mary Rogers. His conclusion smacks of the courtroom:

> Since it is morally certain that Mary's death occurred on an abortion table, the concept of a naval officer has no validity, except as a euphemism for 'abortionist'.[47]

The phrase 'morally certain' is, of course, a legal phrase, and one which, moreover, describes the kind of proof which belongs to the adversarial system. The critic has turned counsel, and in doing so, he reveals exactly the assimilation which Poe has performed between different contexts of probability.

I make this point, not so much to call into question Walsh's excellent research as to underline the nature of the problem for interpretation here: criticism itself is also based, or based partly, on 'evidence' and the problem becomes a reflexive one: the colour of probability, as it were, flows back. Nowhere is this more evident than in the legalistic discussions of Henry James's *Turn of the Screw*, amply recorded in the Norton Critical Edition of that work. From a literary-critical point of view, there is something fundamentally wrong-headed about asking the question: 'Did the governess *really* see the ghosts, or is she lying?' Yet the power of the case format is associated with the need to answer that very question. And no matter how much one appeals to James as a parodist, the question does not go away. Edmund Wilson, with his famous appeal to the unconscious sexuality of the governess, did nothing to resolve it: instead, he merely added to the kinds of evidence which can be brought into play in the 'case'.

Dickens was very interested in Poe's 'Marie Roget' story; and when he went to America, he met with Poe in a hotel in New York to discuss the case and the story with him. Here at the outset, in discussing Dickens's place in this tradition, we meet with an interesting paradox: that the author of *Bleak House* the book that, more than any other in the English language, supports Bentham's indictment of the Blackstonian tradition, reducing the comfortable 'Gothic' castle of the legal system to a black labyrinth of fictions, was not interested in matching the 'Gothic' of this theme in the formal structure of his books. Both Dickens and Poe had the Blackwoods circle in common; Dickens knew them through his father-in-law, George Hogarth, who also edited *Bentleys*. As early as 1823, the Blackwoods writers had been exploiting the powerful effect of terror produced by a certain kind of medical report. Dickens was certainly acutely aware of the reforms necessary in the law of evidence, as his concern in *Bleak House* with the confusion between the competence and the credibility of witnesses shows; but he was not interested in case format from an aesthetic point of view. As an editor of *All the Year Round*, he disliked notes or any apparatus which 'stood between the reader and the text', as he wrote to Collins. Dickens associated 'immediacy' with a third person narrator's voice, not with the direct reproduction of testimony. And, although Esther

Summerson's narrative is an exception to the frame of testimony, in general he preferred, temperamentally, to use a third person. So, for example, in the case where we know he used a Blackwoods tale as a source for his own work, he changed the first person testimony to third-person narrative.[48]

Collins, on the other hand, was irresistibly drawn to the reproduction of direct testimony. He builds his fictional method on the model of evidence-giving in a quite self-conscious fashion. The opening of one of his most famous novels, *The Woman In White*, for example, is presented explicitly as an experiment in the use of legal process for fictional purposes. The technical aspect of the hearsay rule comes into play on the first page of the famous Preface:

> If the machinery of the Law could be depended on to fathom every case of suspicion, and to conduct every process of inquiry with moderate assistance only from the lubricating influences of oil and gold, the events which fill these pages might have claimed their share of the public attention in a Court of Justice.
>
> But the Law is still, in certain inevitable cases, the pre-engaged servant of the long purse; and the story is left to be told, for the first time, in this place. As the Judge might have once heard it, so the Reader shall hear it now. No circumstance of importance, from the beginning to the end of the disclosure, shall be related on hearsay evidence. When the writer of these introductory lines (Walter Hartright, by name) happens to be more closely-connected than others with the incidents to be recorded, he will describe them in his own person. When his experience fails, he will retire from the person of narrator; and his task will be continued, from the point at which he has left it off, by other persons who can speak to the circumstances under notice from their own knowledge, just as clearly and positively as he has spoken before them.
>
> Thus the story here presented will be told by more than one pen, as the story of an offence against the laws is told in court by more than one witness – with the same object, in both cases, to present the truth always in its most direct and most intelligible aspect.[49]

The notion that third-person narrative is a form of hearsay is an amusing implication here, which would not have amused Dickens; but Browning, whose *Ring and the Book* appeared in the same year, would surely have appreciated it, for his poetic method is also a form of direct testimony which has many of the effects of the prose tradition I have been discussing. Here, the social purpose of Collins's opening declaration is a serious one: he does not proceed in a covert or unacknowledged fashion. The fiction is presented as occurring in a cultural gap and the author is merely extending legal method in order to cover that gap. The claim is thus that this fiction is a case which has been excluded from the law by the corrupt nature of that institution. The reader is to be the judge (and, it is assumed, jury), who *might* have been, if the system were fair: the appeal to the *boni homines*, the 'palladium of civil liberty' is accompanied by an hypothesis which contains a rather neat inversion of 'probability' in the aesthetic sense, but which retains it in a more technical, 'legal' sense.

But the whole passage is also founded, paradoxically, on an exploitation of the truth-value of the law. It even employs the very exclusionary rules, which Bentham and others had recommended sweeping away; for in his second paragraph, Collins assumes quite clearly the connection which legal historians have afterwards pointed out, between the hearsay rule and the adversary system; not only the connection, it should be added, but also its virtue. The law's own existing methods are being used and assimilated to narrative; those methods include another 'hidden' acceptance of a legal maxim, that is, the theologically founded *unus testis, nullus testis*; so that fragmentation becomes essential, once one has invoked the principle of corroboration. The passage is at once a defence of the system of evidence-giving, since it rests upon it, and an attack on the corruption of the Law.

I am not simply suggesting that Collins is a tricky and self-conscious writer here. The paradox I am pointing to is only visible if we have access to the cultural meaning of the assumption which the text rests upon. However, Collins was trained as a lawyer in the Inns of Court; and thus he was aware of the relative differences in the English and continental systems. It is interesting to note, therefore, that the source of *The Woman in White* is French – the case of Madame de Douhault, from Maurice Méjan's *Receuil des causes célèbres*, a book which Collins had in his own library. The content of an eighteenth-century case which had been originally tried under French law has been grafted on to a mock-up of English legal procedure.

Collins was extremely fond, like his friend Dickens, of police and medical reports. He was not, however, if the evidence of his works is anything to go by, an orthodox Christian.[50] The theological overlap, nevertheless, creeps into this method of direct witnessing. Much of his work is concerned with a sense of danger to the individual, which can shade over into a suggestion of evil in a fashion that is reminiscent of the double scale of judgement in Mrs Radcliffe. The method of bringing witness after witness forward frees the author to confine the reader to *process*, often slowing up time, for example, in the most outrageous way. This is a familiar effect in Richardson's *Clarissa*, and we get something similar, I think, marooned as we are in a vista of endless testimony, in Collins. The following is a typically teasing passage, which raises the possibility that there is a supernatural explanation of what Hartright sees:

> I started up from the ottoman, before Miss Halcombe could pronounce the next words. A thrill of the same feeling which ran through me when the touch was laid upon my shoulder on the lonely highroad, chilled me again.
>
> There stood Miss Fairlie, a white figure, alone in the moonlight; in her attitude, in the turn of her head, in her complexion, in the shape of her face, the living image, at that distance and under those circumstances, of the woman in white! The doubt which had troubled my mind for hours and hours past, flashed into conviction in an instant. That 'something wanting' was my own recognition of the ominous likeness between the fugitive from the asylum and my pupil at Limmeridge House.[51]

The coincidence is inexplicable, yet doubt rushes into certainty. Hartright is producing testimony to the existence of something which, though it *will* be unravelled, cannot be, for the reader or for himself, at this moment, so that the suggestion, supported by the very isolation of the act of witnessing, is left open to the reader's judgement. Another moment, and Collins dispels the threat in a series of jokes, though the jokes have a characteristic unease about them:

> '. . . Call her in, out of the dreary moonlight – pray call her in!'
>
> 'Mr Hartright, you surprise me. Whatever women may be, I thought that men, in the nineteenth century, were above superstition.'
>
> 'Pray call her in!'

'Hush, hush! She is coming of her own accord. Say nothing in her presence. Let this discovery of the likeness be kept a secret between you and me. Come in, Laura; come in, and wake Mrs Vesey with the piano. Mr Hartright is petitioning for some more music, and he wants it, this time, of the lightest and liveliest kind.'[52]

Hartright is Catherine Morland here, to Marian's Henry Tilney, as Collins, characteristically, inverts the stereotyped sex-roles. But also superstition is *named*, and the notion of a relationship between direct testimony and faith, the thrill of the inexplicable, the crack in the general counter-testimony that 'guarantees' that such intuitions are the mere survival of bygone superstition, is raised in the mind of the reader, and lingers there, after the dissolution of the bantering dialogue: Laura Fairlie in the 'dreary moonlight' is the ghost of a ghost, a metaghost.

The comic scene in the schoolroom which follows this incident reworks the isolation of testimony. The appeal to the 'rational' is offset, displaced, by the corroborative principle itself. As Marian and Walter Hartright approach the schoolroom, they and the reader see a quite different 'explanation', in the scene which they overhear, from the schoolmaster:

The schoolmaster was sitting at his high desk, with his back to me, apparently haranguing the pupils, who were all gathered together in front of him, with one exception. The one exception was a sturdy white-headed boy, standing apart from all the rest on a stool in a corner – a forlorn little Crusoe, isolated in his own desert island of solitary penal disgrace.

The door, when we got round it, was ajar; and the schoolmaster's voice reached us plainly, as we both stopped for a minute under the porch.

'Now boys,' said the voice, 'mind what I tell you. If I hear another word spoken about ghosts in this school, it will be the worst for all of you. There are no such things as ghosts; and, therefore, any boy who believes in ghosts believes in what can't possibly be; and a boy who belongs to Limmeridge School and believes in what can't possibly be, sets up his back against reason and discipline, and must be punished accordingly.'[53]

The satire on the conjunction of reason and discipline, and the ludicrous dogma which purports to override individual testimony to the marvellous, does not require the fragmentation of the novel's form for its effect – the schoolmaster is quite Dickensian in this way. But the reader's knowledge that the solitary testimony of the boy *confirms* that intuitional rush that Walter and Marian have already separately agreed upon, however 'irrational' it might be, gives another undercurrent to the scene here. The comic reference to Crusoe emblematises the conjunction between the different sense of 'witnessing' and the novel's own 'legalistic' method. What is discredited from the official point of view, is fast becoming a 'fact' (though a secret one) for the reader.

Collins reserves the right, however, to renegotiate his relationship with his reader. Despite the *credo* of the opening, and its obvious appeal to the oral process of the adversary system, Walter Hartright takes it upon himself, at the beginning of Volume 3, to condense and render into a written deposition the experiences of Marian and Laura. This act of censorship is based on love, and it can only be thought of, *after* Walter has found the two women, and finally declared his love for Laura:

> My position is defined; my motives are acknowledged. The story of Marian and the story of Laura must come next.
> I shall relate both narratives, not in the words (often interrupted, often inevitably confused) of the speakers themselves, but in the words of the brief, plain, studiously simple abstract, which I committed to writing for my own guidance, and for the guidance of my legal adviser.[54]

In fact, the corroborative principle, which defines 'action' in the book, has run ahead of the 'plot', in the sense of its causal structure, so that the reader needs to have certain events explained. But even the third-person, and its appeal to 'reasonable probability', quite different in essence from the structure of individual testimonies which has been building up, is presented here as 'evidence' of a sort, and is therefore framed by the rest of the book, instead of representing any 'outside' point. It is, in fact, one of the many records proffered us, in which we may discern the thread of future justice. When Walter has obtained his fresh evidence in the case, he is able, finally, to force a written confession from Count Fosco, to which he is a helplessly fascinated witness. For Fosco produces this final, vital evidence, which makes Walter, Laura and Marian safe, in an orgy of *writing*:

> Each slip as he finished it, was paged, and tossed over his shoulder, out of his way, on the floor. When his first pen was worn out, *that* went over his shoulder too; and he pounced on a second from the supply scattered about the table. Slip after slip, by dozens, by fifties, by hundreds, flew over his shoulders on either side of him, till he had snowed himself up in paper all round his chair. Hour after hour passed – and there I sat watching; and there he sat, writing. He never stopped, except to sip his coffee; and when that was exhausted, to smack his forehead, from time to time. One o'clock struck, two, three, four, – and still the slips flew about all round him; still the untiring pen scraped its way ceaselessly from top to bottom of the page; still the white chaos of paper rose higher and higher all round his chair. At four o'clock, I heard a sudden splutter of the pen, indicative of the flourish with which he signed his name. 'Bravo!' he cried – springing to his feet with the activity of a young man, and looking me straight in the face with a smile of superb triumph.[55]

This is, in one sense, the image of the novelist himself – and the image of Fosco as the inspired *alter ego* of Collins, pouring out his confession like a three-decker, must have amused him. But again, the thrust of this structure is towards confession as the final piece of evidence; and, as jury, we must therefore know its contents:

> The reader will have an opportunity, ere long, of forming his own opinion of the document. It will be sufficient to mention here that it answered my purpose.[56]

Its value, as evidence, is unquestionable; but Walter prefers not to plant suppositions as to its truth or falsity into the reader's mind. Even at this late stage, we are not allowed to take the dénouement on trust.

We tend to underestimate the latter-day career of Social Darwinism, I feel; and certainly my final example of the use of testimony for the purposes of articulating horror and anxiety is twentieth-century and is quite as concerned as Bram Stoker's *Dracula* with the question of atavistic regression. On this point,

Lombroso's modern editor, Savitz, makes some very interesting observations:

> Lombroso had his greatest impact in the United States. In the Introduction to this book (*L'uomo deliquente*), he specifically mentions that his theories have become an object of 'almost fanatical adherence', especially in America. . . . The traditional sociological approach to crime that developed before Lombroso in France, and to a lesser extent in England, acted as a bulwark against a complete capitulation to Lombrosianism and offered viable alternatives to his formulations. Then, America had no central sources of continuously collected national crime statistics such as existed in England and France.[57]

Stoker, as I have suggested elsewhere, loved Americans; and he believed that the future of Europe depended on a kind of joint Anglo-American imperialism. He puts an important prophetic speech on this matter into the mouth of his madman, Renfield.[58] Written by an American, Guy Endore, in 1933 and reprinted in 1943, my final example is, to my mind, an extraordinary piece of work: *The Werewolf of Paris*. In 1963 Panther reissued it in paperback. The book is, like *Dracula*, intermittently pornographic, tissued in layer upon layer of documented testimony, powerful and obsessed with the notion of atavistic regression. Guy Endore, who wrote film scripts in Hollywood at one stage and in particular for horror films, is a prolific author whose choice of work deliberately confounds fiction with fact. A francophile, he specialises in 'biographies' of retold life-stories – the Dumas brothers, Casanova and *The Heart and the Mind: The Story of Rousseau and Voltaire*. He also translated Pierre Loti's *Pêcheur d'Islande* in 1931. Two things are evident in his output: an interest in 'history' (and particularly in French culture) and also an interest in horror and sado-masochistic sexuality. Endore also wrote a book called *Satan's Saint: A Novel about the Marquis de Sade*, which was issued by Panther Books in 1967.

The Werewolf of Paris is a *tour de force* of the Gothic, as interesting and certainly as disturbing and unpleasant as *Dracula*. Its importance here is to show how the labyrinthine form of the Gothic persists. The anonymous narrator is a PhD student, writing his dissertation on MS F.2839, which necessitates living in Paris. The dating of this outside frame is 'modern' – not necessarily exactly contemporary with the writing of the book, 1933, but certainly either in the late 1920s or early 1930s. The narrator is visited by Eliane, a pretty, sassy, young American acquaintance from back home, who wants to take out the poor scholar to Zelli's and drink champagne. A Bacchanalian scene ensues in which, bored by the conversation of the narrator and his rather unpleasant friend about insect mimicry, Eliane gets up and does a strip-tease:

'I'm hot,' she said, and quickly loosening her dress she slipped out of it and began to pirouette in her silken panties and brassiere. The proprietor came running out and began to upbraid her and all of us as sales Americans. But Eliane was not to be stopped so easily. She cast herself into the arms of a strange man and said: 'Take me; I'm yours. I want to belong to you. To you only.'

He put his arms round her and led her over to his table, where she was at once at home on his lap, her arms slung tightly around his neck and their mouths as if glued together.

I went over to him and expostulated. Eliane promptly abandoned him and said to me, 'Don't be jealous, I'll be yours. Yes, I'll be yours. Take me with you quick.'

Right there I made my mistake. For what I said was:

'Now come along, Eliane, get your clothes on and let me take you home.' I should have pretended to fall in with her plans. Instead I summoned her to be decent. That was precisely what she did not want to be.

'If you won't have me, then anyone can have me. Who wants me?' she shouted, 'Who wants me? I want a man? I'm virgin and free and white and good-looking too. I'll show you,' and she began to tug at her brassiere.[59]

Eventually, she leaves with the man in a taxi, and the two friends walk home, pursuing a rather irritable conversation. They are accosted by a prostitute who claims to be rich, showing them a roll of banknotes. This gives their conversation another turn, as they speculate about the two events: the narrator is the disbeliever, the sceptic, while his garrulous friend offers him 'explanations':

'It's a disease,' he went on to say. 'They are as if possessed by a beast. Did you know that there is a new school of psychology that is returning to the old belief in possession?'

He waited for an answer so I said briefly: 'No'. It would have done no good to say yes, he would have continued to impart his information to me anyhow.

'You've heard of Hyslop, of course?' he said. 'Well, I should think he would have thought the two examples we saw tonight evidences of possession by the spirits of beasts.'

'Are you sure you're right?' I asked. I was slightly skeptical of the security of his knowledge. It threatened like the Tower of Pisa.[60]

The last image has something odd about it, however: is the account threatening to collapse on its own, or is it threatening to collapse *on* the narrator? Certainly, the surface meaning is the former. The narrator, however, is pretty obviously a marker for our scepticism as they develop the conversation. He lets his garrulous friend ramble on about his 'ridiculous' theories, and then dismisses them with a flourish:

'That was the ancient psychology, too. The Romans, for example, thought of insatiable sexual appetite as due to possession by a wolf.'

'I thought the billygoat was the symbol of sexual insatiability.'

'You are wrong,' he answered. 'The word wolf is to be recognized in the Latin vulva, and in the word lupanar, a brothel, lupus being Latin for wolf. You know the Roman festival of the Lupercales. It would correspond to our carnival and was characterized by a complete abandonment of morals.'

'Wasn't Lupercus another name for the God Pan?' I asked.

'So it was, but the name means protector against the wolves. It had something to do with the nursing of Romulus and Remus by a she-wolf, but its sexual significance is shown by the fact that at the sacrifice of goats during this festival, the women who wished to be fruitful allowed themselves to be beaten with bloody strips cut out of the goat's hide.'

'I find those theories usually built on too shallow a foundation,' I objected. 'It sounds like Frazer and there's nothing I care for less. Besides, there are theories for which I don't care no matter how good they are.'[61]

Again, the last remark reveals that, in the narrator's 'scepticism', there also lurks a feeling of being threatened by the idea. The 'flourish' is a piece of bravado, if looked at in this way; and the whole 'narrative' is, in fact, inserting the theory of atavism into the head of the reader, even as the narrator is 'dismissing' it.

The apparent inconsequentiality of this series of events is preserved in the bored, dismissive air of the narrator, who sits at dawn on a bench by the Seine, vacantly watching two 'beachcombers', while the night's events ring in his head:

> Two men came along, each with a sack slung across his shoulder, and they began to lay out on the ground the spoils of a morning's tour of inspection of the city's rubbish. They broke electric light bulbs, separated the brass base from the glass, and took out the tungsten filament. They had bottles and bits of string, and pieces of rag and buttons, and one of them had a roll of paper, bound with a ribbon. He untied the ribbon and spread out the roll. There were several sheets laced together and evidently covered with writing. That was as much as I could see from where I was sitting.[62]

This is the magic moment: the document has made its appearance. But the author still teases the reader, as we edge nearer to grab and look, with the possibility that this is a non-event. The narrator looks, all the machinery of providential coincidence swings into operation, yet to possess the Manuscript he has to appear not to want it:

> One look, however, had made me keen to own the manuscript. That look had happened upon the words: *The lupercal temples became the later brothels or lupanars. Still today in Italian, lupa signifies both wolf and wanton.*
>
> I offered one franc. The men shrugged their shoulders. They went on separating their bits of metal and rag and exchanged a few rapid remarks, in argot, which I could not catch.
>
> Then I did a brave thing, though my heart pounded in fear. I threw the manuscript down at their feet and saying: 'Bonjour, messieurs,' I walked off. I had taken ten steps, and with difficulty had restrained my desire to look back, when I heard one of them cry out:
>
> 'On vous le vend pour cinq, monsieur.'
>
> I turned back, took the manuscript and said as calmly as I could: 'Va, pour cinq,' and handed them a little bill of five francs.
>
> Thus through Eliane, in a way, I came into possession of the Galliez report: thirty four sheets of closely written French, an

unsolicited summation of the case of Bertrand Chaillet at the latter's court-martial in 1871.[63]

The Eurydice-act here indicates just how self-consciously the author is using this moment to *show* the seams in the text. The occurrence is providential, the inconsequentiality of the rambling opening is shown to have a proleptic thread running through it. The testimony of the narrator to his own 'modern' experience is about to receive corroboration from the past. Yet all this is done with a light touch: the connection between the girl's drunken sexuality in the bar, and the dismissed anthropological theories of the student is not made evident: it is only hinted at in the act of disconfirmation by the narrator. But the idea of 'evidence', and written evidence here, is very strong. We have entered the labyrinth. The play, as in Stoker, is between the shallow idea of 'modernity', and the atavistic threat of the past. The whole idea of research and documentation is used to promote this counterpoint: the 'unsolicited summation' of the case opens up the idea that this is fresh 'evidence', it yields the thrill of historical research; while at the same time invoking the notion of the authority of a real legal case. The American in Paris is a sociological cliché, and the author conveys his knowingness very effectively about this: but it actually functions in the traditional 'Gothic' fashion: it is a journey away from a centre of security into an alien culture, redolent of superstition. The iron match between ancient beliefs and modern psychology is about to be reopened by the Galliez report. The jocular unease of this opening feels brittle to the reader; and it is connected with an ambiguity about whether we are encountering historical fact or not, which persists throughout the text in a very dislocative fashion: the author uses an angular, privatised selection of historical facts to throw the reader off-balance: the text bristles with the signs of authority, used in a fashion that reminds one of the bibliophilic jokes of Swift on this matter. The rhetoric of the manuscript is firmly 'placed' as a form of florid 'Gothic' by the narrator, yet it introduces the theological undertow into the testimony we are being offered, as surely as any traditional nineteenth-century horror story:

> From its very first words, the manuscript exerts a curious fascination. Its wisdom is as strange as that of the pyramidologists of our day, those strangely learned men who prove at length that

the pyramids of Egypt were built to be a permanent storehouse of a scientific knowledge greater than that which we possess at present.

Galliez begins:

'The vast strides of our generation in the conquest of the material world must not mislead us into thinking that when we have plumbed the physical world to its depths we shall thereby have explained all there is to explain. The scientists of a former day strove mightily to fathom the depths of the spiritual world and their successes and conquests are all but forgotten.

'Who can estimate what thanks we owe to those courageous priests of old who went into the forbidding Druidic forests and with bell and book, and swinging censer, exorcised the sylvan spirits, banished the familiars, expelled the elementals, cast out the monsters and devils of old Gaul? Who can estimate the debt we owe to them for helping to slay all the strange and unnatural beasts that formerly cowered in every dark cranny and recess, under ferns and moss-covered rocks, waiting to leap out at the unwary passerby who did not cross himself in time? Not all of these monsters were equally evil, but all constituted unwelcome interferences in the destiny of man.'[64]

The reader is apparently twice-removed from this language: once by the Narrator who finds and introduces the Galliez report, and once by 'Galliez', who is himself to introduce us to the case of Sergeant Bertrand which took place at the time of the Paris Commune. To understand this legal 'case', however, we need to go much further back in time, into the 'superstitions' of the past . . . .

The final resting point is a tiny piece of corroborative evidence in a learned disquisition about hygiene in cemeteries during the Commune period, when the secular 'progressive' attitude towards burial inherited from the French Revolution was at its height. Among the bodies exhumed in a scientific experiment is the following:

Sieur   C . . .   (Bertrand)   Cerebral   hemorrhage   (Not illustrated).

Died Aug 9, 1873 – Buried Aug 10, 1873. – Exhumed June 10, 1881. – Length of inhumation: 8 years, 2 months. The following case was reported to the conservateur of the cemetery and by him forwarded to the department of criminal justice. Evidently a case of grave robbery, or a grim prank of the fossayeurs [gravediggers].

The body of Sieur C . . . was not found in the coffin, instead, that of a dog, which despite 8 years in the ground was still incompletely destroyed.

The fleshy parts and the furry hide are found mingled in a fatty mass of indistinguishable composition (adipocere). A nauseous odour spreads from the body.

No insects.[65]

The 'rational' explanation is clearly discredited: if there is anything this is a 'case' of, it is not grave robbery. The evidence reveals a quite different explanation for the knowing reader: the documentary mode yields the true *frisson* of a profane (hideously material) resurrection in the stubbornness with which the 'true' form of Sergeant Bertrand clings to life.

Postscript

Clearly, I am suggesting that a good deal of the writing I have been describing has both a greater unity and a greater rhetorical sophistication than readers sometimes give it credit for. But I am not claiming that this is a form of literary self-consciousness. We must call a political reflex into play if we are to think and speak of heresy; and often the images of the monstrous, the proscribed and the alien are precisely this – an imaginative play with heresy. But heresy in political terms is not the defiling pitch it may appear to be from a merely emotional or psychological point of view. It is part of the way the culture witnesses itself. Much of the horror novel's concern with 'superstition' in one form or another carries the implication of unstated orthodoxy. The typical rhetorical 'feint' of the Gothic writer is to provide striking images of the unthinkable with a false discredit: in the middle of a barrage of obsessively managed manoeuvres about the relative nature of the credible will come a flash of horror usually from an earlier, sometimes from a more primitive, part of contemporary culture. The peculiar rhetorical form of the horror tradition discredits and authorises the unthinkable at the same time. The values of the proscribed are presented to the reader in terms that *would*, by all the admitted canons of 'rationality' (often deliberately paraded before the reader) invalidate them – the reader's problem or consolation is that they do not. The gap is deliberately invoked in the redundancy of the rhetorical form: 'explanation' discredits itself, or one layer of explanation will discredit another in a series that does not manage to imply its end-point or limit. The key to this form is what it reveals about this particular concept of 'rationality', which unpacks into a form of objective theology. Thus the concern with epistemology and faith at the same time. Traditionally, epistemological doubt remains the hallmark of Protestant faith from the eighteenth century onwards, with the assimilation of 'faith' to 'reason' accomplished as a result of the attacks of Hume and the Deists. This is a 'popular' tradition, in the sense that it provides a common language for the culture – the concept of 'popular' is a vertical, not a horizontal and stratified one.[1] And the questions raised about the nature of belief by the form of the horror novel, as a part of its rhetorical tactics, are genuinely difficult philosophical questions which every reader has

233

to face. In this sense it is not a marginal literary genre at all, a matter of extreme 'sensibility', but an essential and continuous affirmation of the cultural experience of the nineteenth-century reader. Hence, the best and subtlest writing of the tradition is continuous throughout the nineteenth and early twentieth century: Poe, Hogg, Stevenson, Stoker and M. R. James.

Horror fiction is, essentially, fantasy about history. It is a special form of the historical romance, in one sense. But the narrative form is characteristically fragmented. The function of this is to concentrate and locate the reader's experience in particulars, whose *dis*continuity is deliberately invoked. Professor Walzer, discussing the Calvinist attitude towards history, makes a very interesting point about the relation between fragmentation and providential modes of thinking:

> Organic imagery . . . rarely reappears in Huguenot writing. History is as unnatured in its usual treatment by Protestant publicists as is nature itself in Calvin's work. Each historical event, like each breath of wind, is particularly and specially willed by God. History is the casuist's case-book; it is not a continuous development, but a collection of discrete facts, examples and precedents.[2]

I think there is a strong implication in the analyses I have presented above that the narrative form of horror fiction is *itself* symbolic of a resistance to the organic process of history. The reader's responses are *confined* by the methods I have discussed throughout this book to discrete particulars. But, as Walzer implies, the breaking down of experience is a method of revealing its essential unity. Hence perhaps, the frequent puzzling feeling that these writers are very close in their methods of thought to empiricism, almost satirically close. Certainly a lot of the accompanying mediation in the horror novel turns almost automatically about the nature of the empirical.

Even a relatively crude and popular Methodist like Hervey can explain the doctrine of Providence to his readers in such a way that demands a concentration on random or accidental events which reveal an invisible structure. About death, he writes:

> When the king of Israel was mortally wounded, it seemed to be a casual shot. 'A certain man drew his bow at a venture.' (1 Kings xxii. 34) At a venture, as he thought. But his hand was

strengthened by an omnipotent aid; and the shaft levelled by an unerring eye. So that, what we term casualty, is really Providence, accomplishing its deliberate design, but concealing its own interposition.[3]

This is a complicated idea very simply expressed here. It is a doctrine which is common to almost everyone in the horror tradition, and is, I think, a major determinant of narrative form in the nineteenth-century novel in general. The doctrine which generates this notion of providential irony is totally elastic in its literary manifestations. It can dictate retrospective sequence in a lyric poem or a novel equally. In the horror tradition it is essential, because it forces the reader to take the step from the fragments to the whole, the invisible, proleptic thread that runs through a tissue of apparently aimless documentation.

Notes

Notes to the Preface

1. A. Breton, 'Limits not Frontiers of Surrealism', trs. and repr. in *Surrealism*, ed. Sir Herbert Read (London, 1936) pp. 108–9.
2. The handiest recent account of this position is R. Jackson, *Fantasy: The Literature of Subversion* (London, 1981) pp. 171ff.
3. See, for example, F. Jameson, 'Magical Narratives: Romance as Genre', *New Literary History*, vol. 7, no. 1 (Autumn 1975) pp. 133–63.
4. M. Levy, *Le Roman 'gotique' anglais* (Toulouse, 1968) pp. 600ff.
5. See A. Parreaux, *The Publication of 'The Monk': A Literary Event, 1796–1798* (Paris, 1960) p. 139; for the legal history of the crime, see G. D. Noakes, *A History of the Crime of Blasphemy* (London, 1928).
6. J. Bunyan, *Grace Abounding to the Chief of Sinners*, ed. R. Sharrock (Oxford, 1962) p. 55.
7. M. Walzer, *Revolution of the Saints* (London, 1966) p. 84.
8. See W. R. Inge, *Protestantism* (London, 1935). For comment on the Scottish context, see A. Drummond and C. Bullock, *The Scottish Church 1688–1843* (Edinburgh, 1973).
9. By the time Calmet died in 1757, there were at least two editions in circulation in England. For some bibliographical information and a Protestant interpretation of the book, see *The Phantom World, or The Philosophy of Spirits, Apparitions etc.*, by Augustine Calmet, ed. with an introduction by the Revd Henry Christmas (London, 1850).
10. Sigmund Freud, 'The Uncanny', *Collected Papers*, authorised translation under the supervision of Joan Riviere, vol. iv (London, 1957).

Notes to Chapter 1: Dark House

1. C. Drelincourt, *A Christian Man's Consolations against the Fears of Death*, 28th edn (Liverpool, 1811) p. 55.
2. *Ibid.*, p. 57.
3. *Meditations and Contemplations by the Rev. James Hervey AM* (London, 1815) pp. xxxix–xxxxii.
4. In particular 1 Cor. 15 and, for the metaphor of the 'house not built with hands', see 2 Cor. 5:1–6. One of the most important sources for the opposite, literal interpretation of these passages from St Paul is Tertullian:

   But very many also who maintain the resurrection of the soul from death, interpret 'coming out of the tomb' as meaning 'escaping from the world', because the world also is a dwelling-place of the dead, that is of those that know not God, or even 'from the body' itself, because the body also like a tomb holds the soul fast closed up in the death of worldly life.

This for Tertullian is the 'figurative' position, and is a heretical mystification. See *Tertullian Concerning the Resurrection of the Flesh*, ed. B. A. Souter (London, 1922) pp. 47–8.

5. Hervey, *Meditations and Contemplations*, p. 31.
6. *Ibid.*, p. 31n.
7. *Ibid.*, pp. 59–60.
8. Isaac Watts, *Reliquae Juveniles* (London, 1734) p. 107.
9. William Cowper, *The Poetical Works*, ed. H. S. Milford, 4th edn (Oxford, 1963) p. 290.
10. See J. W. Draper, *The Funeral Elegy and the Rise of Romanticism* (New York, 1929) *passim*.
11. Eleanor Sickels, *The Gloomy Egoist: Moods and Themes of Melancholy from Gray to Keats* (New York, 1932) p. 158.
12. Hervey, *Meditations and Contemplations*, p. 28.
13. Jane Austen, *Northanger Abbey*, ed. R. W. Chapman (Oxford, 1969) p. 197.
14. Ann Radcliffe, *The Mysteries of Udolpho* (London, 1794; repr. 2 vols, London, 1962) vol. i, p. 230.
15. Charles Maturin, *Melmoth the Wanderer* (London, 1820; repr. Oxford, 1968) p. 25.
16. Emily Brontë, *Wuthering Heights* (London, 1847; repr. Harmondsworth, 1967) p. 46.
17. *Ibid.*, p. 367.
18. Edgar Allan Poe, *Selected Writings*, ed. D. Galloway (Harmondsworth, 1967) p. 140.
19. *Ibid.*, pp. 141–2.
20. *Ibid.*, p. 161.
21. Repr. from *All the Year Round* (1866), in *The Supernatural Omnibus*, ed. Montague Summers (1931; repr. London, 1974) p. 202.
22. *Ibid.*, p. 202.
23. Charles Dickens, *The Mystery of Edwin Drood* (Oxford, 1963) p. 7.
24. *Ibid.*, pp. 19–20.
25. Wilkie Collins, *The Black Robe*, 3 vols (London, 1871; repr. London, 1885) pp. 235–6. Collins toys in this novel with the traditional myth that a curse attaches to the owners of monastic lands.
26. R. L. Stevenson, *The Strange Case of Dr Jekyll and Mr Hyde*, repr. in *Minor Classics of Nineteenth-Century Fiction*, ed. W. E. Buckler, 2 vols (Boston, Mass., 1967) vol. ii, p. 62.
27. *Ibid.*, pp. 69–70.
28. John Russell Taylor, *Hitch* (London, 1978; repr. London, 1981) p. 290.
29. Mervyn Peake, *Titus Groan* (Harmondsworth, 1968) p. 498.
30. David Storey, *Radcliffe* (Harmondsworth, 1965) p. 20.
31. *Ibid.*, p. 111.
32. Angela Carter, *Heroes and Villains* (London, 1969; repr. Harmondsworth, 1981) pp. 31–2.
33. J. G. Farrell, *Troubles* (London, 1970; repr. Harmondsworth, 1975) p. 15.

34. *Ibid.*, p. 112.
35. *Ibid.*, p. 408.

Notes to Chapter 2: The Unwritten Tradition

1. H. Newman, *Lectures on the Present Condition of Catholics in England* (London, 1851; repr. 1892) p. 328.
2. *Ibid.*, p. 88.
3. See William Haller, *Fox's Book of Martyrs and the Elect Nation* (London, 1963).
4. Newman, *Lectures on the Present Condition of Catholics in England*, p. 141.
5. See O. Chadwick, *The Victorian Church*, 3rd edn (London, 1971) vol. 1, p. 297n.
6. Radcliffe, *The Mysteries of Udolpho*, vol. i, p. 252.
7. *Ibid.*, vol. ii, p. 334.
8. *Ibid.*
9. *Ibid.*, vol. i, p. 251.
10. Ann Radcliffe, *Gaston de Blondeville* (London, 1826) vol. i, p. 70. For further information, see P. Arnand, *Anne Radcliffe et le Fantastique* (Paris, 1976).
11. See D. Gwynn, *The Struggle for Catholic Emancipation, 1750–1820* (London, 1928); and E. R. Norman, *Anti-Catholicism in Victorian England* (London, 1968) pp. 129ff.
12. Ann Radcliffe, *The Italian* (London, 1797; repr. Oxford, 1968) p. 81.
13. Maturin, *Melmoth the Wanderer*, p. 83.
14. *Ibid.*, pp. 83–4.
15. B. J. Armstrong, *Norfolk Diaries* (London, 1949) p. 43.
16. Alvin S. Ryan (ed.), *Newman and Gladstone: The Vatican Decrees*, with an Introduction by Alvin S. Ryan (Notre Dame, Ind., 1962) p. 61. This metaphor is transferable from one socio-religious group to another. For dissenters, the established Protestant church was made up of actors – i.e. hypocrites and pharisees. The evidence for this is scattered throughout the Puritan pamphlets on the theatre from Prynne onwards, where the reader is constantly reminded of the Greek origin of the term 'hypocrite' – i.e. 'stage-player'. Here is a striking example from a dissenting minister, a follower of George Whitefield, in which one can clearly see the extension of the term:

   In England, no gentleman can enter upon any public office in the nation, without professing his belief of the articles of the established religion, and taking the sacrament as a proof of his sincerity. Every officer in the army, or navy, enters this way. Every gentleman employed in the excise or custom house, enters by the same door. . . . Now, if any gentleman, to enter on a lucrative place, subscribe to articles *he does not believe*, and take the sacrament of the Lord's supper, as a proof of his piety, while his life is notoriously wicked before all, he *plays the hypocrite*, in a very particular manner.

He professes to believe what he *does not* believe; and puts on *an appearance* of piety at the sacrament, while his heart and life witness against him. And are there not many hypocrites of this description in these nations? (Alexander Kilham, *The Hypocrite Detected and Exposed* (Aberdeen, 1794) p. 13.)

17. Ryan (ed.), *Newman and Gladstone*, p. 46.
18. Maturin, *Melmoth the Wanderer*, p. 114.
19. H. Trevor-Roper, *Historical Essays* (London, 1957); repr. as *Men and Events* (New York, 1976) p. 230.
20. For a brief account of Gallicanism, see P. Spencer, *Politics of Belief in Nineteenth-Century France* (London, 1954) p. 83.
21. Eugene Sue, *The Wandering Jew* (London, 1868) ch. xv, p. 49. See Spencer, *Politics of Belief in Nineteenth-Century France* for the background to this novel.
22. J. S. Le Fanu, *The Purcell Papers*, 3 vols (London, 1880) vol. i, p. 2.
23. *Ibid.*, p. 3.
24. *Ibid.*, pp. 99–100.
25. *Ibid.*, p. 100n.
26. J. S. Le Fanu, *Uncle Silas* (London, 1864; repr. London, 1966) p. 31.
27. *Ibid.*, p. 41.
28. *Ibid.*, p. 137.
29. S. T. Coleridge, *Biographia Literaria* (London, 1817; repr. London, 1960) p. 262.
30. Le Fanu, *Uncle Silas*, p. 175.
31. *Ibid.*
32. *Ibid.*
33. *Ibid.*
34. See Norman, *Anti-Catholicism in Victorian England*, p. 116.
35. W. H. Mallock, *Doctrine and Doctrinal Disruption* (London, 1890) p. 138.
36. Haller, *Fox's Book of Martyrs and the Elect Nation*, p. 200.
37. C. Maturin, *Five Sermons on the Errors of the Roman Catholic Church* (Dublin, 1824) pp. 41–2.
38. D. Farson, *The Man Who Wrote Dracula* (London, 1975) pp. 124–5.
39. Bram Stoker, *Dracula* (London, 1897; repr. New York, 1965) p. 15.
40. *Ibid.*, pp. 38–9.
41. *Ibid.*, pp. 76–7.
42. *Ibid.*, p. 112.
43. *Ibid.*, pp. 181–2.
44. Farson, *The Man Who Wrote Dracula*, pp. 223–4.
45. Stoker, *Dracula*, p. 222.
46. See B. and M. Pawley, *Rome and Canterbury through Four Centuries* (London, 1974); and E. E. Reynolds, *The Roman Catholic Church in England and Wales* (Wheathamstead, Herts., 1978).
47. See H. M. Burge (ed.), *The Doctrine of the Resurrection of the Flesh; Documents relating to the question of heresy, raised against the Rev. H. D. Major, Ripon Hall, Oxford* (London, 1922).
48. See note 4 to Chapter 1, and B. A. Souter (ed.), *Tertullian Concerning the Resurrection of the Flesh*; see also G. Burnet, *A Treatise Concerning the State*

of *Departed Souls* (London, 1730); A. Sykes, *An Enquiry when the Resurrection of the Body, or Flesh was First Inserted into the Public Creeds* (London, 1757); E. M. Goulbourn, *The Doctrine of the Resurrection of the Body* (Oxford, 1850); and Burge (ed.), *The Doctrine of the Resurrection of the Flesh*.

49. Trevor-Roper, *Historical Essays*.
50. G. C. Coulton, *Fourscore Years* (London, 1944) pp. 18–19.
51. G. C. Coulton, *Sectarian History* (Cambridge, 1938) p. 2.
52. G. C. Coulton, *The Reformation and British Liberty* (Cambridge, 1936) pp. 16–17.
53. B. Crick, *George Orwell* (London, 1980; repr. Harmondsworth, 1982) p. 583. I owe this point to a conversation with Professor Paul Kennedy.
54. *The Ghost Stories of M. R. James* (London, 1925) Introduction, p. iv.
55. *Ibid.*, p. 125.
56. *Ibid.*, pp. 140–1.
57. *Ibid.*, pp. 147–8.
58. *Ibid.*, p. 150.
59. *Ibid.*, p. 568.
60. *Ibid.*, p. 569.
61. *Ibid.*, p. 579.
62. *Ibid.*, p. 585.
63. *Ibid.*, p. 503.
64. *Ibid.*, p. 511.

Notes to Chapter 3: Criminals and Christians

1. Samuel Richardson, *Pamela* (London, 1741; repr. London, 1931) vol. I, p. 56.
2. Ian Watt, *The Rise of the Novel* (London 1963) p. 75.
3. *Ibid.*, p. 83.
4. V. Cunningham, *Everywhere Spoken Against: Dissent in the Victorian Novel* (Oxford, 1975) p. 9.
5. H. Marcuse, *Studies in Critical Philosophy* (London, 1972) p. 63.
6. *Ibid.*, p. 62.
7. 'The Freedom of a Christian', trans. W. A. Lambert, rev. Harold J. Grimm, in *Martin Luther: Selections from his Writings*, ed. John Dillenberger (New York, 1961) p. 58. This passage is much more anodyne in the German text, and the authority from Timothy is omitted, ostensibly for the easier understanding of the common man. For a discussion of the origin and rhetorical structure of the Latin and German texts, see Birgit Stolt, *Studien zu Luthers Freiheitstraktat* (Stockholm, 1968) pp. 104 and 113–16.
8. 'Freedom of a Christian', p. 58.
9. William James, *The Varieties of Religious Experience* (New York, 1925) p. 244. See also his chapter on 'The Divided Self', pp. 166ff.
10. *Ibid.*, p. 245.
11. Jean Calvin, *The Institutes of the Christian Religion*, trs. H. Beveridge

(Edinburgh, 1845) vol. 2, p. 347. Calvin frequently describes the mind as a labyrinth, and he is well aware of the horrors of the inner journey, which, in its ultimate form, he regards as superstitious. Cf. the following passage, for example, in which he tries to invoke the indifference of external observances, and the liberty of the individual Christian to use or omit them, in the hope of guarding his reader against the infinite regress of conscience:

> For when once the conscience is entangled in the net, it enters a long and inextricable labyrinth, from which it is afterwards most difficult to escape. When a man begins to doubt whether it is lawful for him to use linen for sheets, shirts, napkins, and handkerchiefs, he will not long be secure as to hemp, and will at last have doubts as to tow. . . . Here some must by despair be hurried into an abyss, while others, despising God, and casting off his fear, will not be able to make a way for themselves without ruin. (*Ibid.*, vol. 2, pp. 434–5.)

12. Bunyan, *Grace Abounding*, pp. 64–5.
13. *Ibid.*, p. 67.
14. R. L. Stevenson, *The Works of Robert Louis Stevenson* (London, 1911) pp. 101–2.
15. *Ibid.*, p. 109.
16. Daniel Defoe, *Robinson Crusoe* (London, 1962) p. 50.
17. Wilkie Collins, *No Name* (London, 1864) p. 178.
18. K. Burke, *The Rhetoric of Religion: Studies in Logology* (Berkeley and Los Angeles, Calif., 1970) Ch. II, 'Verbal Action in St Augustine's *Confessions*', pp. 43ff.
19. As Joan Webber has shown in *The Eloquent 'I': Style and Self in Seventeenth-Century Prose* (London, 1968), esp. Ch. II. I am indebted to my colleague Mr A. Gash for drawing my attention to her analysis.
20. William Cowper, *Letters and Prose Writings*, vol. I, ed. James King and Charles Ryskamp (Oxford, 1979) p. 20.
21. *Ibid.*, p. 27.
22. *Ibid.*, p. 28.
23. Bunyan, *Grace Abounding*, p. 46.
24. Poe, *Selected Writings*, pp. 158–9.
25. *Ibid.*, pp. 173–4.
26. *Ibid.*, p. 178.
27. *Ibid.*
28. R. D. Laing, *The Divided Self* (Harmondsworth, 1965) p. 117.
29. Bunyan, *Grace Abounding*, p. 30.
30. *Ibid.*, p. 60.
31. H. R. Warfel, *Charles Brockden Brown* (Gainsville, Fla., 1949); A. Axelrod, *Charles Brockden Brown* (Austin, Tx., 1983).
32. Webber, *The Eloquent 'I'*, p. 273n.
33. Charles Brockden Brown, 'Carwin the Biloquist', repr. in *Great Horror Stories of Europe and America*, ed. P. Haining (London, 1972) vol. II, p. 805.
34. *Ibid.*, p. 807.

35. *Ibid.*, pp. 808–9.
36. Quoted in Warfel, *Charles Brockden Brown*, p. 87.
37. George Fox, *Journal*, ed. N. Penny, 2 vols (Cambridge, 1911) vol. 1, p. 15. Spelling and punctuation modernised for the reader's convenience.
38. Inge, *Protestantism*, p. 86.
39. G. Huehns, *Antinomianism in English History* (London, 1951) p. 47; see also C. Hill, *The World Turned Upside Down* (Harmondsworth, 1975) *passim*, who describes Antinomianism, rather appositely in this context, as 'Calvin's lower-class alter-ego' (p. 161).
40. For an account of this, see Drummond and Bullock, *The Scottish Church*, pp. 217–20. Cf. note 7 above; see also *The Marrow of Sacred Divinity*, trs. William Ames (London, 1642), in particular the following section, 'Of Justification', which gives a biblical source:

   > Justification is a gracious sentence of God, whereby for Christ's sake apprehended by Faith he doth absolve the believer from Sin and Death, and accounts him righteous unto life. Rom. 3: 22, 24. (p. 130)

41. Robert Browning, *Poetical Works, 1833–1864*, ed. Ian Jack (Oxford, 1970) p. 397.
42. *Ibid.*, p. 398.
43. *Ibid.*, p. 399.
44. *Ibid.*
45. Quoted in L. Simpson, *James Hogg: A Critical Study* (Edinburgh and London, 1962) p. 192.
46. James Hogg, *The True Confessions of a Justified Sinner*, repr. in W. E. Buckler (ed.), *Minor Classics of Nineteenth-Century Fiction*, vol. 11, pp. 217–18.
47. *Ibid.*, p. 225.
48. *Ibid.*, p. 229.
49. Laing, *The Divided Self*, p. 106.
50. Bunyan, *Grace Abounding*, p. 65.
51. *The Works of Robert Louis Stevenson*, vol. VIII, pp. 282–3.
52. *Ibid.*, p. 283.
53. *Ibid.*, p. 291.
54. Charles Dickens, *Martin Chuzzlewit* (Oxford, 1951) pp. 726–7.
55. Charles Dickens, *Great Expectations* (Oxford, 1953) p. 391.
56. Quoted in Dickens, *The Mystery of Edwin Drood*, pp. 276–7.
57. *Ibid.*, p. 19.
58. *Ibid.*, pp. 70–1.
59. *Ibid.*, p. 215.
60. *Ibid.*
61. *Ibid.*, p. 217.
62. *Ibid.*, p. 218.
63. Samuel Beckett, *Molloy, Malone Dies, The Unnamable* (London, 1959) p. 88.
64. *Ibid.*, p. 113.
65. *Ibid.*, pp. 151–2.

66. *Ibid.*, p. 167.
67. *Ibid.*, p. 175.
68. *Ibid.*
69. E. Butscher, *Sylvia Plath: Method and Madness* (New York, 1976) p. 21.
70. Sylvia Plath, *Ariel* (London 1965) p. 51.
71. *Ibid.*, pp. 20–1.
72. *Ibid.*, p. 21.
73. *Ibid.*, pp. 45–6.
74. *Ibid.*, p. 40.
75. *Ibid.*, p. 43.
76. *Ibid.*, p. 44.
77. *Ibid.*, p. 76.
78. *Ibid.*, p. 84.
79. *Ibid.*, p. 58.
80. *Ibid.*, p. 59.
81. *Ibid.*, p. 48.
82. *Ibid.*, p. 50.
83. *Ibid.*, p. 56.
84. Storey, *Radcliffe*, p. 267.
85. *Ibid.*, p. 267.
86. *Ibid.*, p. 295–6.
87. *Ibid.*, p. 296–7.
88. *Ibid.*, p. 327.
89. *Ibid.*, pp. 346–7.

Notes to Chapter 4: Commodious Labyrinths

1. Robert D. Mayo, 'Gothic Romance in the Magazines', *PMLA*, vol. 65 (1950) p. 778.
2. John Locke, *The Reasonableness of Christianity*, ed. I. T. Ramsay (London, 1958) p. 65:

   and we know those truths by the strength and native light of our own minds, as they did from whom we received them by theirs, only they had the luck to be before us. Thus the whole stock of human knowledge is claimed by everyone, as his private possession, *as soon as he (profitting by others' discoveries) has got it into his own mind* [my italics].

   The final qualification is a significant one, and gives the tenor of the whole tradition.
3. Sir Leslie Stephen, *A History of English Thought in the Eighteenth Century*, 3rd edn (London, 1927) vol. i, p. 303.
4. *Ibid.*, p. 138.
5. Richard Hurd, *Letters on Chivalry and Romance* (London, 1762; repr. Los Angeles, Calif. 1963) pp. 89–90.
6. See *The Rambler*, no. 4, 31st March 1750; repr. in *Samuel Johnson: Selected Writings*, ed. P. Cruttwell (Harmondsworth, 1968) pp. 149–153.

7. Leslie Stephen, for example, comments acutely on the way in which theologians borrowed their models of rational probability from legal procedure:

> The orthodox reasoners transferred to an inappropriate sphere the presumption of the English law, that a man is innocent until his guilt is proved. They forgot that, in the court of criticism, we are bound to take the most probable opinion without regard to consequences. A judge may not imprison a man, though he thinks it probable that he is a forger; but a critic, with the same evidence before him, would reject the suspicious document. (Stephen, *A History of English Thought in the Eighteenth Century*, p. 189.)

This process of conflation makes the 'legalism' of the theologians an elaboration after the event, though it makes their whole process of argumentation look strict. Whether Sir Leslie is too optimistic about judges or critics is irrelevant; the notion of a 'leakage' from one category of probability to another is the important thing.
8. Hurd, *Letters on Chivalry and Romance*, p. 67.
9. Watt, *The Rise of the Novel*, p. 31.
10. J. Hillis Miller, 'Narrative and History', *ELH*, vol. 41 (1974) p. 456.
11. F. Kermode, *The Genesis of Secrecy* (London, 1979) pp. 113–14.
12. K. Thomas, *Religion and the Decline of Magic* (London, 1971; repr. Harmondsworth, 1978) p. 110.
13. Stephen, *A History of English Thought in the Eighteenth Century*, p. 196.
14. See Coleman O. Parsons, 'Ghost Stories before Defoe', *Notes and Queries*, July 1956, pp. 293–8; Ernest A. Baker, *The History of the English Novel* (London, 1942) vol. 5; see also Moody E. Prior, 'Joseph Glanvill, Witchcraft, and Seventeenth-Century Science', *Modern Philology*, vol. 30 (1932–3) pp. 167–93.
15. C. H. Firth, 'Defoe's *True Relation of the Apparition of Mrs Veal*', *Review of English Studies*, vol. vii, no. 25 (Jan. 1931); see also D. Gardner, 'What Canterbury Knew of Mrs. Veal and her Friends', *Review of English Studies*, vol. vii, no. 26 (April 1931).
16. *The Letters of Edgar Allan Poe*, ed. J. W. Ostram (Cambridge, Mass., 1942) vol. ii, pp. 433–4n.
17. David Hume, *On Religion*, ed. R. Wollheim (New York, 1964) pp. 222–3.
18. Stephen, *A History of English Thought in the Eighteenth Century*, p. 246.
19. Hume, *On Religion*, p. 26.
20. Thomas Sherlock, Bishop of Bangor, *The Tryal of the Witnesses of the Resurrection of Jesus* (London, 1729) p. 60. This was an extremely popular work.
21. Sir William Blackstone, *Commentaries on the Laws of England*, rev. edn (London, 1829) vol. iii, p. 268. This is the revised text. In the original, the stress is on direct inheritance of the 'castle', not analogy. There is a discussion of this passage in Leon Radzinowicz, *A History of Criminal Law* (London, 1948) vol. i, p. 353.
22. S. Kliger, 'The *translatio imperii* and the Fall of Rome', *Modern Philology*, vol. xlv, no. 2 (Nov. 1947) p. 73.

23. G. R. Y. Radcliffe and G. Cross, *The English Legal System* (London, 1937) p. 16.
24. A. Esmein, *A History of Continental Criminal Procedure*, trs. J. Simpson (London, 1913) p. 11.
25. M. G. Lewis, *The Monk* (London, 1796; repr. London, 1974) pp. 335–6.
26. *Ibid.*, p. 336.
27. *Ibid.*, pp. 336–7.
28. Sir James Stephen, *A Digest of the Law of Evidence* (London, 1874; repr. London, 1948) p. 38.
29. *Ibid.*, p. 38n.
30. See Chapter 2 above, and W. Walsh, *The Secret History of the Oxford Movement* (London, 1898) *passim*.
31. This does not necessarily mean that they are practised, as the following recent account makes clear. The conclusion of this modern writer is positively Benthamite:

> our modern courts in dealing with hearsay, while giving lip-service to the reasons which impelled their predecessors to create the rule, have in fact entirely disregarded them. The oath and opportunity for cross-examination, and even oath and actual cross-examination do not save the utterance from exclusion as hearsay: the absence of both does not require its exclusion. The decisions indicate a realisation that emphasis upon the theoretical value of oath and cross-examination as instruments for the discovery of truth (a) has obscured the limits of their value in day-to-day practice in ordinary litigation, and (b) has created an entirely unrealistic assumption of naive credulity of jurors and their incapacity to evaluate hearsay as distinguished from first-hand testimony. (Edmund Morris Morgan, *Some Problems of Proof under the Anglo-American System of Litigation* (New York, 1956) pp. 164–6.)

32. Sir Richard Eggleston, *Evidence, Proof and Probability* (London, 1978) pp. 48–9.
33. These examples are quoted in G. D. Nokes, *An Introduction to Evidence*, 4th edn (London, 1967) pp. 317–18.
34. Lewis, *The Monk*, p. 289.
35. *Ibid.*, p. 291.
36. *Ibid.*
37. Radcliffe, *The Italian*, pp. 321–2.
38. *Ibid.*, p. 322.
39. *Ibid.*, p. 326.
40. *Ibid.*, p. 327.
41. *Ibid.*, p. 352.
42. Esmein, *A History of Continental Criminal Procedure*, p. 368.
43. *Ibid.*, p. 251.
44. *Ibid.*, p. 422.
45. Radcliffe, *The Italian*, p. 397.
46. *Ibid.*, pp. 397–8.
47. E. Halévy, *The Growth of Philosophic Radicalism* (London, 1952) p. 79.

48. Anon., 'On Vampyrism', *New Monthly Magazine*, vol. 7 (1823) pp. 144–5.
49. Esmein, *A History of Continental Criminal Procedure*, p. 473.
50. *Ibid.*, p. 107.
51. Eggleston, *Evidence, Proof and Probability*, p. 35.
52. J. G. Phillimore, *The History and Principles of the Law of Evidence* (London, 1850) pp. 157ff., quotes extracts from the records of the trial.
53. J. B. Thayer, *A Preliminary Treatise on Evidence at the Common Law* (Boston, Mass., 1898; repr. New York, 1969) p. 506.
54. C. K. Ogden, *Bentham's Theory of Fictions* (London, 1932) pp. xii–xiii. For Bentham's susceptibility to horror, see p. xiii.
55. Jeremy Bentham, *A Treatise on Judicial Evidence*, ed. and trs. M. Dumont (London, 1825) p. 267.
56. *Ibid.*, p. 276.
57. *Ibid.*
58. *Ibid.*, p. 277.
59. *Ibid.*, pp. 271–2.
60. *Ibid.*, p. 270.
61. *Ibid.*
62. Mary Shelley, *Frankenstein* (London, 1818; rev. edn, London, 1831); repr. in *Three Gothic Novels*, ed. M. Praz (Harmondsworth, 1968) p. 283.
63. *Ibid.*, pp. 286–7.
64. *Ibid.*, pp. 311–12.
65. *Ibid.*, p. 312.
66. *Ibid.*, pp. 318–19.
67. *Ibid.*, p. 313.
68. *Ibid.*, p. 364.
69. *Ibid.*, p. 379.
70. Bentham, *A Treatise on Judicious Evidence*, pp. 28–9.
71. *Ibid.*, p. 144.
72. *Ibid.*, p. 282.
73. Stoker, *Dracula*, p. 11.
74. *Ibid.*, pp. 198–9.
75. *Ibid.*, p. 199.
76. *Ibid.*, pp. 345–6.
77. *Ibid.*, p. 288.
78. Cesare Lombroso-Ferrero, *Criminal Man*, ed. Savitz (Mont Claire, N.J., 1972) pp. xxiv–xxv.
79. *Ibid.*, p. 234.
80. *Ibid.*, pp. 64–5.
81. *Ibid.*, p. 18.
82. Count Cesare, Lombroso-Ferrero, *The Man of Genius* (London, 1891) p. 2.
83. Stoker, *Dracula*, p. 346.
84. Max Nordau, *Degeneration*, 2nd edn (London, 1895) pp. 53–4.
85. *Ibid.*, p. 55.
86. *Ibid.*, p. 540.
87. Stoker, *Dracula*, p. 44.
88. *Ibid.*, p. 46.

Notes to Chapter 5: Strange Cases

1. Eggleston, *Evidence, Proof and Probability*, pp. 106–7.
2. Thomas, *Religion and the Decline of Magic*, p. 187.
3. See, for example, Bishop Joseph Hall, *Resolutions and Decisions of Divers Practical Cases of Conscience* (London, 1649), a book which was still popular enough in the eighteenth century for the hawk-eyed Mrs Thrale to recognise in Hall the source for Horace Walpole's sensational new drama of incest, *The Mysterious Mother*. See *Thraliana: The Diary of Mrs Hester Lynch Thrale*, ed. K. C. Baldestone, 2 vols (Oxford, 1951) vol. II, p. 786.
4. Poe, *Selected Writings*, p. 350.
5. Brian Inglis, *Natural and Supernatural* (London, 1977) p. 216.
6. Poe, *Selected Writings*, p. 353.
7. *Ibid.*, p. 356.
8. *Ibid.*, pp. 356–7.
9. *Ibid.*, p. 357.
10. Drelincourt, *A Christian Man's Consolation against the Fears of Death*, pp. 562–3.
11. Stevenson, *The Strange Case of Dr Jekyll and Mr Hyde*, p. 108.
12. Poe, *Selected Writings*, p. 359.
13. Drelincourt, *A Christian Man's Consolation against the Fears of Death*, pp. 36–7.
14. Quoted in Leon Lemmonier, *Edgar Poe et la critique française* (Paris, 1828) p. 21.
15. *Ibid.*
16. Eggleston, *Evidence, Proof and Probability*, p. 6.
17. W. B. Gallie, *Philosophy and the Historical Understanding* (London, 1964) pp. 38–9.
18. Ambrose Bierce, *Can Such Things Be?* (London, 1926) p. 218.
19. *Ibid.*, p. 220.
20. *Ibid.*, p. 223.
21. Esmein, *A History of Continental Criminal Procedure*, comments on the source for this notion:

> This is a traditional rule, 'Testis unus, testis nullus', or, as Loysel said, 'The voice of one is the voice of none'. Paul Viollet, in his 'Histoire du droit civil française', (Paris, 1893), p. 30, has shown that this rule, which 'has dominated the whole matter of testimonies and enquiries during the whole of the Middle Ages and down to modern times', is undoubtedly derived from Scripture. It is formulated in St John and St Matthew (St John, viii, 17). 'And we may affirm', adds Viollet, 'that this rule of two, invariable in the Middle Ages, and retained in the 1800s in several legal systems of the United States of America, is of Hebraic origin.' (p. 623n)

22. Bierce, *Can Such Things Be?*, p. 223.
23. *Ibid.*, p. 224.
24. *Ibid.*, pp. 226–7.

25. *Ibid.*, pp. 230–1.
26. See A. Hughes, 'Science in English Encyclopaedias, 1704–1875', *Annals of Science*, vol. vii (1951) p. 345.
27. *Ibid.*, pp. 355–7.
28. Repr. in Buckler (ed.), *Minor Classics of Nineteenth-Century Fiction*, vol. ii, p. 29.
29. *Ibid.*, pp. 31–2.
30. For comment on the controversy over literal or figurative interpretations of St Paul, see note 4 to Ch. 1, and note 48 to Ch. 2.
31. Buckler (ed.), *Minor Classics of Nineteenth-Century Fiction*, vol. ii, p. 53.
32. *Ibid.*, p. 55.
33. *Ibid.*, p. 61.
34. *Ibid.*, pp. 62–3.
35. *Ibid.*, p. 58.
36. See G. W. Keeton and O. R. Marshall, 'Bentham's Influence on the Law of Evidence', in *Jeremy Bentham and the Law* (London, 1948); and Sir Frederick Holdsworth, *A History of English Law* (London, 1944) vol. viii, p. 132.
37. Stephen, *A Digest of the Law of Evidence*, pp. xi–xii.
38. Thayer, *A Preliminary Treatise on Evidence at the Common Law*, p. 266.
39. *Ibid.*, p. 273.
40. Lord Maugham, *The Problem of Judicial Proof* (Birmingham, 1939) p. 2.
41. *The Collected Works of Edgar Allan Poe*, ed. T. O. Mabbott, 3 vols (Cambridge, Mass., 1978) vol. iii, p. 747 and n. The editor's foreword contains further bibliographical and historical information about the case of Mary Rogers.
42. Lemmonnier, *Edgar Poe et la critique française*, p. 157.
43. *Ibid.*, p. 142.
44. J. Walsh, *Poe: The Detective* (New Brunswick, 1968) pp. 72–3.
45. Poe, *The Collected Works of Edgar Allan Poe*, p. 723.
46. *Ibid.*, p. 772. See the editor's note on this passage.
47. Walsh, *Poe: The Detective*, p. 77.
48. See H. P. Sucksmith, 'The Secret of Immediacy: Dickens's Debt to the Tale of Terror in *Blackwoods*', *Nineteenth-Century Fiction*, vol. 26 (1971–2) pp. 145ff.
49. Wilkie Collins, *The Woman in White* (London, 1860) vol. i, pp. 3–4.
50. Compare, however, the following youthful outburst in *The Leader*, which seems revealing. Collins's friend, Piggott, the editor, began early in the 1850s to include religious articles in the magazine, a policy which provoked protest from Collins:

> I go with you in your judgement on Literature – but, in regard to your mixing up the name of Jesus Christ with the current politics of the day, I am against you – against you with all my heart and soul. I will expose and condemn as heartily as any of you the corruptions and abuses of Church politics, as the inventions of man – but if one of the things you understand by 'freedom of religious thought' be the freedom of mingling Our Saviour's name with the politics of the day – I protest against that 'freedom', as something irredeemably bad in

itself; and utterly useless for any good purpose whatever. . . . I am neither a Protestant, a Catholic – or a Dissenter – I do not desire to discuss this or that particular creed; but I believe Jesus Christ to be the son of God; and believing that, I think it a blasphemy to use his name, as it is used in [recent articles].

Quoted in Sue Lonoff, *Wilkie Collins and his Victorian Readers: A Study in the Rhetoric of Authorship* (New York, 1982) pp. 216–17.

51. Collins, *The Woman in White*, vol. i, p. 93.
52. *Ibid.*, pp. 93–4.
53. *Ibid.*, p. 132.
54. *Ibid.*, vol. iii, p. 8.
55. *Ibid.*, p. 308.
56. *Ibid.*, p. 309.
57. Lombroso-Ferrero, Count Cesare, *Criminal Man*, ed. Savitz (Mont Claire, N.J., 1972), p. xix.
58. The following remarks, heavily ironic, give the reader some insight into the religio-political affiliations of 'sanity' in this novel:

Mr. Morris, you should be proud of your great state [Texas]. Its reception into the Union was a precedent which may have far-reaching effects hereafter, when the Pole and the Tropics may hold alliance to the Stars and Stripes. The power of Treaty may yet prove a vast engine of enlightenment, when the Monroe Doctrine takes its true place as a political fable. (Stoker, *Dracula*, p. 249.)

59. Guy Endore, *The Werewolf of Paris* (New York, 1933) p. 7.
60. *Ibid.*, p. 9.
61. *Ibid.*, p. 10.
62. *Ibid.*, p. 11.
63. *Ibid.*, pp. 12–13.
64. *Ibid.*, pp. 13–14.
65. *Ibid.*, pp. 324–5.

Notes to Postscript

1. I have in mind here the use of the concept 'popular' as a form of stratification in Louis James, *Fiction for the Working Man* (Harmondsworth, 1974) *passim*.
2. Walzer, *Revolution of the Saints*, p. 78.
3. Hervey, *Meditations and Contemplations*, pp. 16–17.

Bibliography

Ames, William (trs.), *The Marrow of Sacred Divinity* (London, 1642).

Anon., *The Awful Disclosures of Maria Monk* (London, 1839).

Anon., 'On Vampyrism', *New Monthly Magazine*, vol. 7 (1823) pp. 144–5.

Armstrong, B. J., *Norfolk Diaries* (London, 1949).

Austen, Jane, *Northanger Abbey*, ed. R. W. Chapman (Oxford, 1969).

Axelrod, A., *Charles Brockden Brown* (Austin, Texas, 1983).

Bachelard, G., *La Poétique de l'espace* (Paris, 1957).

Baker, E. A., *A History of the English Novel*, 12 vols (London, 1942).

Beattie, James, *An Essay on the Nature and Immutability of Truth, in Opposition to Sophistry and Scepticism* (Edinburgh, 1770).

Beckett, Samuel, *Molloy, Malone Dies, The Unnamable* (London, 1959).

Bentham, Jeremy, *A Treatise on Judicial Evidence*, ed. and trs. M. Dumont (London, 1825).

Bierce, Ambrose, *Can Such Things Be?* (London, 1926).

Blackstone, Sir William, *Commentaries on the Laws of England*, 4 vols (revised edn, London, 1829).

Breton, A., 'Limits not Frontiers of Surrealism', trs. and repr. in *Surrealism*, ed. Sir Herbert Read (London, 1936).

Brontë, Emily, *Wuthering Heights* (London, 1847; repr. Harmondsworth, 1967).

Browning, Robert, *Poetical Works, 1833–1864*, ed. Ian Jack (Oxford, 1970).

Buckler, W. E. (ed.), *Minor Classics of Nineteenth-Century Fiction*, 2 vols (Boston, Mass., 1967).

Bunyan, John, *Grace Abounding to the Chief of Sinners*, ed. R. Sharrock (Oxford, 1962).

Burge, H. M. (ed.), *The Doctrine of the Resurrection of the Flesh; Documents relating to the question of heresy raised against the Rev. H. D. Major, Ripon Hall, Oxford* (London, 1922).

Burke, K., *The Rhetoric of Religion: Studies in Logology* (Berkeley and Los Angeles, Calif., 1970).

Burnet, G., *A Treatise Concerning the State of Departed Souls* (London, 1730).

Butscher, E., *Sylvia Plath: Method and Madness* (New York, 1976).

Calmet, Augustin, *The Phantom World, or the Philosophy of Spirits, Apparitions, etc.*, ed. with an introduction by the Revd Henry Christmas (London, 1850).

Calvin, Jean, *The Institutes of the Christian Religion*, trs. H. Beveridge, 3 vols (Edinburgh, 1845).

Carter, Angela, *Heroes and Villains* (London, 1969; repr. Harmondsworth, 1981).

Chadwick, O., *The Victorian Church*, 3rd edn, 2 vols (London, 1971).

Coleridge, S. T., *Biographia Literaria*, 2 vols (London, 1817; repr. 1960).

Collins, Charles, 'The Compensation House', first pub. *All the Year Round*, ed. Charles Dickens (London, 1866); repr. in *The Supernatural Omnibus*, ed. M. Summers (London, 1931; repr. 1971).

Collins, Wilkie, *The Woman in White*, 3 vols (London, 1860).
——, *No Name* (London, 1864).
——, *The Black Robe*, 3 vols (London, 1871).
Coulton, G. C., *The Reformation and British Liberty* (Cambridge, 1936).
——, *Sectarian History* (Cambridge, 1938).
——, *Fourscore Years* (London, 1944).
Cowper, William, *The Poetical Works*, ed. H. S. Milford, 4th edn (Oxford, 1963).
——, *Letters and Prose Writings*, vol. ı, ed. James King and Charles Ryskamp (Oxford, 1979).
Crick, B., *George Orwell* (London, 1980; repr. Harmondsworth, 1982).
Cunningham, V., *Everywhere Spoken Against: Dissent in the Victorian Novel* (Oxford, 1975).
De Beer, E. S., ' "Gothic": the Origin and Diffusion of the Term', *Journal of the Warburg and Courtauld Institute*, vol. xı (1948).
De Foe, Daniel, *A True Relation of the Apparition of One Mrs. Veal* (London, 1706); repr. in *Daniel Defoe*, ed. J. T. Boulton (London, 1965).
——, *Robinson Crusoe* (London, 1962).
——, *The History and Reality of Apparitions* (London 1727).
Dicey, A. V., *Lectures on the Relation between Law and Public Opinion in England* (London, 1905).
Dickens, Charles, *Martin Chuzzlewit* (Oxford, 1951).
——, *Great Expectations* (Oxford, 1953).
——, *The Mystery of Edwin Drood* (Oxford, 1963).
Douglas, Mary, *Natural Symbols* (London, 1970).
Draper, J. W., *The Funeral Elegy and the Rise of Romanticism* (New York, 1929).
Drelincourt, Charles, *A Christian Man's Consolation against the Fears of Death*, 28th edn (Liverpool, 1811).
Drummond, A., and Bullock, C., *The Scottish Church, 1688–1843* (Edinburgh, 1973).
Eggleston, Sir Richard, *Evidence, Proof and Probability* (London, 1978).
Ellis, S. M., *Wilkie Collins, Le Fanu, and Others* (New York, 1931).
Endore, Guy, *The Werewolf of Paris* (New York, 1933).
Engelmann, A., *et al.*, *A History of Continental Civil Procedure* (Boston, Mass., 1927).
Esmein, A., *A History of Continental Criminal Procedure*, trs. J. Simpson (London, 1913).
Farrell, J. G., *Troubles* (London, 1970; repr. Harmondsworth, 1975).
Farson, D., *The Man Who Wrote Dracula* (London, 1975).
Fehr, B., 'The Antagonism of Forms in the Eighteenth Century', *English Studies*, vol. xvııı (1936) pp. 115–21, 193–205; vol. xıx (1937) pp. 3–4, 49–57.
Firth, C. H., 'Defoe's *True Relation of the Apparition of Mrs. Veal*', *Review of English Studies*, vol. vıı, no. 25 (Jan. 1931) pp. 3–8.
Fox, George, *Journal*, ed. N. Penny, 2 vols (Cambridge, 1911).
Fox, John, *The Acts and Monuments of the English Martyrs* (London, 1563).
Freud, Sigmund, 'The Uncanny', in *Collected Papers*, vol. ıv (London, 1957).
Gallie, W. B., *Philosophy and the Historical Understanding* (London, 1964).
Gardner, D., 'What Canterbury Knew of Mrs. Veal and her Friends', *Review of English Studies*, vol. vıı, no. 26 (April 1931) pp. 192ff.

Gladstone, W. E., 'The Vatican Decrees and Civil Liberty', repr. in Alvin S. Ryan (ed.), *Newman and Gladstone: The Vatican Decrees* (Indiana, 1962).

Glanvill, Joseph, *Sadducismus Triumphatus* (London, 1689); repr. with Introduction by Coleman O. Parsons (Gainesville, Fla., 1966).

Goulbourn, E. M., *The Doctrine of the Resurrection of the Body* (Oxford, 1850).

Gwynn, D., *The Struggle for Catholic Emancipation, 1750–1820* (London, 1928).

Haining, P. (ed.), *Great Horror Stories of Europe and America*, 3 vols (London, 1972).

Halévy, E., *The Growth of Philosophic Radicalism* (London, 1952).

Hall, Joseph, *Resolutions and Decisions of Divers Practical Cases of Conscience* (London, 1649).

Haller, W., *The Rise of Puritanism* (New York, 1938).

——, *Fox's Book of Martyrs and the Elect Nation* (London, 1963).

Hervey, James, *Meditations Among the Tombs* (London, 1749); repr. as *Meditations and Contemplations by the Rev. James Hervey AM* (London, 1815).

Hill, C., *The World Turned Upside Down* (Harmondsworth, 1975).

Hogg, J., *The True Confessions of a Justified Sinner*, repr. in W. E. Buckler, *Minor Classics of Nineteenth-Century Fiction* (Boston, Mass., 1967).

Holdsworth, Sir Frederick, *A History of English Law*, 14 vols (London, 1944).

Huehns, G., *Antinomianism in English History* (London, 1951).

Hughes, A., 'Science in English Encyclopaedias, 1704–1875', *Annals of Science*, vol. vii (1951) pp. 343–7.

Hughes, W., *The Maniac in the Cellar* (Princeton, N.J., 1980).

Hume, D., *On Religion*, ed. with an introduction by Richard Wollheim (New York, 1964).

Hurd, R., *Letters on Chivalry and Romance* (London, 1762); repr. in facsimile with an introduction by Hoyt Trowbridge (Los Angeles, Calif., 1963).

Inge, W. R., *Protestantism* (London, 1935).

Inglis, B., *Natural and Supernatural* (London, 1977).

Jackson, R., *Fantasy: The Literature of Subversion* (London, 1981).

James, Louis, *Fiction for the Working Man* (Harmondsworth, 1974).

James, M. R., *The Ghost Stories of M. R. James* (London, 1925).

James, William, *The Varieties of Religious Experience* (New York, 1925).

Jameson, F., 'Magical Narratives: Romance as Genre', *New Literary History*, vol. 7, no. 1 (Autumn 1975) pp. 133–63.

Johnson, Samuel, *The Rambler*, no. 4, 31 March 1750; repr. in Samuel Johnson, *Selected Writings*, ed. P. Cruttwell (Harmondsworth, 1968).

Jones, Ernest, *On the Nightmare* (London, 1931).

Keeton, G. W. and Marshall, O. R., 'Bentham's Influence on the Law of Evidence', *Jeremy Bentham and the Law* (London, 1948).

Kermode, F., *The Genesis of Secrecy* (London, 1979).

Kilham, Alexander, *The Hypocrite Detected and Exposed* (Aberdeen, 1794).

Kliger, S., 'The *translatio imperii* and the Fall of Rome', *Modern Philology*, vol. xlv, no. 2 (Nov. 1947) pp. 73–103.

——, *The Goths in England* (Cambridge, Mass., 1952).

Laing, R. D., *The Divided Self* (Harmondsworth, 1965).

Laplace, Pierre Simon, *A Philosophical Essay on Probabilities*, trs. F. W. Truscott and F. L. Emory (New York, 1902).

Lavater, Lewes, *Of Ghostes and Spirites Walking by Nyght*, ed. with an introduction by J. Dover Wilson (Oxford, 1929).

Lea, H. P., *Superstition and Force* (Philadelphia, 1892).

Lecky, W. H., *History of the Rise and Influence of Rationalism in Europe*, 2 vols (London, 1890).

Le Fanu, J. S., *Uncle Silas* (London, 1864; repr. London, 1966).

——, *The Purcell Papers*, 3 vols (London, 1880).

Lemmonnier, Leon, *Edgar Poe et la critique française* (Paris, 1828).

Levy, Maurice, *Le Roman 'gotique' anglais* (Toulouse, 1968).

Lewis, M. G., *The Monk* (London, 1796; repr. London, 1974).

Locke, J., *The Reasonableness of Christianity*, ed. I. T. Ramsay (London, 1958).

Lombroso-Ferrero, Count Cesare, *Criminal Man*, ed. Savitz (Mont Claire, N.J., 1972).

——, *The Man of Genius* (London, 1891).

Lonoff, S., *Wilkie Collins and His Victorian Readers: A Study in the Rhetoric of Authorship* (New York, 1982).

Lubbock, S. G., *A Memoir of Montague Rhodes James* (Cambridge, 1939).

Luther, Martin, *Martin Luther: Selections from his Writings*, ed. J. Dillenberger (New York, 1961).

Macaulay, R., *The Pleasures of Ruins* (London, 1953).

McBryde, G., *Letters to a Friend*, ed. Gwendolin McBryde (London, 1956).

Mallock, W. H., *Doctrine and Doctrinal Disruption* (London, 1890).

Marcuse, H., *Studies in Critical Philosophy* (London, 1972).

Maturin, C., *Melmoth the Wanderer* (London, 1820; repr. Oxford, 1968).

——, *Five Sermons on the Errors of the Roman Catholic Church* (Dublin, 1824).

Maugham, Lord, *The Problem of Judicial Proof* (Birmingham, 1939).

Mayo, Robert D., 'Gothic Romance in the Magazines', *PMLA*, vol. 65 (1950) p. 778.

Miller, Hillis J., 'Narrative and History', *ELH*, vol. 41 (1974) p. 456.

Morgan, E. M., *Some Problems of Proof under the Anglo-American System of Litigation* (New York, 1956).

Newman, H., *Lectures on the Present Condition of Catholics in England* (London, 1851).

Nokes, G. D., *A History of the Crime of Blasphemy* (London, 1928).

——, *An Introduction to Evidence*, 4th edn (London, 1967).

Nordau, M., *Degeneration* (London, 1895).

Norman, E. R., *Anti-Catholicism in Victorian England* (London, 1968).

Ogden, C. K., *Bentham's Theory of Fictions* (London, 1932).

Parreaux, A., *The Publication of 'The Monk': A Literary Event, 1796–1798* (Paris, 1960).

Parsons, Coleman O., 'Ghost Stories before Defoe', *Notes and Queries*, July 1956, pp. 293–8.

Pawley, B., and Pawley, M., *Rome and Canterbury through Four Centuries* (London, 1974).

Peake, Mervyn, *Titus Alone* (Harmondsworth, 1968).

Phillimore, J. G., *The History and Principles of the Law of Evidence* (London, 1850).

254 *Bibliography*

Plath, Sylvia, *Ariel* (London, 1965).
Poe, Edgar Allan, *Selected Writings*, ed. D. Galloway (Harmondsworth, 1967).
——, *The Collected Works of Edgar Allan Poe*, ed. T. O. Mabbott, 3 vols (Cambridge, Mass., 1978).
——, *The Letters of Edgar Allan Poe*, ed. J. W. Ostram, 2 vols (Cambridge, Mass., 1942).
Prior, Moody E., 'Joseph Glanvill, Witchcraft, and Seventeenth-Century Science', *Modern Philology*, 30 (1932–3) pp. 167–93.
Radcliffe, Ann, *The Mysteries of Udolpho* (London, 1794; repr. 2 vols, London, 1962).
——, *The Italian* (London, 1797; repr. Oxford, 1968).
——, *Gaston de Blondeville*, 4 vols (London, 1826).
Radcliffe G. R. Y., and Cross, G., *The English Legal System* (London, 1937).
Radzinowicz, L., *A History of Criminal Law*, 4 vols (London, 1948).
Reynolds, E. E., *The Roman Catholic Church in England and Wales* (Wheathamsted, Herts, 1978).
Richardson, Samuel, *Pamela, or Virtue Rewarded* (London, 1741; repr. 2 vols, London, 1931).
Robson, W. A., *Civilisation and Growth of Law* (London, 1935).
Ryan, Alvin S. (ed.), *Newman and Gladstone: The Vatican Decrees* (Notre Dame, Ind., 1962).
Sade, Marquis de, 'Idee sur Les Romans' (Paris, 1800); repr. in *Les Crimes de l'Amour* (Bruxelles, 1881).
Shelley, Mary, *Frankenstein* (London, 1818; rev. edn, 1831); repr. in *Three Gothic Novels*, ed. and with an introduction by M. Praz (Harmondsworth, 1968).
Sherlock, T., *The Tryal of the Witnesses of the Resurrection of Jesus* (London, 1729).
Sickels, Eleanor, *The Gloomy Egoist: Moods and Themes of Melancholy from Gray to Keats* (London, 1932).
Simpson, L., *James Hogg: A Critical Study* (Edinburgh and London, 1962).
Spencer, P., *Politics of Belief in Nineteenth-Century France* (London, 1954).
Stephen, Sir James, *A Digest of the Law of Evidence* (London, 1874; repr. London, 1948).
——, *A History of English Thought in the Eighteenth Century*, 3rd edn, 2 vols (London, 1927).
Stevenson, R. L., *The Works of Robert Louis Stevenson*, 20 vols (London, 1911).
——, *The Strange Case of Dr Jekyll and Mr Hyde*, repr. in *Minor Classics of Nineteenth-Century Fiction*, ed. W. E. Buckler, 2 vols (Boston, Mass., 1967).
Stoker, Bram, *Dracula* (London, 1897; repr. New York, 1965).
——, *A Glimpse of America* (London, 1886).
Stolt, Birgit, *Studien zu Luthers Freiheitstraktat* (Stockholm, 1968).
Storey, David, *Radcliffe* (Harmondsworth, 1965).
Stuart, Charles (ed.), *The Reith Diaries* (London, 1975).
Sucksmith, H. P., 'The Secret of Immediacy: Dickens's Debt to the Tale of Horror in *Blackwoods'*, *Nineteenth-Century Fiction*, vol. 26 (1971–2) pp. 145ff.
Sue, Eugene, *The Wandering Jew* (London, 1868).

Summers, Montague (ed.), *The Supernatural Omnibus* (London, 1931; repr. 1974).

Sykes, A., *An Inquiry when the Resurrection of the Body, or Flesh was First Inserted into the Public Creeds* (London, 1757).

Taylor, John Russell, *Hitch* (London, 1978; repr. London, 1981).

Tertullian Concerning the Resurrection of the Flesh, ed. B. A. Souter (London, 1922).

Thayer, J. B., *A Preliminary Treatise on Evidence at the Common Law* (Boston, Mass., 1898; repr. New York, 1969).

Thomas, K., *Religion and the Decline of Magic* (London, 1971; repr. Harmondsworth, 1978).

Thrale, Hester, *Thraliana: The Diary of Hester Lynch Thrale*, ed. K. C. Baldeston, 2 vols (Oxford, 1951).

Tompkins, J. M. S., *The Popular Novel in England, 1770–1800* (London, 1932).

Trevor-Roper, H., *Historical Essays* (London, 1957); repr. as *Men and Events* (New York, 1976).

——, *The European Witch-Craze of the Sixteenth and Seventeenth Centuries* (Harmondsworth, 1969).

Von Bar, C. L., *A History of Continental Criminal Law* (London, 1916).

Walsh, J., *Poe: The Detective* (New Brunswick, 1968).

Walsh, William, *The Secret History of the Oxford Movement* (London, 1898).

Walzer, M., *Revolution of the Saints* (London, 1966).

Warfel, H., *Charles Brockden Brown* (Gainsville, Fla., 1949).

Watt, Ian, *The Rise of the Novel* (London, 1963).

Watts, Isaac, *Reliquae Juveniles* (London, 1734).

Webber, Joan, *The Eloquent 'I': Style and Self in Seventeenth-Century Prose* (London, 1968).

Weber, M., *The Protestant Ethic and the Spirit of Capitalism*, trs. Talcott Parsons (London, 1976).

Wimsatt, W. K., Jr, 'Poe and the Mystery of Mary Rogers', *PMLA*, LVI (March 1941) pp. 230–48.

Index